10-13-75

Perceiving Women

Perceiving Women

edited by

Shirley Ardener

A HALSTED PRESS BOOK

John Wiley & Sons
New York

First published in 1975
by Malaby Press Limited
Aldine House, 26 Albemarle Street, London

This book has been set in 11 on 12 point Times New Roman
and was printed in Great Britain by the Aldine Press
Letchworth, Herts

Published in the U.S.A.
by Halsted Press, a Division
of John Wiley & Sons, Inc.,
New York

Library of Congress Cataloging in Publication Data
Main entry under title:

Perceiving women.

'A Halsted Press book.'
Includes index.

CONTENTS: Ardener, S. Introduction.—Ardener, E. Belief and the problem
of women.—Ardener, S. Sexual insult and female militancy. [etc.]
1. Women—Addresses, essays, lectures.   2. Feminism—Addresses, essays,
lectures. I. Ardener, Shirley.
HQ1154. P427   1975   301.41'2   75–12662
ISBN 0-470-03309-6

Contents

SHIRLEY ARDENER

Introduction   vii
The papers
Muted groups and differing orders of perception
Specialized or 'un-natural' female groups and female universals
Conclusion

EDWIN ARDENER

Belief and the Problem of Women   1
The problem
Statement and observation
Man, Mouse, Ape, and Water Spirit
Mermaids and the wild
Symbolism of the mermaid cult
Mankind and womankind

The 'Problem' Revisited   19

SHIRLEY ARDENER

Sexual Insult and Female Militancy   29
The Bakweri
Judicial procedures
The Balong
The Kom
Comparative African material
*Militant techniques in Africa and in the women's liberation
    movements*
Conclusion

JUDITH OKELY

Gypsy Women: Models in Conflict   55
Gorgio view of Gypsy women
Gypsy view of their women
Contradictions

Contents

Pollution
   Sexuality as inherently polluting if mismanaged
   Menstruation as polluting
   Childbirth as polluting
Women's perspectives
Economic role
Physical combat
Political role
Ritual equality and sexual rights

HILARY CALLAN
The Premiss of Dedication: Notes towards an Ethnography
of Diplomats' Wives   87
   Preliminary methodological remarks
   The questions posed
   Protocol and rank
   Official status
   Official duties and informal obligations
   Independent interests
   Paradoxes
   Conclusion

DRID WILLIAMS
The Brides of Christ   105
   Introduction
   Some theoretical considerations
   The daily life of the nuns
   Space–time in the Carmelite Order
   Carmelite semantics
   Carmelite vows
   Conclusion

CAROLINE IFEKA-MOLLER
Female Militancy and Colonial Revolt: The Women's War of
1929, Eastern Nigeria   127
   Introduction
   The Women's War
   The 'why' and the 'how' of the Women's War
   How women became 'as men': Igbo and Ibibio societies, 1880–
      1925
   A decade of protest ends in the Women's War
   Conclusion

NAME INDEX   159
SUBJECT INDEX   162

Shirley Ardener

Introduction

The title selected for this volume has a certain ambiguity. The choice was deliberate, for it was hoped that the alternative readings would draw attention to two major concerns of the papers collected here: how groups of women perceive themselves and the world around them, and how we as observers (whether male or female) are to perceive them. 'Perceiving women' seemed to be appropriate to describe both the subject-matter of the volume and the activity of those who, like the social anthropologists whose studies are offered here, have made the effort to attempt to understand them. The title refers both to substance and to methodology. It might even be thought to describe the activity of any readers who are kind enough to open these pages.

All the writers here share a common interest in these two themes, and we have all, whether bravely or foolhardily others must decide, presented tentative theoretical speculations and interpretations in order to stimulate discussion which might break new ground. Those who do not find such analyses helpful but who welcome new data will, we hope, find the information which is set out interesting of itself. It illustrates well the extraordinary differences between the various ideas about women which communities generate, and under the influence of which women live their lives. Although each paper presented here is focused on different material, differently analysed, there are many points of contact between the contributions which give unity to the volume. It will become clear that the papers have had some influence one upon another. Before discussing them it will be helpful to give some brief historical details of how they came to be written.

THE PAPERS

In 1968 Edwin Ardener was invited by Jean La Fontaine to contribute towards a book in honour of his former teacher Dr Audrey Richards on her formal retirement (although, happily, not from social anthropology altogether). As his tribute to her work on female puberty rites among the Bemba of Uganda, he chose to consider some rituals performed by Bakweri women, living in Cameroon. He prefaced his contribution with some general remarks on the study of women. First read in 1968, the paper appeared in the festschrift in 1972. Since it has influenced other contributions submitted here, we felt that it would be helpful to reprint it in the present volume, and we are grateful to him and others concerned for agreeing.[1] He has also added a new commentary here.

My own paper, originally read in February 1971 at a seminar convened by John Beattie and Peter Lienhardt at the Oxford Institute of Social Anthropology, also discusses some patterns of behaviour of Cameroon women, but links these with certain manifestations of the modern women's liberation movements in the West. Soon after this was given, an informal seminar of women social anthropologists began to meet regularly at Oxford in order to concentrate attention on issues of mutual concern. Among the papers specially prepared for the seminar were those of Drid Williams on nuns and Judith Okely on Gypsies, revised versions of which are now made available here. Subsequently, the Decennial Conference of the Association of Social Anthropologists held in Oxford in 1973 offered an opportunity for some social anthropologists from different academic institutions at home and abroad who were interested in studies of women to meet for informal discussions. At the suggestion of Caroline Ifeka a seminar was arranged outside the official programme of the Conference at which the papers by Drid Williams and myself, and a preliminary version of the one by Caroline Ifeka on Nigerian women published here, were read. It was hoped that a contribution being prepared by another Oxford-trained social anthropologist currently working overseas, Hilary Callan, would be presented *in absentia*, but unfortunately it did not arrive in time; it was subsequently read at the Oxford women's seminar and is now included in this volume. My own paper eventually appeared in *Man* (September 1973). I was persuaded that it might be helpful if it were also made more widely accessible by inclusion in this collection. Having established this sequence of events, an attempt can now be made to outline some of the issues raised, although this brief discussion can by no means do full justice to the papers which, of course, can best speak for themselves.

Edwin Ardener suggested that, with notable exceptions, generally social anthropologists had not studied women with the kind of attention which, as half or more of most populations, they should command. By this statement he hoped to stimulate increased interest in and respect for the study of the female component of society, for at the time this field was relatively neglected and had not everywhere benefited from the current resurgence of interest which has been stimulated by the recent women's social and political movements. He went on to suggest that the inadequate treatment might in part have been due to the fact that in their own societies, and as subjects of research, women are often more 'inarticulate' than men, and thus pose special technical problems for the inquirer. It might be appropriate here to stress that he did not deny that women do 'utter or give tongue'. He was drawing attention to the fact that because the arena of public discourse tends to be characteristically male-dominated and the appropriate language registers often seem to have been 'encoded' by males, women may be at a disadvantage when wishing to express matters of peculiar concern to them. Unless their views are presented in a form acceptable to men, and to women brought up in the male idiom, they will not be given a proper hearing. If this is so, it is possible to speculate further and wonder whether, because of the absence of a suitable code and because of a necessary indirectness rather than spontaneity of expression, women, more often than may be the case with men, might sometimes lack the facility to raise to conscious level their unconscious thoughts. Edwin Ardener suggested that women's ideas or models of the world around them might nevertheless find a way of expression in forms other than direct expository speech, possibly through symbolism in art, myth, ritual, special speech registers, and the like. Following his preliminary theoretical discussion, he drew upon the ethnography of the Bakweri people of Cameroon, in West Africa, in order to extend his argument. He took the Bakweri story of how four friends parted company, to become Water Spirit, Ape, Mouse, and Man, and he set out some implications which can be drawn from this myth. He then described the mermaid cult of the Bakweri women, the various rites performed, and the secret language, and he attempted to interpret the symbolism in the light of his general thesis.

My own paper considers the problem of why Bakweri women, in certain recognizable circumstances, were prepared to act in a manner not usually expected of them. The women, including those who were highly respected in their communities, participated in behaviour which they would normally consider 'shocking', and which we might call 'vulgar' or 'obscene'. It was clear that their participation did not bring them into disgrace as one might expect, but on the contrary, it reinforced their dignity. It is well known, of course, that in some societies behaviour which is normally forbidden may be 'licensed' or prescribed for special occasions (when, for instance, sexual 'liberties' are permitted), but such behaviour could be regarded as having been specially sanctioned or redefined for the occasion by general public opinion as 'permissible' or 'non-obscene'. The difference in the Bakweri case was that the behaviour retained some implication of impropriety—indeed, this was an essential implication—but nevertheless it received the support of otherwise polite and conforming women. Some related material was available from the nearby Balong people, and from a very different group, the Kom, living some hundreds of miles away to the north. Additional information scattered in the social-anthropological literature came to light which also supported the conclusion that the Bakweri women were not as unusual in this respect as might be supposed. On further consideration it also became apparent that certain of these features not only recurred in groups of different African women, they were also exemplified in the words and deeds of certain members of the modern women's liberation movement, in one of its phases, in the West, which I therefore set out.

Judith Okely's paper is based on her experience of living in a caravan alongside Gypsy families. She accompanied the women when they went out calling on houses, selling their handiwork, and on their visits to cafés and public houses. She has taken advantage also of some literature written by them and about them. Quotations are selected which illustrate the ideas which non-Gypsies have had of Gypsies, and these are compared with the notions Gypsies have about themselves and about the host group, the English, among whom live the group which was studied. Of particular interest are her descriptions of the purity rituals which rule the lives of the women.

Although all of us contributing to this volume have had the advantage and the pleasure of living alongside the women described (or, in Caroline Ifeka's case, among their descendants), none has been quite so directly involved in her field as Hilary Callan, who has tackled the difficult task of analysing a group of which she is herself a member. She attempts here to make explicit the implicit and uncodified assumptions of the rights and duties of wives of diplomats. We learn how these wives form part of the diplomatic Mission, and yet at the same time they do not, according to the way in which they are perceived. Their characters, temperaments, and qualifications are supposedly of no concern to the Diplomatic Service because they are private citizens, present in the Mission at the request of their husbands. Yet they are expected to exercise their talents, do their duties, almost as if they were a recognized part of the Service. The delicate subject of the internal organization of the wives' group is also considered. Her study will be of particular value to those who are interested in women who have been brought into association with each other primarily because of a formal, structural relationship between their husbands (wives of dons, or of business or 'company' colleagues, are obvious parallels), but it may also throw light on some features inherent in the situation of all wives.

If most people know little of the expectations of women in far places, or of the thoughts of the Gypsies met on the doorstep, probably even less is known of the preoccupations of those of our countrywomen who live behind the walls of a closed community. Drid Williams introduces us into this world by her study based on fieldwork in a Carmelite Order. We read of the founding of the Order by St Teresa, and of the pattern of the daily life of the nuns. Such is the fascination of the model which she has begun to reveal to us that her paper inspires requests for more data. She has, however, had to resist the temptation to include partial answers to complicated questions (such as those concerning the place given to the body in the life of the nuns, how they come to terms with their sexual identities, and other questions which would also be of particular interest to us in our study of women) since she will be better able to deal with these and other matters more fully in future publications. In the space available here she devotes particular attention to an examination of those intellectual aspects of the nuns' cosmology, or model of the world, which relate to their faith and govern their Rule, matters which are of central concern to them, and which determine the shape of their lives.

Caroline Ifeka's study returns us to West Africa, to the Igbo and Ibibio women of Nigeria. Much of the action of her paper takes place on ground recently fought over in the so-called Biafran War. She takes us back in time to an earlier and less well-known situation of conflict, the women's uprising of the nineteen-twenties. The precolonial system of agricultural production, and certain aspects of the belief system, are recalled, and the changes which took place as a result of the altered circumstances of the colonial period are described. The dramatic events of the women's uprising are sketched, and the various theories which have been put forward to explain the occurrences are reviewed. Caroline Ifeka has brought into the analysis and matched up different sets of information and from this complex material draws her own interpretation of the reasons for the actions of the women and the causes of the war. Although her exposition is centred on one historically documented event, her propositions are of general theoretical interest.

MUTED GROUPS AND DIFFERING ORDERS OF PERCEPTION

Having briefly delineated the ground covered in this volume, some possible theoretical implications of the papers can be drawn out with the aim of providing a tentative general analytical framework in which to view them. Although I have mainly restricted my attention to the material in the volume, I have also made use of some of the ideas on the perception of events developed by Edwin Ardener.[2] His hypothesis is being published elsewhere, so I shall not discuss it in full nor evaluate it here, as I can leave him and others to enter any dialogue which is required. I have, however, applied the theory to the specific data provided in this volume. In so doing I have had to restate it partially, and I must, of course, take responsibility for any distortion which I may have introduced in the process and also for any malformed assumptions which I may have drawn from my consideration of the studies of the other contributors to this volume. These would, of course, be matters for regret.

It might be helpful to note my use of the term 'model' below. By the expression 'model of women', for instance, I mean the set of ideas which together represent women in the minds of those who have 'generated' the model. When the expression 'women's models' is used the reference is to the concepts which women themselves generate in their minds (which will, of course, include 'models of women'). Everyone probably perceives the world in a unique way, but nevertheless people are not so independent that some do not hold some very close ideas, and therefore it is not unreasonable to talk sometimes of a group sharing or generating a common model of society or common models of its components.[3]

As we have noted, Edwin Ardener's paper suggests that women may not have been given the kind of attention by anthropologists which is their due as half of most populations partly because their own societies, and also the world of academic social anthropology, have viewed them under the influence of dominant male systems of perception. The implications are that a society may be dominated or overdetermined by the model (or models) generated by one dominant group within the system. This dominant model may impede the free expression of alternative models of their world which subdominant groups may possess, and perhaps may even inhibit the very generation of such models. Groups dominated in this sense find it necessary to structure their world through the model (or models) of the dominant group, transforming their own models as best they can in terms of the received ones. Individual members of the dominant group will vary, of course, in their competence to express verbally and in other ways the articulation of their model, but there may be presumed to be a considerable degree of 'fit' between the dominant model and their structural position in society. This gives them a great advantage over those in the sub-dominant groups for whom the 'fit' might be very imperfect. As a result, the latter might be relatively more 'inarticulate' when expressing themselves through the idiom of the dominant group, and silent on matters of special concern to them for which no accommodation has been made in it. Although he has suggested that women characteristically form such a relatively 'inarticulate' group in any situation where the interests of the group are at variance with those of men, he also identifies other groups in society, defined by criteria other than sexual, which may also be effectively 'mute'. His views have received considerable support, particularly from younger female social anthropologists, one of whom, Charlotte Hardman, proposed the useful term 'muted group' to describe the kind of conformation in mind, and the term 'counterpart model' for any alternative model such a group may generate.[4]

Judith Okely's paper is of particular relevance in this wider context. In Great Britain the Gypsy population (male and female) is a sub-dominant group, and *prima facie* 'muted' in relation to the dominant structure. Often thought of as 'underprivileged' and to be ripe for 'retraining' and 'resocialization' by some well-meaning Britons (an idea sometimes appearing to gain support from the Gypsies when they adopt 'a subservient and humble posture' in compliance with the expectations of the dominant model) the Gypsies are seen to possess a private view of the world, a counterpart model, in which members of the dominant group are not only *not* ideals to be respected or emulated, but, on the contrary, are seen as polluting. Inside those littered Gypsy encampments are found notions of purity and cleanliness which would be completely perplexing to the typical house-proud member of the surrounding dominant group who might consider the Gypsies to be 'dirty'.

Judith Okely's example introduces another complication, for we see that a subdominant structure which is muted and must operate only in terms acknowledged in the dominant structure may itself overdetermine its own internal substructures, which are thereby made muted. Thus, Gypsy women may be seen to compose a group which is relatively muted within Gypsy society, which in turn is itself relatively muted in a universe which includes the surrounding housedwelling society.[5] An interesting feature, just to complicate matters further, is that seen from the standpoint of the dominant male Gypsy model, non-Gypsies (both men and women) and Gypsy women are, in certain respects, all seen as potentially destructive of or dangerous to the dominant Gypsy structure. Gypsy women, while openly subscribing to the dominant Gypsy model, are able to exploit this feature and other ambiguities in their placing in the structures, as Judith Okely's paper will show. They conduct their lives with an independence for which no recognition is allowed in the dominant Gypsy model, having themselves generated a counterpart model of possible behaviour, not admitted to the general public domain and therefore 'muted', all of their own. Judith Okely's paper also illustrates the fact that counterpart models (whether generated by women or by ethnically or otherwise defined groups) are not generated independently of those of the dominant structure, but are to some extent shaped by them, a point also made by Caroline Ifeka.

In a number of papers [6] Edwin Ardener has suggested that we should not imagine that the models which any group generates should all be thought of as of the same theoretical order. He envisages that most of the models which quickly come to mind are built up from the ingredients which daily life provides (*à la* 'bricolage' of Lévi-Strauss) from whatever resources are available at any given time. Our ideas thus depend on what the context of the moment produces. We arrange what we perceive into some sort of order, pattern, or model. For instance, we identify a number of conjoined pieces of wood as a 'table', we interpret a series of actions and collection of artifacts as a 'hijack', an assembly of bricks and mortar once classified as a slum we may perceive to be a 'bijou residence', and so forth. The process of making order out of those selected elements of which we make ourselves aware is continuous. We can see that if this is so it must also be circular because we tend to register most easily those 'bits' of perception which we recognize to be potentially capable of being related to each other.

Although today's events are always unique, nevertheless there seem to be some underlying continuities, which may be summed up by the common tag *plus ça change, plus c'est la même chose*. To explain this Edwin Ardener suggests in his theory of structures of thought that we should envisage the human perceptual process to be of more than one order. The changing categories of society at the surface of events, which he terms the 's-structures' (from 'syntagmatic'—the terminology need not detain us here), are themselves shaped by other more fundamental, more persistent structures, which he calls 'p-structures' (from 'para-digmatic'), which are located in the programmatic aspects of the particular society. These may be regarded as frameworks, or models, or sets of ground rules, which are linked in certain ways to those categories and ideas which we generate to help us order our experience of daily life. So-called 'stereotypes' belong to the class of 's-structures': by definition the term implies specific form. The underlying continuities or 'p-structures' are more general, usually unconscious, ideas which are realized in life only in various guises which depend for their specificity on the context of the moment, that is, in the form of 's-structures' which change with the fashions, circumstances, and times.

If we accept the proposed distinction between dominant and muted groups as a basis for discussion, it may well be that while both groups generate ideas of social reality at the deepest ('p-structural') level, muted groups find that, unlike dominant groups, they must inhibit the generation of ideas close to or at the level of the surface of events ('s-structures'), since the conceptual space in which they would lie is over-run by the dominant model of events generated by the dominant group. It has been suggested by Ardener that in an autonomous (dominant) system the two orders of structures (dominant 'p' and dominant 's') are linked by certain transformational rules. If this is so we should expect a muted system composed of the 'p-structures' of a muted group and the imposed 's-structures' of a dominant group to be held together by more complex logical relationships. If such a system is to be envisaged without a collapse, some adequate binding relationships must nevertheless obtain, so perhaps we must assume that generally muted groups manage to forge rickety or cumbersome links between the two orders of structures.

It might help to understand this if we imagine a dominant system in which recognition is given to an 's-structure' which we shall label '4', which is a transformation of a given 'p-structure' labelled, say, '2 + 2', with which it is considered to be in an equal relationship. Let us summarize this and say the dominant system is: '2 + 2' (equals) '4'. Then suppose that the 'p-structure' which an associated muted group generates is not '2 + 2' but '3 + 3'. In order to come to terms with the required 's-structure' '4', this group must adjust its perceptual process so that instead of the simple '2 + 2' (equals) '4' it must generate the system '3 + 3' (if 2 is taken away equals) '4', or the like. Thus the dominant and the muted groups may each generate different structural premises, and still come to accept a common statement of perception.

In such systems, of course, only the dominant concept '4' is normally perceived. This might have a number of alternative realizations (for instance '6 − 2', or '2 × 2' or '10 − 7 + 1') according to circumstances. We could further imagine that the dominant group might never generate, and recognition might never be given to '6', nor its alternatives '5 + 1', '3 × 2', etc. (that is: to those statements which the subdominant group might most economically generate), and the group is thereby 'muted'.

It is difficult to give apt illustrations from life without overconcretization ('p-structures', as I understand them, are not casily describable since once we clothe them in words they tend to take the form of 's-structures' and thus our purpose is defeated). We have to rely upon imperfect analogies, such as the one just given. But we might, nevertheless, venture to express the problem with which Hilary Callan's paper grapples in these terms. The prime importance of the furtherance of the interests of the Embassy is a concept presented to the wives by the dominant group. For the wives to generate other overriding objectives is not acceptable in the ideology of the Mission. A wife who wishes to establish an independent career must therefore 'encode' or 'transform' her objective in terms of its value to the Mission. Her clear perception of purpose may be clouded or overdetermined in this way by the dominant ideology; the process of generation of her ideas is thus made more complicated. The 'premiss of dedication' which concerns Hilary Callan may be analogous to an adjustment in the system of members of a muted group which transforms their own unconscious perceptions into such conscious ideas as will accord with those generated by the dominant group. The 'premiss of dedication' is like that part of the transformation or mode of specification which effects the stifling of unacceptable statements in the discourse of a muted group. Most of the wives of diplomats seem to accept this situation without stress, although as Hilary Callan's paper hints, there are inconsistencies and incompatibilities which still trouble some.

But if, to continue our speculations, we may imagine that, generally, muted groups do manage to establish transformational links between their own perceptual structures and those of the world of events presented to them by the dominant ideology, perhaps there are times when they cannot, and then various repercussions are made manifest. Caroline Ifeka's case study of the Igbo women's war may possibly be understood as an example where such links became so overstrained that orderly conduct became impossible. Thus, if one were to put her argument in terms of structures or models of different orders of generation, one might see her paper as an attempt to explain the effects of a disjuncture between the underlying 'p-structures' of women's model of women (which persisted from the time when traditional Igbo patterns of production existed at the surface of events) and the new ephemeral models encountered in a changing system of production. Perhaps the two could not be satisfactorily related one to another, the links could not be forged. Caroline Ifeka's paper demonstrates that the introduction of taxation for women, supposedly one of the main causes of the militancy, is to be seen as a contingent event only. In terms of our discussion, it acted as a trigger on the tensions created by the disjuncture.

The data set out by Caroline Ifeka suggest that the traditional system

xv

of subsistence agriculture, which was a major preoccupation in the women's lives, offered them an analogy with themselves. It sustained the physical continuity of the group, and it thus exemplified their *raison d'être*. Their identities were therefore closely linked in their minds to the land and its fertility. But when women entered large-scale cash-crop production, processing, and distribution, their activities did not merely ensure the health and continuity of the group. They produced surpluses which could be transformed into power, prestige, and the like, thus involving them with factors of quite a different kind. Igbo men and women had traditionally operated in different political conceptual spaces. Unlike men, women could move about freely in times of conflict between villages: a very important distinction and advantage. In the different political space in which men operated, power and prestige could change hands, concessions could be extorted and conceded; political advantage was balanced by political loss in the overall male system. Women were not directly concerned with either; they operated in another 'space'.

When taxation was introduced for men, although disliked it did not fundamentally challenge the underlying male political system, the gains and losses in the colonial confrontation were compatible with it. But when women were suddenly thought to be about to be taxed, the integrity of the women's model of women was threatened, their distinctive space was intruded upon. Dragged out of it, the women felt their separate identity to be challenged. It seems that it was not merely that they objected to the 'cost' of taxation (as Caroline Ifeka suggests, they may even have been contributing towards the taxes paid by the men anyway) although this may well have been an irritant. More important seems to have been the fact that they were to be defined as persons liable for tax. One witness used the telling phrase that the conviction that women were to be taxed 'stirred them to the depths of their being' (see below p. 150). The taxation issue, therefore, while being, as Caroline Ifeka suggests, a trigger able to fire an already potentially explosive situation, was a singularly apposite one. It reminded women that the new circumstances gave them an identity which placed them in the male system, depriving them of some female advantages while putting them at a disadvantage compared to men. As Caroline Ifeka points out, they were turned into men as far as the penalties went without appearing to get any equivalent political gains. If the taxation or another catalytic issue had not arisen, the Igbo women might or might not have been able to forge a bridge across the disjuncture between their own deep models of women and the new models generated at the surface of events until the models could be mutually reconciled. Caroline Ifeka's paper is valuable in focusing our attention beyond contingent events, beyond economic considerations of real importance in themselves, to the underlying perceptual and symbolic systems which give them significance.[7]

We could envisage, perhaps, that the construction and maintenance

xvi

of any coherent conceptual system conjoining the deep models of a muted group with the surface models of the dominant group would require from the members of the muted group the investment of a great deal of disciplined mental energy. This investment may be one reason why they are often seen to be more conservative than members of dominant groups, even clinging to models which seem to disadvantage them. It is often the most insecure and underprivileged sections of societies (so defined according to classifications drawn from the dominant system) which seem to resist change most strongly. But after lifetimes of adapting in order to achieve a precarious accommodation, should we be surprised if the prospect of beginning again should be resisted? For some muted groups whose members seem to exhibit an acceptance of, even apparent contentment with, their lot in situations which those outside the system, or even sometimes those within the dominant structure, imagine would be intolerable, another explanation is possible. While professing to support the values and codes of behaviour embodied in the dominant system, perhaps their own sense of value derives from a muted counterpart system, of which they may not themselves even be completely aware. For instance, the principal measure for social success or for other satisfactions in the counterpart model may differ from that of the model of the dominant group, and therefore their acquiescence at being placed low down on the latter's scale for success may occur because the placing seems unimportant or irrelevant to them, since they may not necessarily be 'unsuccessful' or 'unsatisfied' according to the logic of their own muted model.[8]

SPECIALIZED OR 'UN-NATURAL' FEMALE GROUPS AND FEMALE UNIVERSALS

Some of the studies here concern groups whose membership is ascribed by birth. Hilary Callan's group of wives, and the community of nuns described by Drid Williams, are not biologically self-reproducing. They are groups which must be joined, to which recruits must come from outside. Membership is not the automatic outcome of the line of least resistance: a conscious choice must be made. While they share this characteristic, there is a major difference between the two cases in their attitudes to recruitment. Not all the women who become wives of diplomats can be assumed to do so primarily because they want to be diplomats' wives as such (although this might possibly be a consideration for some, others may even dislike conforming): the determining model for most is probably associated with the marriage union. In the case of the nuns we may more confidently presume that recruitment is determined primarily by the desire of the would-be novices to become nuns, and to conform to their model and expectations of a nun.

Whatever logical necessity is envisaged by the nuns themselves, to outsiders the group seems essentially artificial or 'un-natural'. The

xvii

group exists as a creation generated by the thoughts and the consequential actions of the nuns. The nuns could make void their Order whenever they wish. It endures because the nuns think it should; it is essentially a creation of the intellect; it exists because of the ideal model in the minds of the nuns. If the Order of nuns may seem in one sense artificial (that is, it is not found in 'nature'), the nuns themselves are certainly not 'unnatural' in their model-making process, and in the way they order their world according to their own system; on the contrary, they apply themselves with more conscious dedication and precision than is usual for most of us to processes which with varying degrees of unawareness we all implement continuously.

Since Drid Williams's study has so powerfully reminded us of the primacy of the model in the case of the nuns, we may wonder whether our category 'women' might not also be entirely an intellectual creation which one day may disappear. At the least its realization on the surface of events may change in due course so radically that it would be almost unrecognizable to many alive today. As it is now, since there is so much variation in our present-day models of women, we may well wonder whether they have anything in common which makes them distinctly female. If there is so much variation, wherein lies their womanhood? It would be very easy to conclude that, since models of women are so very different in detail one from another, there are no specific common characteristics.

Clearly there are some biological bases used for the definitions of women in society, but the extent and influence of the biological differentiations between men and women are matters on which as yet we know very little. We do not really understand how supposedly measurable biological differences are related to those we cannot yet easily analyse, such as emotional and intellectual processes. There may or may not be social correlates which vary, in some regular way that we cannot yet perceive, with measurable physical characteristics. Of course, even when discussing the biological bases that have been used for defining women in society, we still come up against problems because various societies may not allocate the same physical properties to women, and in any case 'measurement' itself is determined by an arbitrary set of distinctions. It may also be possible that physical differentiations (whether 'real' or 'socially perceived') are merely arbitrary markers which have been found useful for setting up *social* oppositions, and it is the opposition to men that is the basis of womanhood, however characterized in the world of events. Because of this opposition, women *experience* the world differently from men, regardless of whether or not innate differences are significant. There is no space here to enter the wide debate on the relationship between the categories identified as 'sex' and 'gender'.[9] It is enough to note that our present ideas about women seem to require the accommodation of both concepts.

The scale of the task of understanding 'women' (or any other defined group in society) is daunting, but it should not prevent us from taking such steps as we can in the hope that surer ways forward can be found in the future. By open-minded examination of as many women's models as we are able, we may not only locate interesting differences between them, but may also stumble upon possible points of congruence. We should not be disappointed if, should women's models of the world (or those of any other muted group) be elicited, they were found to resemble in the main those of the dominant structures with which they are associated. It is the small deviations from any norm which may be crucial. Just as the pinch of caraway seed may transform a basic recipe, or a drop of dye may alter a hue, so any small unique differences in world-views may make 'all the difference'.

Given the welter of differing social manifestations, how, it may be asked, can we hope to identify any underlying structures? The possibility of eliciting a common model from phenomena which do not exactly match in all details appeared credible after having considered certain selected patterns of activity and modes of expression exhibited by several culturally distinct groups of women, as described in my paper below. Although none of the sets of information on the different groups were exactly the same, there were enough common elements to make me suspect that there might be some possible underlying common pattern, which would be available to us if we could but elicit it. At the level of the surface of events, there were differences in the way these features were made manifest, of course, due to the differences in circumstances, but these isolated groups of women seemed nevertheless to share some responses. The patterns of behaviour, although not one was exactly like another, each seemed to display parts of a model which they possessed in common. To understand this one may imagine a set of screens in which gaps appear in different places. Through one screen an eye and an ear can be discerned, through another a different ear and a nose, and through another an eye, a nose and mouth, and so forth. Each glimpse is different in detail, but given enough evidence we can construct the structure of a face lying behind each screen. No two screens are alike, no two mouths are alike, and yet a hidden model of a face is common to all. So, in trying to discern common underlying features in patterns of thought and behaviour in society, we must reconstruct a model from a series of partial manifestations. In the end we have to risk an imaginative leap, to make a guess at the underlying structure, making adjustments as more 'screens' become available for study, more insights are gained or better logic prevails. Sometimes, as seems to have happened to me since some of my propositions were first outlined, there is the pleasure of coming across the generation of new statements of thought, or of events, which provide further examples of what has already been seen, or, more excitingly, give examples of features whose possible forms have been deduced; sometimes one must abandon cherished hypotheses altogether or make crucial realignments. It is by these methods that we attempt to elicit those underlying continuities termed 'p-structures'. They cannot be directly perceived and have no independent existence since they can only take form when 'clothed' in models at the surface of events (the 's-structures'), and it is by the study of the latter that we reveal the former. The one is inherent in the other.[10]

Of course, the process is a little more complex than just described, because we are not provided with discrete screens each displaying manifestations from only one model. Our perceptual experience is continuous. It is as if elements from innumerable conceptual models are presented to us, as each instance dissolves into the next. We sort out our perceptual experience and arrange it into manageable orderings or models as best we can and as best serves our purposes. The 'models' which anthropologists put forward in order to share their analyses are themselves only deliberate attempts to do this.

In my own study of militant women I have described certain patterns of behaviour and techniques of communication which have been employed at certain times by different groups of women. I have made certain analytical distinctions in order to sort out the mass of material available and to focus attention on particular aspects. I make a distinction between 'women's rights' and 'women's liberation', for instance. This might not seem controversial to some now, but, despite my having said that militant women are usually concerned with both aspects, some have assumed that I intended the dichotomy to be a rigid one. Of course, women, both in Africa and elsewhere, pursue what they see as their 'rights', not only through the institutions available to them, but also, when these fail, by attacking them. The position taken here in isolating certain special features does not conflict with the present-day militancy. Rather it should illuminate it while remaining to some degree able to detach itself from the particular demands of any single conflict. Some of the manifestations on which I concentrate in my paper seem to appear with less frequency, or in other guises, in England at least, at the present time; others seem more prevalent. The manner in which women communicate changes according to circumstances. My general appreciation of the literature of the modern movement will be evident in my paper. It is not my purpose to review all the recent work here. Many of the approaches are very interesting (e.g. Sheila Rowbotham, 1973, among others), and are often in harmony with some of the discussions in this volume. When my paper was first conceived, the introduction of the new literature into it was intended to place these writings more evidently on the academic map, as academic data, as social phenomena worthy of dispassionate study. They seemed hardly to be taken seriously in some intellectual circles at the time. In a further work now in hand I hope to show correspondences between the modes of expression of hostility employed by the women described and those used by other groups in society, defined by religious and other criteria.

CONCLUSION

The general theoretical approaches in this volume seem to offer possible ways forward in our particular field of research. The 'position of women' type of study often documents how women are placed in an 'inferior' position in the received system of such-and-such a society *vis-à-vis* men. These studies can be very valuable and further research along these lines will continue to be fruitful. Nevertheless, after we have located the model of women in the overall ideological framework of a dominant structure we are still left with many features requiring analysis, and not least of them is, as has been stressed, the often little defined and seemingly vague, possibly repressed, alternative ideas which women may have about the world, including those about themselves, which may easily be overlooked. We need to examine carefully the models of both the dominant and the muted groups in any society in order that we may learn more about the relationship between them and how this became established.[11] It is important to remember that the relationship will not necessarily be a constant one. Neither may we assume that the relationship between any particular members of the groups will necessarily be direct images of the relationship between the groups to which they are assigned.

We might note that the present way of distinguishing a 'dominant' from a 'muted' or ill-articulated model, does not impose upon us an obligation to talk in terms of 'domination by men' or 'the oppression of women' where this is taken to be a purposeful male activity, although of course such interpretations might well be appropriate in many situations. Clearly, the bee crushed by the passing elephant is at a relative, indeed a fatal, disadvantage compared to the larger beast, but merely to say that it has been 'oppressed' by the elephant seems to be missing some essential points. The same would, of course, be true if similar statements were made about a bee which fatally stung an elephant. We should note that a dominant group may not necessarily be demographically more populous than a muted group, which may provide the majority of a population. It should also be possible to discuss the relationship between models in terms of dominance, without any necessary implication that the group generating the dominant model has been able to do so only through a monopoly of sin (or, for that matter, by possessing special virtue).

We should beware of assuming, as some might have done in the past, that greater theoretical interest must lie in a dominant model than in one generated by a muted group: a society could be envisaged (and such may well exist) where knowledge of the dominant model would be less helpful in understanding what is happening at any given time than would a knowledge of the less well-articulated models of the muted groups in that world, were this information accessible to us. A study of muted groups is certainly not a subordinate kind of social anthropology, although we may concede that it may be a difficult one. At a time when it is being proclaimed that many assumptions and values which have dominated our own lives in recent years are being challenged, the study of other values and assumptions present in obscured models will, it is hoped, find a responsive reception. This is a task, which is only at the beginning, for to perceive beyond the reflective screens of a dominant structure is a difficult challenge.

Notes

The contributors to this volume would especially like to thank Diana Burfield for help in seeing this volume through the press, and Malcolm Crick for preparing the index.

1 To Audrey Richards herself, to the editor Jean La Fontaine, and to Tavistock Publications.

2 Within the limited aims of this introduction I have confined my remarks to the works of contributors to this symposium. The approaches presented here are intended to increase the number of possible ways of considering women in society, not to impose further constraints. Our field of research has been, as it were, momentarily held still to allow possible significant patterns to be discerned, one or two at a time. That societies are more complicated than can be expressed in any single short paper should be evident. Other writers have done work which is pertinent to our chosen field; because it has not been reviewed here, does not mean that it is considered to be irrelevant.

3 The use of the term 'model' is not entirely satisfactory, and I make no attempt here to define the term. It is intended to refer not only to our ideas about so-called 'real' 'things' and 'people' as discrete entities, but also ideas about such abstract categories as 'greed', or 'pride', or 'nationhood', and so forth. Others may prefer and have used different terminology when considering this field of study, and some may apply the term 'model' differently. There is a considerable body of literature which discusses the term, but this does not seem to be the place to enter into the discussion. Readers may make their own substitutions should they wish to translate into terminology more to their approval.

4 In Ardener's terms, the *dominant group* and the *dominant model* together form the *dominant structure*. It follows that the *muted group* and the *counterpart model* together form a *muted* or *subdominant structure*. It should be noted that one dominant structure may overdetermine a number of muted structures. He gives attention on pages 19–27 below to some critical comments which were recently published and clarifies certain misinterpretations and other matters.

5 Just as Gypsy men may be 'muted' in one context and 'dominant' in another, women who tend to be 'muted' relative to men may be 'dominant' in certain circumstances. Their opportunities for generating a dominant ideology of their own, seem, however, generally to be more infrequent than is the case for men. Women may sometimes be in a dominant position, to find that the only ideology which they have acquired any competence in handling has not been generated independently by themselves, but is one acquired from the group most commonly dominant.

6 Ardener (1970, 1971, 1973).

7 Ifeka places greater emphasis on the symbolic weight of the female powers of reproduction in women's identity than I do in my paper. In the Igbo case, this is shown to be a result of male control. Some of the material I present illustrates women asserting their claim to an honour which does not depend solely on their reproductive capacity, and I lay particular stress upon certain 'non-functional' aspects of the feminine sense of self.

8 For members socialized in terms of the dominant model to force recognition of the values of the dominant group in such a way as further to obscure their muted counterpart model, even if done with the best intention of helping individuals to improve their placing in the dominant structure, might sometimes be a disservice. This would be especially true if after the muted group has accepted the value system of the dominant group, the latter abandons it and generates another one similar to that from which the muted group has just been weaned!

9 See, for instance, Anne Oakley (1972).

10 They are 'simultaneities' (Ardener 1973).

11 Some interesting biographical and other work has begun in the field of English social history which concentrates on sections of the population previously largely neglected in the mainstream of historical writings. Members of the women's anthropology group seminar at Oxford, like those in other comparable groups, have also produced a substantial number of new analyses recently. Besides those of us represented in this volume, Juliet Blair, Helen Callaway, Kirsten Hastrup and Harriet Sibisi, for instance, have papers in the *Journal of the Anthropological Society of Oxford*. Further publications by members of the seminar are forthcoming.

References

ARDENER, E. W. 1970. Witchcraft, Economics, and the Continuity of Belief. In M. Douglas (ed.), *Witchcraft Confessions and Accusations*. London: Tavistock.
— 1971. The New Anthropology and its Critics. *Man* (N.S.) **6**: 449–467.
— 1973. Some Outstanding Problems in the Analysis of Events. Paper presented at the Decennial Conference of the ASA (publication forthcoming).
BLAIR, J. 1974. An Apparent Paradox in Mental Evolution. *Journal of the Anthropological Society of Oxford*, V (2).
CALLAWAY, H. 1975. Review Article: African Women in Towns. *Journal of the Anthropological Society of Oxford*, VI (1).
HASTRUP, K. 1974a. The Sexual Boundary—Purity: Virginity and Hetero-sexuality. *Journal of the Anthropological Society of Oxford*, V (3).
— 1974b. We Men and Women. Unpublished monograph. University of Copenhagen.
— 1975. The Sexual Boundary—Danger: Transvesticism and Homosexuality. *Journal of the Anthropological Society of Oxford*, VI (1).
LA FONTAINE, J. S. (ed.) 1972. *The Interpretation of Ritual*. London: Tavistock.
OAKLEY, A. 1972. *Sex, Gender, and Society*. London: Temple Smith.
ROWBOTHAM, S. 1973. *Woman's Consciousness, Man's World*. Harmondsworth: Penguin.
SIBISI, H. 1975. Some Notions of 'Purity' and 'Impurity' among the Zulu. *Journal of the Anthropological Society of Oxford*, VI (1).

Edwin Ardener

Belief and the Problem of Women

THE PROBLEM

The problem of women has not been solved by social anthropologists. Indeed the problem itself has been often examined only to be put aside again for want of a solution, for its intractability is genuine. The problem of women is not the problem of 'the position of women', although valuable attention has been paid to this subject by Professor Evans-Pritchard (1965). I refer to the problem that women present to social anthropologists. It falls into (1) a technical and (2) an analytical part. Here is a human group that forms about half of any population and is even in a majority at certain ages: particularly at those which for so many societies are the 'ruling' ages—the years after forty. Yet however apparently competently the female population has been studied in any particular society, the results in understanding are surprisingly slight, and even tedious. With rare exceptions, women anthropologists, of whom so much was hoped, have been among the first to retire from the problem. Dr Richards was one of the few to return to it at the height of her powers. In *Chisungu* (1956) she produced a study of a girls' rite that raised and anticipated many of the problems with which this paper will deal.[1] While I shall illustrate my central point by reference to a parallel set of rites among the Bakweri of Cameroon, through which women and girls join the world of the mermaid spirits, this paper is less about ethnography than about the interpretation of such rites through the symbolism of the relations between men and women.

The methods of social anthropology as generally illustrated in the classical monographs of the last forty years have purported to 'crack the code' of a vast range of societies, without any direct reference to the female group. At the level of 'observation' in fieldwork, the behaviour of women has, of course, like that of men, been exhaustively plotted: their marriages, their economic activity, their rites, and the rest. When we come to that second or 'meta' level of fieldwork, the vast body of debate, discussion, question and answer, that social anthropologists really depend upon to give conviction to their interpretations, there is a real imbalance. We are, for practical purposes, in a male world. The study of women is on a level little higher than the study of the ducks and fowls they commonly own—a mere bird-

1

watching indeed. It is equally revealing and ironical that Lévi-Strauss (1963: 61) should write: 'For words do not speak, while women do.' For the truth is that women rarely speak in social anthropology in any but that male sense so well exemplified by Lévi-Strauss's own remark: in the sense of merely uttering or giving tongue. It is the very inarticulateness of women that is the technical part of the problem they present. In most societies the ethnographer shares this problem with its male members. The brave failure (with rare exceptions) of even women anthropologists to surmount it really convincingly (and their evident relief when they leave the subject of women) suggests an obvious conclusion. Those trained in ethnography evidently have a bias towards the kinds of model that men are ready to provide (or to concur in) rather than towards any that women might provide. If the men appear 'articulate' compared with the women, it is a case of like speaking to like. To pursue the logic where it leads us: if ethnographers (male and female) want only what the men can give, I suggest it is because the men consistently tend, when pressed, to give a bounded model of society such as ethnographers are attracted to. But the awareness that women appear as lay figures in the men's drama (or like the photographic cutouts in filmed crowd-scenes) is always dimly present in the ethnographer's mind. Lévi-Strauss, with his perennial ability to experience ethnographic models, thus expressed no more than the truth of all those models when he saw women as items of exchange inexplicably and inappropriately giving tongue.

The technical treatment of the problem is as follows. It is commonly said, with truth, that ethnographers with linguistic difficulties of any kind will find that the men of a society are generally more experienced in bridging this kind of gap than are the women. Thus, as a matter of ordinary experience, interpreters, partial bilinguals, or speakers of a vehicular language are more likely to be found among men than among women. For an explanation of this we are referred to statements about the political dominance of men, and their greater mobility. These statements, in their turn, are referred ultimately to the different biological roles of the two sexes. The cumulative effect of these explanations is then: to the degree that communication between ethnographer and people is imperfect, that imperfection drives the ethnographer in greater measure towards men.

This argument while stressing the technical aspect does not dispose of the problem even in its own terms, although we may agree that much ethnography (more than is generally admitted) is affected by factors of this type. It is, however, a common experience that women still 'do not speak' even when linguistic aspects are constant. Ethnographers report that women cannot be reached so easily as men: they giggle when young, snort when old, reject the question, laugh at the topic, and the like. The male members of a society frequently see the ethnographer's difficulties as simply a caricature of their own daily case. The technical argument about the incidence of interpreters and so on is therefore really only a confirmation of the importance of the analytical part of the problem. The 'articulateness' of men and of ethnographers is alike, it would appear, in more ways than one. In the same way we may regard as inadequate the more refined explanation that ethnographers 'feed' their own models to their male informants, who are more susceptible for the same technical reasons, and who then feed them back to the ethnographer. That something of this sort does happen is again not to be doubted, but once again the susceptibility of the men is precisely the point. Nor is it an answer to the problem to discuss what might happen if biological facts were different; arguments like 'women through concern with the realities of childbirth and child-rearing have less time for or less propensity towards the making of models of society, for each other, for men, or for ethnographers' (the 'Hot Stove' argument) are again only an expression of the situation they try to explain.

We have here, then, what looked like a technical problem: the difficulty of dealing ethnographically with women. We have, rather, an analytical problem of this sort: if the models of a society made by most ethnographers tend to be models derived from the male portion of that society, how does the symbolic weight of that other mass of persons—half or more of a normal human population, as we have accepted—express itself? Some will maintain that the problem as it is stated here is exaggerated, although only an extremist will deny its existence completely. It may be that individual ethnographers have received from women a picture of a society very similar to the picture given by men. This possibility is conceded, but the female evidence provides in such cases confirmation of a male model which requires no confirmation of this type. The fact is that no one could come back from an ethnographic study of 'the X', having talked only *to* women, and *about* men, without professional comment and some self-doubt. The reverse can and does happen constantly. It is not enough to see this merely as another example of 'injustice to women'. I prefer to suggest that the models of society that women can provide are not of the kind acceptable at first sight to men or to ethnographers, and specifically that, unlike either of these sets of professionals, they do not so readily see society bounded from nature. They lack the metalanguage for its discussion. To put it more simply: they will not necessarily provide a model for society as a unit that will contain both men and themselves. They may indeed provide a model in which women and nature are outside men and society.

I have now deliberately exaggerated, in order to close the gap in a different way. The dominance of men's models of a society in traditional ethnography I take to be accepted. However, men and women do communicate with each other, and are at least aware of each other's models. It has been furthermore the study by ethnographers of myth and belief, collected no doubt, as formerly, largely from men, that has provided the kinds of insights that now make it possible to reopen the

3

problem of women. Much of this material still discusses women from a male viewpoint. Women are classed as inauspicious, dangerous, and the like. But models of society as a symbolic system made from this kind of data are (it is no surprise to note) of a rather different type from the ethnographic (male) models deriving from the older type of fieldwork (e.g. Needham 1958, 1960, 1967). So much so that many social anthropologists are unable to accept them as 'true' models, that is 'true to reality', where 'reality' is a term of art for what fieldwork reveals. I suggest, on the contrary, that a fieldwork problem of the first magnitude is illuminated. Indeed the astounding deficiency of a method, supposedly objective, is starkly revealed: the failure to include half the people in the total analysis.

STATEMENT AND OBSERVATION

At the risk of labouring the obvious, but to avoid being buried in a righteous avalanche of fieldnotes, I say this yet again with a diagram (*Figure 1*).

Because of an interesting failing in the functionalist observational model, statements *about* observation were always added to the ethnographer's own observations. To take a simple case:

Figure 1

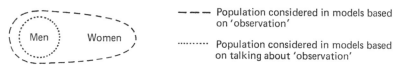

— — — Population considered in models based on 'observation'

·········· Population considered in models based on talking about 'observation'

typically an ethnographer 'observed' a number of marriages and divorces, and heard a number of statements about the frequency of divorce, and then cumulated these quasi-quantitatively into a general statement about divorce frequency. So he did in other less easily detectable ways, and in some of those ways he may still do so today. This confusion had many serious consequences; in particular the difficulty of dealing with statements that were not about 'observation' at all (relegated to 'belief' or the like). For our purposes here, it is enough to note that statements made by the male segment were *about* both males and females. The functionalist confusion of the two levels at any time obscured the inadequacy of the total analysis as far as women were concerned. Since the analysis was always thought to represent observation, or to be checked by observation, it was hard for anyone with fieldnotes on women to see that they were effectively missing in the total analysis or, more precisely, they were there in the same way as were the Nuer's cows, who were observed but also did not speak.

The students of symbolism cannot be accused of any functionalist bias towards the primacy of observation. Functionalist fieldwork was

unhappy with myths precisely because they made statements that conflicted with, could not be cumulated to, objective measures of economic
or political status. Not being faced with this mistaken necessity, the
symbolists, almost incidentally, rediscovered women, who loom rather
large in their material. In view of the absence of conscient women from
the older models, this gains further significance, and suggests a further
step, which is taken here. The study of symbolism uncovers certain
valuations of women—some of which make more sense if women, not
men, had made them (they conflict with the social models of men). Old
women ('old wives' tales') or mothers (we may extend this analysis even
to the lore and language of children) acquire in the world of symbolism
something more like their demographic conspicuity. Furthermore, in a
field situation poor communication with women in this area is not so
often complained of. I here contend that much of this symbolism in fact
enacts that female model of the world which has been lacking, and
which is different from the models of men in a particular dimension: the
placing of the boundary between society and nature.

I suppose in Lévi-Strauss's terms this would place women in an
ideologically more primitive position than men. It is not a necessary
conclusion. It means something like this: the notion of themselves in
society is imposed by its members upon a relatively unbounded continuum in ways which involve the setting up of a multitude of bounded
categories, the bounds being marked by taboo, ridicule, pollution,
category inversion and the rest, so ably documented of late by social
anthropologists (Douglas 1966; Leach 1961, 1964). The tension between
'culture' and 'nature' (the 'wild') is to be understood as an outcome of
this struggle, from which no human beings are free. The appreciation of
the symbolic stress on the division between society and nature derives
from Lévi-Strauss (1949), and lies behind much of his later work,
including the three volumes of *Mythologiques* (1964, 1966, 1968). Lévi-
Strauss now prefers the terminology 'nature' and 'culture' (1967: 3;
trans. 1969: 3). Of late he has also been concerned to state that the
distinction lacks objective criteria (1967: 12). This concern seems surprising since it is easily resolved as Lévi-Strauss himself shows:

> [T]he contrast of nature and culture would be neither a primeval fact,
> nor a concrete aspect of universal order. Rather it should be seen as
> an artificial creation of culture, a protective rampart thrown up around
> it because it only felt able to assert its existence and uniqueness by
> destroying all the links that led back to its original association with
> the other manifestations of life (1967: xvii; trans. 1969: xxix).

Within this wider task men have to bound themselves in relation both
to women and to nature.

Since women are biologically not men, it would be surprising if they
bounded themselves against nature in the same way as men do. Yet we
have seen that the men's models are characteristically dominant in

5

ethnography. If men are the ones who become aware of 'other cultures' more frequently than do women, it may well be that they are likely to develop metalevels of categorization that enable them at least to consider the necessity to bound themselves-and-their-women from other-men-and-their-women. Thus all such ways of bounding society against society, including our own, may have an inherent maleness. The first level is still recognizable, however, in the tendency to slip back to it from the metalevel: that is, to class other men and their wives with nature; as the Germans say, as *Naturmensch* (cf. Lévi-Strauss 1967: xvi). If men, because of their political dominance, may tend purely pragmatically to 'need' total bounding models of either type, women may tend to take over men's models when they share the same definitional problems as men. But the models set up by women bounding themselves are not encompassed in those men's models. They still subsist, and both sexes through their common humanity are aware of the contradictions. In the social anthropologist's data the process can be more clearly viewed.

MAN, MOUSE, APE, AND WATER SPIRIT

According to a story of the Bakweri of Cameroon (in a male recension): 'Moto, Ewaki, Eto, and Mojili were always quarrelling and agreed to decide by a test which of them was to remain in the town and which should go into the bush. All were to light fires in their houses in the morning and the person whose fire was still burning on their return from the farms in the evening was to be the favoured one. Moto being more cunning than the others built a fire with big sticks properly arranged, whereas they only built with small dry sticks, and so his was the only fire that was still alight on their return in the evening. Thus Moto remained in the town and became Man. Ewaki and Eto went into the bush and became the Ape and the Mouse. Mojili was driven into the water and became a water spirit.' [2] *Moto* (Common Bantu **muntu*) is the ordinary Bakweri word for 'human being of either sex', and thus includes 'woman'. Ewaki, Eto, and Mojili, who are opposed to Moto by reason of his special skill with fire, lack of which relegates them to the bush, are in Bakweri belief all associated with women and their children, whom they attract into their domain. Mojili is responsible for young girls becoming mermaids (*liengu*, plural *maengu*) who are dangerous to men, and whose husbands are *eto* (pl. *veto*), the rats; while the attraction of human children to the apes of the forest is so great that the word *ewaki* must not be mentioned in front of children under seven, in case they fall sick and die. Mojili's name has the same effect. Rites exist to control these manifestations (E. Ardener 1956).[3]

The possible marginality of women when men are defining 'the wild' is evident. Thus the idea of the denizens of the wild, outside Moto's village, being a danger or attraction to women and their offspring is comprehensible in a male model of the universe, in which female reproductive powers do not fall under male control. This is, however, inadequate. Bakweri women themselves bound their world as including the wild that Moto excluded. They go through rites by which they become *liengu* mermaid spirits, or spirits of the forest, generally in adolescence, and retain this feature of womanhood throughout their lives. The story of Moto gives the clue, for the three excluded 'animal' brothers all have the human gift of fire. Although the men bound off 'mankind' from nature, the women persist in overlapping into nature again. For men among the Bakweri this overlapping symbolic area is clearly related to women's reproductive powers. Since these powers are for women far from being marginal, but are of their essence as women, it would seem that a woman's model of the world would also treat them as central. When we speak of Bakweri belief we must therefore recognize a man's sector and a woman's sector, which have to be reconciled. Thus the myth of Moto states the problem of woman for Bakweri men: she insists on living in what is for them the wild.

MERMAIDS AND THE WILD

The wild for the male Bakweri is particularly well differentiated, because of the many striking forms in which it expresses itself. This people occupies the southeastern face of the 13,000 foot Cameroon Mountain, on the West African coast of Cameroon—an environment of romantic contrasts. The mountain rises straight from a rocky sea coast through zones of forest, grass, and bare lava to the active volcanic craters of the peak. The Bakweri proper occupy the forest, and hunt in the grass zones. A deity or hero, Efasamote, occupies the peak. Congeners of the Bakweri (Mboko, Isubu, and Wovea Islanders) occupy the rocky strand, and fish. The Bakweri proper are agriculturists; the staple crop was traditionally the male-cultivated plantain banana, although since the introduction of the Xanthosoma cocoyam in the last century, this female crop has become the staple (E. Ardener 1970). It should be added that the whole area is now greatly fragmented by plantations and a large migrant population now lives in the Bakweri area (Ardener, Ardener, and Warmington 1960). The mountain is an extremely wet place, and visibility is often reduced to a few yards because of the clouds that cover it for much of the time.

The villages are traditionally fenced—people and livestock living inside the fence, the farms being outside the fence. This way of looking at it is not inaccurate. In the light of the subject of this paper it is, however, just as true to say: the men live inside the fence with their livestock (goats, cows, and pigs) and most of their plaintains; the women go outside the fence for their two main activities—firewood-collecting and farming the Xanthosoma. The men and their livestock are so closely associated that the animals have characteristically lived in the houses themselves. I have myself visited in his hut an elderly man on his bed, so hemmed in by dwarf cows (still the size of ponies) that it was difficult to reach him. The women are all day in the forest outside the fence, returning at evening with their back-breaking loads of wood and cocoyams, streaming with rain, odds and ends tied up with bark strips and fronds, and screaming with fatigue at their husbands, with the constant reiteration in their complaints of the word *wanga* 'bush', 'the forest'. The Bakweri men wait in their leaking huts for the evening meal. It is no wonder that the women seem to be forest creatures, who might vanish one day for ever.

At the coast, the 'wild' *par excellence* is the sea, and its symbolism is expressed through the *liengu* water-spirits. The Cameroon coast provides a kaleidoscope of beliefs about *liengu*. They are found among the Kole, the Duala, the Wovea, the Oli, the Tanga, the Yasa, and many other peoples. Ittmann (1957) gathers together material from numbers of such sources.[4] The common theme is, however, used in the different belief systems of the various peoples in different ways. As I have tried to demonstrate elsewhere (1970), from a consideration of the Bakweri zombie belief, the *content* of a belief system can be analysed as a specific problem, by methods of the type used by Lévi-Strauss in *Mythologiques* (1964, 1966, 1968), as well as through those of more humdrum ethnographic aim. Among the latter, it is possible to discuss the geographical distribution of parts of the content of the belief, and consider, in the *liengu* case, questions such as whether the mermaids 'are' manatees or dugongs, which will not concern us here. The *realien* of the belief for each people are the elements plundered by the *bricoleur*: dugongs, mermaids are all to hand, but what dictates the particular disposition of elements in each system, the 'template' of the belief?

The Bakweri incorporate the *liengu* mermaids into a damp tree-ridden environment in which the sea is not visible, or is seen only far off on clear days, and in which the forest is the dominant external embodiment of the wild. The *liengu* beliefs and rites are in detail marked as a result by the inconsistency of a marine iconography with a non-marine environment. We have various different combinations producing a patchwork of several women's rites all of which are linked by the name *liengu*, some of which have content that links them with certain other West African rites. They are all enacted, however, as a response to a fit or seizure that comes mainly upon adolescent girls but also upon older women. For those men who participate in the rites, the stress is laid upon the 'curing' of the women. For, as we shall see, the men have their own view of the rites. *Liɛngu la ndiva* (*ndiva*: 'deep water') appears to retain the closest connection with the water spirits.[5] The sickness attacks a girl or woman, characteristically, by causing her to faint over the fireplace, so that she knocks out one of the three stones that are used to support the cooking pots. A woman versed in this form of *liengu* then comes and addresses her in the secret *liengu* language. If she shows any signs of comprehension, a *liengu* doctor (male or female) is called and given a black cock, on which he spits alligator pepper; he then kills it and sprinkles its blood in the hole made when the girl knocked out the hearth-stone, and replaces the stone. The patient then enters a period of seclusion. Drummers are called on a fixed evening, the girl herself staying in an inner room, dressed only in a skirt made of strips of bark of roots of the *iroko* tree, hung over a waist string. The doctor then makes her a medicine which she vomits, bringing up the black seeds of the wild banana; these are then threaded on a string and worn like a bandolier. The drummers stay all night and they and the doctor receive a fee. There are usually a number of visitors, especially *liengu* women, and these are given food.

During the period of seclusion which then follows, the girl has a woman sponsor who teaches her the secret *liengu* language, and gives her a *liengu* name. She is subject to a number of conventions and taboos during this period, which will be summarized later. After several months, the *liengu* doctor is called again, and, in the darkness before dawn, she is picked up and carried in turn, one by one, by men chosen for their strength, until they reach the deep part of a stream where the doctor pushes her in. Women who accompany them sing *liengu* songs, and the company try to catch a crab, representing the water spirit. After this rite, the girl is regarded as being a familiar of the water spirits and one of the *liengu* women. On the return of the party, the *liengu* drummers play and food is provided for the guests. After the visit to the stream the girl stays in her house for a further period. On the occasion when she finally comes out the doctor and the drummers, and other women and visitors, come to the house, where she is dressed in new clothing. Traditionally she was rubbed with camwood. There is another feast, and she is regarded by the men as finally immune from any attack by the water spirits.

Liɛngu la mɔngbango differs from *ndiva* in several respects. For example, the first symptom is sometimes said to be the girl disappearing into the bush as if attracted by spirits. She is then sought by a group of female relatives singing to her in *liengu* language, and when she is found, is taken to the seclusion room. There the doctor makes the vomiting medicine as in *Liɛngu la ndiva*. Details of the seclusion show little difference, but in this case it does not last the whole period of the rite. After a few months, a feast is made which is traditionally all eaten on the ground, after which the girl is allowed to go out, although still subject to taboos. After a further period of about nine months, a sheep is killed and a similar feast made, the girl and her *liengu* woman sponsor being secluded in an enclosure in the bush. She is now dressed in fern-fronds (*senge* or *njombi*) rubbed with camwood, and led through the village tied to the middle of a long rope held by her companions in front and behind. Outside her house, both sets of people pull the rope, as in a tug of war, until the rope comes apart, when the girl falls down, as if dead.

9

She is revived by being called nine times in the *liengu* language, after which she gets up, and is dressed in new clothing. A few weeks later, she is washed in a stream by the doctor to show that she is free from the taboos she observed during the rites. Both with *ndiva* and *mongbango* the rites extend over about a year.

A third version of the rite, *liɛngu la vefea*, reduces the procedure essentially to the killing of a goat and a young cock, and the drinking of the vomiting medicine followed by food taboos. The medicine is the same in all three rites. Among the upper Bakweri who live furthest from the sea, an even more generalized *liengu* rite seems to have existed in which the simple *rite de passage* aspect is very noticeable. It is said that formerly every daughter was put through *liengu* at about 8 to 10 years of age so that she would be fertile. She would wear fern-fronds and be secluded for a period, apparently shorter than in the above examples. Other variations in detail appear to have existed in different places and at different times.[6]

The reduced rites were, at the time of my first acquaintance with the Bakweri (in 1953), the commonest. The people had, during the previous generation, been overwhelmed by their belief that they were 'dying out' —a belief not without some slight demographic justification. Their economy was stagnant. Public rites of all kinds had gone into decline. The people blamed the general conditions of their country on witch-craft. The decline of the *liengu* rites was further blamed by many for the fertility problems of Bakweri women. Nevertheless, a celebration of the *mongbango* ceremony occurred in that same year. In 1958 a Bakweri *liengu* girl was even brought, with a *liengu* mother, to grace a Cameroon Trade Fair. Since then there has been a revival of all kinds of *liengu* rites (I was asked to contribute to the expenses of one in 1970). How-ever, the great rites of *mongbango* and *ndiva*, because of their expense, were probably always relatively rare, compared with *vefea* and other reduced rites. The latter are also common now, because so many *liengu* celebrations are 'remedial', for women who did not pass through them in their adolescence—during the long period of decline. Nevertheless, even such women are told the ideology of the great rites: the immersion (of *ndiva*), the tug-of-war (of *mongbango*), the seclusion, and the secret language. Since we are concerned here with the dimension of belief, it may be added that the image of the *liengu* is a powerful one even for the many Christian, educated, and urban Bakweri women. Scraps of the secret language are common currency. It is as if the *liengu* rites are always 'there' as a possibility of fulfilment; and also as if the rites are themselves less important than the vision of women's place in nature that appears in them: the template of the belief.

Despite the fact that *liengu* is a woman's rite, men are not immune to the precipitating sickness, especially if there are no women left in a man's extended family, and rare cases are cited in which men have gone through at least part of the rite. The fertility associations of the rite are uppermost in such cases, and the *liengu* mermaids have had to work through a male in the absence of viable females. *Liengu* doctors may be men or women. As we shall see, the participation of men does not obscure the symbolism of the rites for women. It does assist their symbolism for men. Thus the men who carry the *ndiva* girl have to be strong. Although men from her matrilineage (in practice, perhaps, her full brothers) would be favoured, a man from her patrilineage, or just a fellow-villager would be acceptable. Men see themselves as helping out with the treatment of morbidity (social and physical) in women. The domination of men as doctors in Bakweri medical rites means that the specialization as *liengu* doctors by men presents few problems. The major rites (*ndiva* and *mongbango*) have a public aspect, because of their relative expense, and a male doctor is likely to be involved. The female *liengu* doctors are associated with the less expensive, reduced rites. The 'medical' aspects of the rite have thus a somewhat 'male' aspect.

The female significance of the rites lies in the girl's acceptance by her fellow *liengu* women. In the fuller *ndiva* and *mongbango* forms, as already noted, it is customary for her to have a sponsor (*nyangb'a liengu*, '*liengu* mother') to teach her the mysteries. For the periods of seclusion, in both rites, the girl is not allowed to plait her hair but must must let it grow uncontrolled, and rub it, as well as her whole body, with charcoal mixed with palm-kernel oil, so that she is completely black. This is supposed to make her resemble a spirit. She is forbidden to talk to visitors, but greets them with a rattle, of different types in *liengu la ndiva* (*njola*, made of wicker-work) and in *mongbango* (*lisonjo*, made of certain tree-seed shells). This is also used night and morning, when she has to recite certain formulae in the *liengu* language. While in the house, the *liengu*, as the girl herself is now called, treats rats (*veto*) with special respect as they are regarded as her husbands (compare the story of Moto above). If a rat is killed she must cry all day and wash it and bury it in a cloth; killing rats in her compound is forbidden. No man or boy can enter the *liengu* house wearing a hat or shoes, or carrying a book (all introduced by Europeans) or she will seize them, and return them only on the payment of a fine. If a person dies in the village the *liengu* must not eat all day. In *liengu la mongbango*, after her period of seclusion, and before the completion of the rite, the girl may go out only with her rattle, and should turn away if she sees any person not a Bakweri. If anyone wishes to stop her he has only to say the word *yowo* ('magical rite') and she must do whatever he says. However, the *liengu* has an effective retaliation if molested, as any male whom she knocks with her rattle is thought to become permanently impotent. The *liengu* may not go into any room but her own and dogs must not go near her. She should always be addressed by her special *liengu* name. Truncated forms of these requirements are also followed by women in the *vefea* rite. After all rites the participant is henceforth known by one of a standard series of *liengu* names.

11

SYMBOLISM OF THE MERMAID CULT

It has been the intention here merely to indicate those aspects of the symbolism that are peculiar to the *liengu* corpus. This is not the place for an extended analysis, which I hope to attempt elsewhere. The male interpretation is that the *liengu* rites cure a spiritual illness. That is why male doctors take part. The women nod at this sort of interpretation in male Bakweri company, but there is a heady excitement when the *liengu* subject is raised in the absence of Bakweri men. It is accepted that the *liengu* mermaid spirits do 'trouble' the women, and cause them physical symptoms. The trouble is solved when a woman becomes a *liengu*. The mermaid world is one of Alice through the looking-glass—no manmade objects, garments only of forest products; no imported goods, traded through men.[7] For the edible plantain banana, a male crop and consciously seen as clearly phallic, we find the inedible seed-filled, wild banana—a total symbolic reversal whose effect is a 'feminization' of the male symbol. The male doctor, who is perhaps only a half-aware participant in this, makes the medicine in an integument of (male) plantain leaves to him in its harmful effects. The rites see the women as attracted away into the wild. The domestic hearth-stone (*lio*) is the popular symbol of the household (a unit in the essentially patrilineal residence pattern). It is dislodged. In *mongbango* food is eaten on the earth, and not on the customary (male) plantain leaves. The mermaid's rattle destroys the potency of males. The men are reduced to the scale of little rats, her 'husbands'. She returns to the world through the symbolic tug-of-war at which she is in the middle. She falls senseless. The men assume the world has won. Yet she is revived by nine calls in the *liengu* language. There is surely little reassuring to men in her final incorporation in the wild outside the fence of the village.[8]

The interpretation of the Bakweri *liengu* rites as 'nubility rites', because they often (but not always) precede marriage, is not exactly an error, since it does not say anything. It merely draws attention to the question 'what after all *is* a nubility rite?' Passage through *liengu* rites shows that a girl is a woman; her fellow-women vouch for it. The men feel a danger has been averted; she has been rescued from the wild and is fitted for marriage with men. But she still continues to bear a spirit name, and converses with fellow-women in the mermaid language. The term 'nubility rite' implies for some that the rites have a social 'function'; the girl takes her place in the system of relations between corporate kin-groups. The rites no doubt can be shown to 'validate' this and that aspect of the structure in the normal 'functionalist' manner. Alternatively they prepare the girl for the role of exchangeable unit in a system of alliance. These are good partial statements, but we are left asking questions like 'why did she vomit the seeds of the wild banana?' The terms 'puberty rite' and 'fertility rite' would be just as useful and just as partial. 'Puberty' stresses the biological basis that 'nubility' obscures, but of course even when the rites are not delayed until after marriage, they may take place some years after the onset of puberty—the rigid association of puberty with the menarche is a result of our mania for precision. 'Fertility' at least takes account of the association of the rites with a whole period of the woman's life. They are also 'medical rites' because they 'cure' sickness, and share features in common with Bakweri medical rites for men and women. A set of over-lapping analyses such as Richards makes for *Chisungu* (1956) would clearly be equally fruitful here.

The rites are open to analysis in the manner of Van Gennep as classical rites of passage. They fall like all such rites into stages of separation, transition, and incorporation, but the notion of passage is either self-evident (through the rite) or inadequately defined. An analysis in the manner of Turner (1967) could also be attempted, and it is evident that there is the material for such an analysis. The Turnerian method assumes that symbolism is generated by society as a whole. This is of course in a sense true: the very contradiction of symbolic systems, their 'multivalency', 'polysemy', 'condensation', and the like, derive from the totalitarian nature of symbolism. But as the Moto story shows, its surface structure may express the male view of the world, obscuring the existence at deeper levels of an autonomous female view. I feel also that Turner does not perceive the 'bounding' problem that male/female symbolism is about, and which introduces an element of ordering into the symbolic sets.

I have argued that Bakweri women define the boundary of their world in such a way that they live as women in the men's wild, as well as partly within the men's world inside the village fence. In modern times the world outside the fence has included the 'strangers', migrants who are allowed to settle there. Sometimes the strangers' quarter is larger than the Bakweri settlement. Bakweri women have long travelled from stranger-quarter to stranger-quarter, entering into casual liaisons, while the men have complained (Ardener *et al.* 1960: 294–308; E. Ardener 1962). This fortuitous overlap of the old wild with the new urban jungle may well account for the peculiar sense of defeat the Bakweri showed for so many years, which made them come to believe that zombies were killing them off (E. Ardener 1956 and 1970). For the women's part, it is possibly not sufficient to account for their notable conjugal freedom, as I have argued elsewhere (1962), merely on the grounds that there are nearly three males to every woman in the plantation area. The Bakweri system of double descent similarly expresses the basic dichotomy. The patrilineage controls residence (the village), the inheritance of land and cattle, succession to political office—the men's world. The matrilineage controls fertility, and its symbolic fertility bangle is found on a woman's farm outside the village fence (E. Ardener 1956).

13

MANKIND AND WOMANKIND

The Bakweri illustration can only briefly document my theme. Men's models of society are expressed at a metalevel which purports to define women. Only at the level of the analysis of belief can the voiceless masses be restored to speech. Not only women, but (a task to be attempted later) inarticulate classes of men, young people, and children. We are all lay figures in someone else's play.

The objective basis of the symbolic distinction between nature and society, which Lévi-Strauss recently prematurely retreated from, is a result of the problem of accommodating the two logical sets which classify human beings by different bodily structures: 'male'/'female'; with the two other sets: 'human'/'non-human'. It is, I have suggested, men who usually come to face this problem, and, because their model for *mankind* is based on that for *man*, their opposites, *women* and *non-mankind* (the wild), tend to be ambiguously placed. Hence, in Douglas's terms (1966), come their sacred and polluting aspects. Women accept the implied symbolic content, by equating *womankind* with the men's wild.

Figure 2

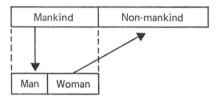

The topic of this paper is 'the problem of women'. Women, of course, have 'a problem of men', who may indeed live in a part of the wild that women bound off from themselves. With that world of hunting and war, both sexes are familiar. The men's wild is, of course, a threat to women. The *liengu* taboos of the Bakweri express some of this. The secluded mermaids hate European goods, which have increased male power. The tabooed 'male' animal, the dog (used in the chase), is an added danger because it can see the spirit world. Dogs walk purposefully on their own, although they have nowhere to go, and they frequently stare attentively into space. Bakweri men have their own symbolic zone of adventure and hunting beyond that of the women, on the mountain-top away from all villages and farms. This is ritually expressed in the men's elephant dance (E. Ardener 1959). Elephants sometimes emerge from the remote parts of the mountain and destroy the women's farms. Men and boys in many villages belong to an elephant society, a closed association that claims responsibility for the work of elephants, through the elephant-doubles (*naguals*) of its more powerful members. In their annual dance they enact their control over the elephant world. Women

14

on such occasions form the audience, who clap out the rhythm for the men's virtuoso dancer. Some women rather half-heartedly claim the role of bush-pigs, but like Dames in an order of chivalry or girls at Roedean, they are performing a male scenario.[9]

It is a tragedy of the male life-position that, in the modern age, the men's wild is not now so easily accessible to them. For modern Bakweri as for American males the hunting fantasy at least is no longer plausible. For if women still symbolically live in their wild, men have tried to ignore their own in the official symbolism of civilization. It will have emerged that the argument of this paper as it applies to women is a special but submerged case of the mode whereby self-identification is made. Obviously the different classes of men and of women, and individuals of all ages and both sexes contribute to that totality of symbolism—which merely appears a 'forest' when one fails to look at the trees.

To return, then, to the limited problem of my title, we need not doubt that the societies from which ethnographers come share the problem of all societies. If, as I suggest is the case, men's models of society accommodate women only by making certain assumptions that ignore or hold constant elements that would contradict these models, then the process may be traced further back into the ethnographer's own thinking and his own society. Our women ethnographers may then be expressing the 'maleness' of their subject when they approach the women of other societies.[10] It may well be, too, that their positive reluctance to deal with the problem of women is the greater because they sense that its consideration would split apart the very framework in which they conduct their studies.

Notes

1 This paper was read at Dr Kaberry's seminar in University College London in late 1968. In presenting it for Dr Audrey Richards's festschrift, I acknowledged my debt to her for the main part of my early anthropological training. Her astringent humour and basic open-mindedness are qualities that I have respected ever since. I also thanked Dr Jean La Fontaine for her appreciative remarks on the paper, and for entering into the spirit of the analysis in her comments as editor.

2 This version was given in 1929 by Charles Steane, a Bakweri scholar, to B. G. Stone (MS. 1929).

3 *Moto, eto*, and *ewaki* are the ordinary words for 'person', 'rat', and 'ape'. *Mojili* or *Mojele* is to the coastal Bakweri a spirit. For inland Bakweri his name is a euphemism for 'ape'. It is likely that the term belongs to the animal world, but is borrowed from the fishing peoples. Possibly it is the manatee.

4 When the term is used *in isolation* the spelling *liengu* will be used (not, that is, the 'Africa' alphabet spelling *liɛngu*, nor the occasional spelling with orthographic subscript *liɛngu*). The belief appears to be of coastal origin. There it is concerned with men, fishing, and the dangers of the deep. This paper is concerned with the

15

liengu belief as utilized by the Bakweri. Elements of content are differently combined even between the coast and the mountain. Ittmann's rich material (1957) is to be used with caution because it combines several different systems. The pidgin English translation for water spirit is 'mammy water'. The 'mammy water' myth has wide currency in West Africa in urban contexts. The ambiguity of the position of women in African towns makes this secondary elaboration of the belief very appropriate.

5 See also Ardener, E. (1956).

6 Various forms cited by myself (1956) and Ittmann (1957) are closer to 'fattening room' seclusion rites of the Cross River area in form and content. Their assimilation to the *liengu* belief is explicable because the latter belief most clearly organizes the women's world-view for the Bakweri.

7 Here is a subtle case of identical content yielding different meaning. The Duala mer-people hate European objects, but the *maengu* are often male. There they symbolize men's domination of the deep; they particularly detest paper (conceived of as the bible).

8 For the *liengu* language, see Ardener (1956) and Ittmann (1957). It is a code calqued upon Bakweri with vocabulary from various sources.

9 Dr La Fontaine commented on this paper that men plus wild = death, destruction; women plus wild = agriculture, fertility. She, a woman, thus expresses that faith in the female civilizing mission shared by so many reflective members of her sex!

10 For some unresolved puzzles of a new woman fieldworker see Bovin (1966). For a resolution through literature see Bowen (1954).

References

ARDENER, E. W. 1956. *Coastal Bantu of the Cameroons*. London: Oxford University Press for International African Institute.
— 1959. The Bakweri Elephant Dance. *Nigeria* (60): 31–8.
— 1962. *Divorce and Fertility*. London: Oxford University Press.
— 1970. Witchcraft, Economics, and the Continuity of Belief. In M. Douglas (ed.), *Witchcraft Confessions and Accusations*. ASA Monograph 9. London: Tavistock.
ARDENER, E. W., ARDENER, S. G., and WARMINGTON, W. A. 1960. *Plantation and Village in the Cameroons*. London: Oxford University Press.
BOVIN, M. 1966. The Significance of the Sex of the Field Worker for Insights into the Male and Female Worlds. *Ethnos* 31 (supp.): 24–7. Stockholm.
BOWEN, E. S. 1954. *Return to Laughter*. London: Gollancz.
DOUGLAS, M. 1966. *Purity and Danger*. London: Routledge & Kegan Paul.
DOUGLAS, M. (ed.) 1970. *Witchcraft Confessions and Accusations*. ASA Monograph 9. London: Tavistock.
EVANS-PRITCHARD, E. E. 1965. The Position of Women in Primitive Societies and in Our Own. In *The Position of Women and Other Essays in Social Anthropology*. London: Faber & Faber.
ITTMANN, J. 1957. Der kultische Geheimbund djĕngú an der Kameruner Küste. *Anthropos* 52: 135–76.
LEACH, E. R. 1961. Two Essays concerning the Symbolic Representation of Time. In *Rethinking Anthropology*. London: Athlone Press.
— 1964. Animal Categories and Verbal Abuse. In E. H. Lenneberg (ed.), *New Directions in Language*. Cambridge, Mass.: MIT Press.

LENNEBERG, E. H. (ed.) 1964. *New Directions in Language*. Cambridge, Mass.: MIT Press.

LÉVI-STRAUSS, C. 1949. *Les Structures élémentaires de la parenté*. Paris: Presses Universitaires de France (2nd edn 1967).

— 1963. *Structural Anthropology*. New York: Basic Books.

— 1964. *Mythologiques: Le Cru et le cuit*. Paris: Plon.

— 1966. *Mythologiques: Du Miel aux cendres*. Paris: Plon.

— 1967. *Les Structures élémentaires de la parenté*. Paris: Mouton.

— 1968. *Mythologiques: L'Origine des manières du table*. Paris: Plon.

— 1969. *The Elementary Structures of Kinship*. London: Eyre & Spottiswoode.

NEEDHAM, R. 1958. A Structural Analysis of Purum Society. *American Anthropologist* **60**: 75–101.

— 1960. The Left Hand of the Mugwe. *Africa* **30**: 20–33.

— 1967. Right and Left in Nyoro Symbolic Classification. *Africa* **37**: 425–52.

RICHARDS, A. I. 1956. *Chisungu: A girls' initiation ceremony among the Bemba of Northern Rhodesia*. London: Faber & Faber.

STONE, B. G. 1929. Assessment Report of Buea District. MS. Victoria Divisional Office, Cameroons.

TURNER, V. W. 1967. *The Forest of Symbols*. Ithaca, NY: Cornell University Press.

Edwin Ardener

The 'Problem' Revisited

The paper reprinted above is now somewhat old, and as composed just antedated the main impact of the new feminist literature. It is important to stress therefore that it was not seen as a contribution to that literature. Most of what it says seems quite commonplace at the present. In its rather long unpublished existence it was orally delivered in various places in the context of a discussion of the nature of dominant structures. It is not exactly the paper I would now write, if indeed I would write it at all. It has been a genuine pleasure to me, as a result, that it has not been rejected in its entirety by women social anthropologists concerned with the social differentiation of men and women. There have, however, been questions, and one or two misunderstandings, most of which occur in a critique by Nicole-Claude Mathieu called 'Homme-Culture et Femme-Nature?' (1973).

First of all, it should not be necessary for a social anthropologist, male or female, to offer any particular explanation for writing on 'the problem of women' as I presented it. One of the greatest statements of it was made by Virginia Woolf in 1928. She noted the great gulf between the saliency of women in symbolism and literature and their position until recently in the official structure. 'Imaginatively she is of the highest importance; practically she is completely insignificant. She pervades poetry from cover to cover; she is all but absent from history' (Woolf 1928: 45). Perhaps there were certain coincidences, for what they are worth, that at least did not place any obstacles of experience to my attempt on the question. My first fieldwork was among the Ibo, in the area in which the Women's Uprising of 1929 occurred. This was followed by studies among the Bakweri of Cameroon, who were portrayed, and who portrayed themselves, as riven by marital conflict. Among the latter, studies from the male point of view (Part III of Ardener, Ardener, and Warmington 1960) were followed by a study from the women's side (Ardener 1962).[1] The difference in atmosphere was extremely striking. For the men, society was in chaos, even breaking down. For the women, life was a periplus of adventures, in which the role of independent 'harlot' was often viewed as objectively a proud one. I admit that the paper may be affected by ethnographic experiences that particularly highlight the 'separate realities' of men and women. There will be societies in which the gap is greater or smaller, confined to one area of life or another. Alternatively the gap should be seen as an exemplification of all discontinuities in the experience of groups in society, however defined.

Still, the necessity to interview women in such numbers as is required in a fertility and marital survey provides a considerable body of data for an anthropologist, which it has not always been fashionable to see in other than statistical terms. In the general social-anthropological world, I do not think it an exaggeration to say that by 1960 studies of women had declined to a fairly low theoretical status. Temporarily even the standard books by Margaret Mead had receded into the background. No doubt my recollection can be contested. Nevertheless, I recall the remark then being made (by a woman): 'No anthropological book with "women" in the title sells.' The writings were there, as some critics point out, but (to modify the pre-nineteenth-century motto of the Russians about their literature): 'De mulieribus—sunt, non leguntur.'

I have been asked whether women anthropologists 'raised my consciousness'. Although this hints at a characteristic modern paradox,[2] the question is relevant and deserves a careful answer. Because in both Eastern Nigeria and Cameroon, women had caused 'trouble' to the male population and to the administration, there had already been women anthropologists in these areas. In Iboland Sylvia Leith-Ross and M. M. Green had been deliberately invited to make studies in the aftermath of the Women's Riots, or what Caroline Ifeka terms the Women's War. It was Miss Green who in later years taught me the first elements of Ibo. In Cameroon, Phyllis Kaberry at one time nearly studied the Bakweri but eventually studied 'women' on the inland Plateau. She had already written *Aboriginal Woman*, and was to write *Women of the Grassfields*. Then through all phases of both the Nigerian and Cameroon studies, the last of which are still not finally completed, I worked with Shirley Ardener who must be the female anthropologist of the most continuous and subtle influence on me. Later she and Phyllis Kaberry and I collaborated on studies in Cameroon history with Sally Chilver— now one of the most distinguished ethno-historians in the study of the region. If in retrospect I note that my first teacher was Audrey Richards, and that the paper appeared in her festschrift, edited in its turn by Jean La Fontaine, there is a galaxy of female talent enough here to reassure any who might view with regret and suspicion the presence of a male anthropologist in this field.

Yet what was the precise nature of their influence on this paper? None of them, certainly of the senior ones, were particularly of a 'feminist' turn of mind. None appeared to be then students of 'women' except fortuitously, as part of their general anthropological work. Thus arose the paradox that a 'problem of women anthropologists' began to present itself unbidden to my mind. It had two components: (1) That they did not seem to be in a much more privileged position in interpreting the women of their fields than was a male anthropologist. (2) That the women anthropologists themselves, although they were loth to differentiate themselves from male anthropologists, did have significantly different academic pasts, presents, and (it looked likely) futures, in the anthropological profession itself.

It is easy nowadays to criticize me for needing these insights. A critic (Mathieu 1973) has stated that only one who believes in 'woman' as a universal category could have fallen into the error of entertaining such an expectation as is implied in the first point. That reading is not quite exact: the problem was that women anthropologists did not themselves then reject the expectation, even though uncomfortable with it. Of course, in the last few years all this has changed—or begun to change. My second point is also a mere commonplace among militant women. Nevertheless, an independent perspective is not without its value. During the 'sixties it did sometimes look as if women anthropologists had even more academic vitality in relation to their numbers than had their male colleagues. At long anthropological conferences their contributions frequently threw brave, short-lived beams of light into the gloom before being overwhelmed by it. Nevertheless no woman became until recently a Professor of Anthropology in a British University.[3] It was quite apparent, however, that women formed only an easily recognizable part of a class of social anthropologists in the same condition. Yet while male anthropologists of a 'destructured' tendency were generally conscious of the nature of the situation which enveloped them, the women anthropologists seemed 'muted' on their own position. Publicly, at least, they did not 'see' or 'perceive' themselves within the structure of academic anthropology; so, inevitably, they did not 'see' other women clearly in their own fields. That is the reason why 'Belief and the Problem of Women' ends with the challenge to women anthropologists 'to split apart the very framework in which they conduct their studies'. Nicole-Claude Mathieu asks, should not men do likewise? Precisely. No one who knows my general position will imagine that this conclusion was to be seen as an achievement of male complacency. I have taken the 'woman' case in order to *de*sexualize it. When I say that it is a special case of a situation applying to other social classes and individuals, both men and women, this is not a casual aside as Mathieu again seems to think—it is the intended conclusion of the paper, which has been merely illustrated by the case of women.

In the light of the foregoing it may be worth noting for the chronological record that in July 1973 at the Session on Marxism of the ASA Decennial Conference I made an oral contribution to the discussion of class:

If we look at those classes which are usually considered to be the exploiting or dominant classes, and then we consider those others which are supposedly the exploited or suppressed classes, there is this dimension that hasn't been mentioned yet: which is [that] of relative articulateness. One of the problems that women presented was that they were rendered 'inarticulate' by the male structure; that the domi-

21

nant structure was articulated in terms of a male world-position. Those who were not in the male world-position, were, as it were, 'muted'.

I repeated my suggestion that this applied to other social groups and also to individuals, and stated its relevance to the question of the universality or otherwise of the concept of class:

> We may speak of 'muted groups' and 'articulate groups' along this dimension. There are many kinds of muted groups. We would then go on to ask: 'What is it that makes a group muted?' We then become aware that it is muted simply because it does not form part of the dominant communicative system of the society—expressed as it must be through the dominant ideology, and that 'mode of production', if you wish, which is articulated with it. (From transcript of discussion 7 July 1973.)

Nevertheless, the point must be made that not all phenomena of mutedness can be linked simply and directly to a 'mode of production'. Dominant/muted alternations, as we shall see, occur at too many levels to actualize themselves always in these terms. The definition of 'mode of production' itself would suffer extraordinary transfigurations if it were so. Nevertheless, those alternations which are tied to a mode of production certainly acquire a special kind of salience or stability—an institutionalization—that will be familiar to marxist analysts.

The approach is already being provisionally applied to other muted groups, such as children (Hardman 1973) and criminals (Maguire 1974). We owe the convenient term 'muted' itself to Charlotte Hardman. But the phenomenon of 'mutedness' (it must be warned) is a technically defined condition of structures—not some condition of linguistic silence.[4] There is also an ambiguity about the term 'muted' in this connection—for in English we mean by it both 'dumb' and 'of a reduced level of perceptibility'. The muted structures are 'there' but cannot be 'realized' in the language of the dominant structure (see above, pp. xii–xv).

The operation of a dominant structure from the point of view of a subdominant may be likened to a pin-table in which the very operation of the spring, to propel the ball, itself moves the scoring holes some centimetres to the side. The more skill the operator uses in directing the ball, the more carefully he ensures that the scoring hole will not be there to receive it. The ultimate negativity of attempts to modify dominant structures by their own 'rules' derives from the totally reality-defining nature of such structures. Because of this essential element the manifold of experience through the social may be usefully termed a 'world-structure', for it is an organization both of *people and of their reality*. It is not my intention to appear to confuse the apparently practical aspects of the perception of woman, and of perceiving by women, by alluding in too much detail to these questions, some of which are at early stage of analysis. But a 'world-structure', in these clearly defined terms, is the nearest congener to the 'society' or (and?) 'culture' of traditional anthropology. The characteristic bounding problem that those terms imply ('Where does a society begin or end?', 'When are cultures the "same", or "different"? In space or in time?') is solved by its resolution in the chief criterion of a 'world-structure': it is a *self*-defining system.

We are now able to examine an unfortunate misunderstanding of my previous paper. I find it difficult to see how any careful reader can deduce that for me it is a simple case of 'man=culture' and 'women= nature'. The fault lies, no doubt, in my citation of Lévi-Strauss. My readers should concentrate upon the 'defining' or 'bounding' problem presented by women in a situation in which the 'bounds' of 'society' are themselves defined by men. In the conceptual act of bounding 'society' there is a fortuitous homology between the purely ideational field or background against which 'society' is defined as a *concept*, and that part of the actual, territorial world which is not socially organized—the 'wild'. The 'wild' = the 'non-social'. It is a mere confusion that it may also be walkable into, and be found to contain sounding cataracts and unusual beasts. A 'society', because it has a geographical *situs*, in one of its defining spaces, or along one of its dimensions, therefore projects an equivalent geographical aspect on to its counter-concept—the 'non-social'. If the world were geographically a uniformly barren surface, the self-defining human entities upon it would thereby merely lack a useful set of topographical differentia for the 'non-social'. Conceptually these differentiae would not cease to exist. In rural societies the equation: non-social = non-human = the wild = 'nature' is easily concretized. There is a powerful metaphor, with a key into experience. This is the source of the triviality as well as the power of the binary opposition 'nature/culture' in Lévi-Strauss's own analyses. Its 'universality' is indeed a powerful triviality. It is 'self/not-self' raised to the level of society's own self-definition, and clothed in 'totemic' and botanical imagery.

My argument was: where society is defined by men, some features of women do not fit that definition. In rural societies the anomaly is experienced as a feature of the 'wild', for the 'wild' is a metaphor of the non-social which in confusing ways is vouched for by the senses.

Figure 1

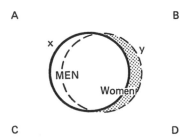

A B C D is an unbounded field against which the two intersecting circles

23

x, y are defined. From the perspective of circle x the shaded portion of y is part of the field A B C D. The circle x, *plus* the unshaded overlap of circle y, is the model of society where the male model is dominant (heavy outline and capital letters). In metaphorical terms, A B C D is 'the wild'. In the diagram, the shaded area of y, which is classified by men with the 'wild', is not confused by women themselves with the 'wild' (save when they speak in the dominant 'language'). Rather, for them there is a zone in circle x which is ambiguously male and 'wild', a zone which men do not perceive.

This confusion of self-definition with geographical reality is avoided when we think not of 'society', but of a world-structure which defines human reality—if you like 'relevant' reality. In these terms if the male perception yields a dominant structure, the female one is a muted structure. It is an empirical contingency that the immanent realizations of muted structures are so often equated in this way with the nullity of the background, of 'nature'; and also that 'nature' itself should thus contain at its core a common metaphorical conceptualization, appearing in Rousseau and Lévi-Strauss, on the one hand, and the Bororo or the Bakweri, on the other.[5]

Mathieu appears to take my own argument to its extreme when she chides me for mentioning the female biology as one of the features males find difficult to tidy away into the perceptions of the dominant structure. Yes, of course, we can say that the very concept of female biology is a product of the dominant structure. But once more I reply that the undoubted anatomical and functional differences become a powerful and convenient metaphor for this, possibly the most ancient and surely the most nearly universal, structural dominance. Hertz similarly showed that a possibly slight anatomical ('biological') discrepancy between a right- and a left-handed tendency became a powerful metaphor for all binary discriminations, including this very one between the sexes; and, as Needham's comprehensive volume on the subject also illustrates (1973), it is also no surprise that spatial concepts (inside–outside, village–wild) should be lined up with these pairs. Mathieu thus is quite mistaken in asserting that I am a 'biological essentialist' and that my analysis demands a theory of biological causation.

Some of her mistakes rest upon subtle difficulties of translation from English into French, and I accept part of the blame for this, as even for an English-speaking reader there are a number of levels of irony and ambiguous nuance in the style of the paper. Still, when I write of 'women overlapping into [the men's view of] nature again' I do not mean 'refaire le saut dans la nature' (Mathieu: 107–8). Women do not 'leap back' into nature: they overlap, protrude beyond the limits set for them by men. When I write of a 'propensity' of males to make models of society of a particular bounded type, I do not mean *une capacité* (ibid: 107) but 'a structural readiness'; nor do I refer to *des modèles bien délimités, modèles discrets de la société* (ibid: 102), but to models of a society bounded (*délimités*) *in a particular way*. Furthermore, when I say that 'all such ways of bounding society against society . . . may have an inherent maleness', the term 'maleness' is of course not here a biological term, a function of male gonads. We cannot draw from it the conclusion that: 'La "dominance politique" des hommes est ainsi conçue comme une charactéristique fixe d'une catégorie biologique fixe: le politique est à l'homme ce que la vertu dormitive est au pavot, une propriété' (ibid: 107). It is strange to be suspected of an ethologistic determinism, even greater than Professors Fox and Tiger are normally accused of.

Lastly, nothing but some basic stereotypical error can account for the sternness of Mathieu's response to my interchange with Jean La Fontaine (note 9, p. 16, above). She detects an irony on my part. There is indeed one: I certainly do not reject (as she suggests) the validity of a female equation of the wild of 'maleness' with death, destruction, and 'non-culture'. I was gently deprecating, however, any hint of a simple 'female utopianism' that would define death and destruction as incompatible with *itself*. But in the end I suspect that 'culture' is for Mathieu an *a priori* category with a high positive marking—whereas, for many of us, a position 'in the wild' (were that actually in question) still has no negative connotations. I am quite prepared to be defined as 'nature' by Mathieu for I detect in her paper the salutary symptoms of one who has begun to 'split apart the very framework of her studies'.[6]

In conclusion I would state my position so: The woman case is only a relatively prominent example of muting: one that has clear political, biological, and social symbols. The real problem is that all world-structures are totalitarian in tendency. The Gypsy world-structure, for example, englobes that of the sedentary community just as avidly as that of the sedentary community englobes that of the Gypsies. The englobed structure is totally 'muted' in terms of the englobing one. There is then an absolute equality of world-structures in this principle, for we are talking of their self-defining and reality-reducing features. *Dominance* occurs when one structure blocks the power of actualization of the other, so that it has no 'freedom of action'. That this approach is not simply a marxist one lies in our recognition that the articulation of world-structures does not rest only in their production base but at all levels of communication: that a structure is also a kind of language of many semiological elements, which specify all actions by its power of definition.

My intervention in the discussion as far as it concerns women was a product of concern with the technical features of socio-intellectual structures which regularly assign contending viewpoints to a non-real status; making them 'overlooked', 'muted', 'invisible': mere black holes in someone else's universe.

Notes

1 See References above, pp. 16–17.

2 The paradox is that studies of the cultural relativity of ideas of 'women' should seem to increase rather than reduce the tendency to see this as a 'women's' subject.

3 I think the date was 1966.

4 For those familiar with this terminology, the following diagram will suffice:

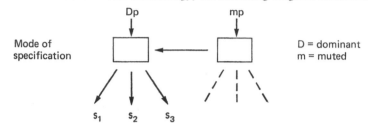

The 'reality' configurations (s-structures) are generated from p-structures. Dominant p-structures generate s-structures relatively directly. Sub-dominant p-structures generate only indirectly—through the mode of specification of the dominant structure.

5 Since the 'wild' is always 'symbolic' it is not surprising that women do sometimes see *themselves* as part of it (cf. Ortner 1973). Her approach, by a greatly different route, complements mine.

6 I should like to add here that I find myself in general agreement with much of Mathieu's own position. In misreading mine she has really done my paper too great an honour: she has judged it by the standards of length of a monograph. To push through an argument in a short paper one begins with certain commonsense categories in order to dissolve them. The terms are redefined between the beginning and the end. I accept then that there are 'generalizations'. But I do not think that the many examples of ethnographers to whom the women *have* 'spoken' (among whom I am after all one!) touch the central point that within social anthropology 'no one could come back from an ethnographic study . . . having talked only *to* women and about men, without professional comment and some self-doubt. The reverse can and does happen constantly.' I have not replied to all points, not because they are without interest or are too compelling, but because the central charge of biologism is so improbable that it distorts all her presentation. As a final exemplification of it I quote from her last words: 'Vouloir rendre la parole aux classes inarticulées en allant rechercher "aux niveaux les plus profonds" du symbolisme ce que, tels des schizophrènes, ils tenteraient d'exprimer, présente le même danger en ethnologie que l'explication constitutionnaliste de la schizophrénie en psychiatrie. . . .' It is astonishing that here the Laingian approaches to the 'meaning' of schizophrenia, with which my approach is most comparable, are interpreted as 'constitutionalist' psychiatry.

References

ARDENER, E. W. 1960. *Divorce and Fertility: an African Study*. London: Oxford University Press.

ARDENER, E. W., ARDENER, S. G., & WARMINGTON, W. A. 1960. *Plantation and Village in the Cameroons*. London: Oxford University Press.

HARDMAN, C. 1973. Can there be an Anthropology of Children? *Journal of the Anthropological Society of Oxford* 4: 85–99.

HERTZ, R. 1909. The Pre-eminence of the Right Hand: a Study in Religious Polarity. Translated and reprinted in R. Needham, *Right and Left: Essays on Dual Symbolic Classification*. Chicago and London: University of Chicago Press, 1973.

KABERRY, P. M. 1939. *Aboriginal Woman: Sacred and Profane*. London: Routledge & Kegan Paul (reprinted Gregg International, 1970).

— 1952. *Women of the Grassfields*. London: HMSO (reprinted Gregg International, 1970).

MAGUIRE, M. 1974. Criminology and Social Anthropology. *Journal of the Anthropological Society of Oxford* 5 (2): 109–17.

MATHIEU, N. C. 1973. Homme-Culture, Femme-Nature? *L'Homme*, July–Sept.: 101–113.

NEEDHAM, R. 1973. *Right and Left: Essays on Dual Symbolic Classification*. Chicago and London: University of Chicago Press.

ORTNER, S. B. 1973. Is Female to Male as Nature is to Culture? *Feminist Studies* 1 (2). Also in M. Z. Rosaldo and M. Lamphere (eds.) *Woman, Culture, and Society*. Stanford, Calif.: Stanford University Press, 1974.

WOOLF, V. 1928. *A Room of One's Own*. London: Hogarth Press (cited from Penguin edition).

27

Shirley Ardener

Sexual Insult and Female Militancy

This article attempts to examine certain manifestations of female militancy in Africa, not only for their own interest, but also to see whether they can throw any light upon the completely independent modern women's liberation movements with which we are now familiar in the West. The African ethnographical material, which is set out first, refers mainly to the Bakweri, the Balong and the Kom of West Cameroon. Besides oral reports collected from Cameroonians about traditional behaviour and on particular occurrences, for the Bakweri there is additional relevant documentation from Court records. For the Kom some published material is available; I have taken the opportunity to include here also information collected by a Kom who had an interest in social anthropology, as well as being the son of one of the principal female actors in the drama which will unfold below. The Cameroon material is followed by some relevant data from other parts of Africa. Discussion is then broadened to include material on the women's liberation movement in America and England.

THE BAKWERI

The Bakweri live on the slopes and around the base of the Cameroon Mountain, which is a volcano of some 13,500 feet lying on the west coast of Africa. They are the largest autochthonous population in the area, numbering near 20,000 persons. They speak a Bantu language, and they distinguish a category which they label *titi ikoli* which is relevant to our discussion of female militancy. It is difficult to give a precise translation of the expression. Bakweri explain it in different ways: *Titi ikoli* is 'beautiful'; *titi ikoli* means something valuable 'as if one married a woman for £1,000'; yet, 'the word refers to an insult'. As we shall see, it is possible to speak of the 'native law of *titi ikoli*' and of things being 'of the nature of *titi ikoli*'. The expression falls into two parts: *ikoli* has the independent meaning of 'thousand'. *Titi* is said to be a childish word for the female vulva, although the normal term for this is *ndondo*. It is sometimes used to refer to young girls. Everyone is said to 'know the implications in [the combination] *titi ikoli*' and usually mention of the expression brings forth embarrassed laughter. It comprehends the following associations: 'a woman's underparts' (the genitals, anus, and

29

buttocks), and the insult of these; and 'women's secrets' and the revealing of these. At the same time it is associated with certain types of mandatory female sanctions which follow upon such insult.

The insult is typically envisaged in the form of an accusation that the sexual parts of women smell. If such an insult has been uttered to a Bakweri woman before a witness, she is supposed immediately to call out all the other women of the village. The circumstances having been recounted, the women then run and pluck vegetation from the surrounding bush, which they tie around their waists. Converging again upon the offender, they demand immediate recantation and a recompense. If their demands are not met they all proceed to the house of the village head. The culprit will be brought forward, and the charges laid. If the insult is proved to have been made, he will be fined a pig of a certain size for distribution to the group of women, or its money equivalent, plus something extra, possibly salt, a fowl, or money, for the woman who has been directly insulted. The women then surround him and sing songs accompanied by obscene gestures. All the other men beat a hasty retreat, since it is expected that they will be ashamed to stay and watch while their wives, sisters, sisters-in-law and old women join the dance. The culprit must stay, but he will try to hide his eyes. Finally the women retire victoriously to divide the pig among them.

The songs the women sing are often obscene by allusion, as for instance, in the song:

> *Na l-umwe njenje, e.*
> (I prick thorn)

Another kind of song would be:

> *Titi ikoli, a senje veoli,*
> *molonga na molonga*
> (*Titi ikoli* is not a thing for insults,
> beautiful beautiful)

Other types of insult are recognized, as we shall see below, but it was said by a youth that offences relating to *titi ikoli* had become less common, since 'people were more clever and would not insult people like that. Not that they would not insult nowadays, but that they were cleverer to do it in the house with no one to be witness'.

Cases of abuse of the type discussed were reported as having occurred, not only in Bakweri villages, but also in the ethnically mixed immigrant-dominated plantation camps and townships lying between them. For instance, in 1953, at a plantation labour camp, a Balundu boy cursed a woman saying she was 'rotten'. The women were all annoyed and they combined, regardless of tribal origin, and attempted to catch the offender. He managed to escape, but they determined to watch out for him.

During the late-colonial period women had largely replaced these traditional direct sanctions by the use of formal Court procedures. Looking through notes taken from old Court records for a number of Bakweri villages for 1956, several cases of abuse of this type were revealed. The records were kept in English or pidgin English, by Court Clerks, and give useful examples of situations which could provoke such insults.

In the dispute taken by Mary Ekumbe and other women of Mafanja against Efende Mwendeley of Mafanja, before the Bonjongo Court, the charge was:

> The plaintiff claims jointly for self and other women of Mafanja Bakweri Native Town the sum of £20, being damages for defamation of character and slander on about the 14th February 1956 at about 2 p.m. In that Defendant did on 14th February 1956 at about 2 p.m. meet with Madam Therisia Ese at Mafanja town and used the following words in Bakweri language: '*Ngwete ja varana isasosa imbondo jawu. Eveli ndi varana vase. Ese nyi? Ema linga ema na mende o vewa. Ndi na suu mwango.*' The above speech in Bakweri language means that the women in this village have smelling bottoms and are not washing their bottoms. You are glad that I have gone to prison. I have won the case.

The defendant, Efende, denied the charge. The leading plaintiff, Mary, gave the following evidence:

> Some months ago defendant had a case of a cap gun with Carl Bweme. This matter was reported to police and a police constable came [from town] to arrest defendant [and took him away]. A few days later defendant returned rejoicing that he had been acquitted. We all were happy to hear that, and we were trying to welcome [him, and] he turned to us and used the words mentioned above on us. We got offended and reported the matter to the village head Kekele where defendant was found guilty and asked to pay £5.0.0 to the women, [but] he refused. Then we took action in the magistrates' court.

The Magistrates' Court had then referred the case back to the local village Court.

The women's case was much strengthened by the support of the defendant's wife, who after reporting what her husband had said about the Mafanja women, remarked sadly: 'Hearing this I was touched' (that is: upset). The Court ruled in favour of the women and awarded them £10 damages, and costs of £4.0.6d. The reasons given by the Court for this decision were:

> Defendant admits that he used insultive words on the people of Mafanja including women. But he has refused to tell court the words

31

on the people. Plaintiff has 3 witnesses to support her statement and defendant's wife is one. Defendant has no witness for his defence. The real damages that would have been awarded to the women according to local customary laws is £5.6.0. The court considers the award of £10.0.0 because defendant has suffered the women by going to Buea Magistrate's Court and to this Court.[1]

In the same Court, Namondo Lokita of Ewongo accused another woman of (as a judge put it) insulting 'the lower part of women'. She claimed £3 'being damages for insult that Plaintiff speaks with the anus'. Namondo's evidence went as follows (I paraphrase where not in quotation marks): The defendant, Sundi, is my sister-in-law. She began to talk against me and I reported this to her sister Misis, who then warned her not to do so. Whereupon the defendant Sundi, in front of witnesses, said 'my disgrace of suing people to court had gone far and wide'. Namondo continued:

> I asked whether suing people to court was a crime. I told her that she should not forget she is so mouthy that she could not stay with the husband in a house for a long period. Then she said I speak with my Anus. Tondi heard this . . .

Sundi's side of the story was as follows:

> It is true [that the] Plaintiff is my sister-in-law. One day her husband came to ask me that I talked ill of Plaintiff that I asked whether plaintiff was wearing high hill shoes. I refused the fact. [Later I was with the Plaintiff and] she began to quarrel [with] me. She said I had a disgrace that I would not stay in any house with my husband because of being too mouthy. I asked whether she was speaking with her anus . . .

Namondo had taken Sundi before the Village Head, Nambele Moka, who supported her complaint. But Sundi would not accept his ruling and had then gone to another elder who supported her instead.

After hearing all the evidence the Court ruled in favour of the plaintiff Namondo, awarding 30/– damages and 12/6 costs. The reasons given were:

1 Defendant admits that she said Plaintiff speaks with the anus.
2 Defendant was found guilty by chief Nambile who heard witnesses. The second elder who found the plaintiff guilty [that is, found Sundi, our defendant, not guilty] did not hear any witnesses.

The Court then added the general principle, with which we are now concerned: 'It is unlawful to insult the lower part of women'.[2]

Another case which was brought before the Lisoka Court is useful because it concerns the definition of *titi ikoli*. The interpretation of the term made by the women plaintiffs was not upheld by the all-male

Court bench. The case was brought by Namondo Keke of 'Wonjia Women Community' against another woman Elisah Ngalle, also of Wonjia. The claim was for £6.10.0 'being compensation for woman "titi Ikolli"'. The plaintiff being ill, was represented by another woman of the same community. Her case was presented thus:

> One day I was in my house and so Defendant and her husband had a dispute. She suspected the husband of adultery. That she met a rag on the bed owned by one Lyona [= Liengu] Ikome. This rag is what we women use for co-habiting. It was a very shameful thing when this was brought out. We then decided to call for Lyengu [Liengu] Ikome. Defendant disagreed. This is why the community of Wonjia women have sued her to Court that she has proven women's secrets.

The rag was produced in Court. The defendant, Elisah, did not in fact deny the circumstances, but said as part of her evidence:

> Very soon woman said I have offended them by native law of 'titi ikoli'. This was at my surprise. 'Titi ikoli' means a person who has abused another the private part. I did not abuse anybody. I wonder to be sued in Court.

Although the plaintiff (acting for the 'women's community') affirmed that 'any rag of this nature is of "*titi ikoli*"', the Court dismissed the case against Elisah. Here, however, we meet the element of 'revealing women's secrets'.[3]

These incidents all involved Bakweri. There are many migrants from other parts of Cameroon in the area, and at Muea Court, in the same year, a woman described as 'Catherine of Yaounde at Muea' sued a plantation worker from the up-country plateau who was known to the Court as 'Thomas of Grassfield at Lysoka Camp'. She asked for £15 'being compensation for immoral insult against Plaintiff in that her private part is watery and hollow since 2 weeks'. Thomas did not show up in Court. Catherine gave her evidence as follows:

> One day while coming from the farm in company of [two Muea women] the Defendant saw me and called me. I kept mute. He began to abuse me to say my private part is hollow and watery. I then held him. The Molyko C[ameroon] D[evelopment] C[orporation] Manager met us and on inquiry, I told him the whole story. He then advised me to sue to Court. Before suing to Court I first of all approached the Overseer and the headman of [the] Defendant['s plantation work gang] was authorized [to hear the complaint]. The defendant was called for hearing but refused. This is why the case has been brought before this court.

The two Muea women witnesses confirmed Catherine's story and the Court ruled in her favour, awarding her £10 damages and costs. A Free Warrant of Arrest of the defendant Thomas was issued.[4]

33

The seriousness with which the Courts regarded insults of this kind is confirmed when we consider the level of damages awarded at that time in other types of defamation case. In Bonjongo during the year under examination, 206 new cases were heard (plus 50 enforcement cases). Fifteen of these (or approximately 7 per cent of new cases) involved defamation of one sort or another. Apart from the two cases we have considered above there were: defamation by accusation of witchcraft, six cases; by accusation of corruption (also in fact a witchcraft case), one case; one case of false accusation of theft; one case where the plaintiff claimed to have been falsely accused of destroying crops; one defamation case where plaintiff (who was to be a selector in a succession dispute) had been accused of not being a citizen of his village. There was one case each of 'scandalizing' or 'traduction' of name, and one where the plaintiff had been insulted by being called a fool. The damages awarded in the cases which were successful were as follows: false accusation of witchcraft, two cases, damages assessed at £1 and £5. False accusation of theft, £6, and for falsely alleging that plaintiff had destroyed crops, damages 10/-. 'Scandalizing my name' was proved, and a recompense of £1 was given; and damages for suggesting that plaintiff was a fool were assessed at 5/-.

The fines in the cases which were discussed earlier were as follows: Namondo, who had asked for £3, received 30/- damages from Sundi. In the case where Efende had to pay damages to the women of Mafanja, the Court assessed the customary charge as £5.6.0, but ordered him to pay £10, for putting the women to the trouble of taking him to Court (the women had wanted £20). The women of Wonjia asked for but did not get £6.10.0, since the case was dismissed. Although Catherine did not get all the £15 she asked for, she was awarded £10. These sums may seem paltry by modern English monetary standards, but they were quite high in Bakweri terms at the time, especially compared to damages paid for other insults. They were surprisingly high when one considers that damages demanded of co-respondents in divorce cases were set as low as £2.2.6 (a sum known as 'an adultery fee'), and that where divorce was not involved compensation paid by an adulterer was likely to be in the order of £5: only half the sum which Efende had to pay the Mafanja women.

What can be teased out of the evidence so far considered? In *titi ikoli* we find a semantic field which includes 'beautiful and above price', the female genitals and, possibly by extension, the neighbouring area of the anus and buttocks, and is associated with 'women's secrets'. It includes the serious offence of stating publicly that the private parts of women smell. Both men and women may commit the offence. Such insults concern not only the woman directly abused, but all women. Mandatory militant action follows which overrides allegiance to kin and tribal groups. Women demonstrate, not on behalf of the victim of the abuse, but on behalf of themselves as a sexual group. Traditionally on these occasions they dress as the 'wild' in green vegetation. Judicial procedures controlled by men may be invoked in both traditional and modern circumstances.

In stressing the particular association of *titi ikoli* with women, the possibility of an association of the term with men has not been excluded. In response to questions it was said that men would resent insults of the kind under discussion, but it was agreed that there would be no question of men coming out to demonstrate *en masse* or to dance or to sing indecent songs. The only alleged evidence of such insults being directed against men that I have, was the attempt by Efende to escape the wrath of the women of Mafanja by saying he had 'insulted all people both women and men . . . I did not call one's name'. He hoped, it seems, thus to desexualize the insults, but no offence seems to have been taken by the men if he did so. Young brides are particularly warned not to insult their husbands in certain ways: these include spitting, and a certain gesture made with the hand, but no mention is made of *titi ikoli* insults.

THE BALONG

The Balong are a people numbered in hundreds only, who live in four villages at the foot of the mountain, about forty miles inland, sharing a boundary with the Bakweri. In all four villages immigrants are very conspicuous. Although there are differences Balong also share many features with the Bakweri. Balong women too are prepared to come out in defence of their sex:

> When a man insults his wife and says 'Your ass de smell' it is like insulting all women, and all women will be angry. Even if a brother curses his sister like that it will be the same. The women will tell other women and in the evening they will go to that man and demand a fine of £5 and one pig and soap for all to wash their bodies because he has said that women smell. If the man refuses, the women will send a young woman round the village with a bell to warn men to stay indoors. They [the women] will be angry and they will take all their clothes off. They will shame him and sing songs. They will sing *Ndungu fumwe figa wa* (I knock my toe, it hurts, meaning 'man curse me, I vex').

Usually the man will pay the fine, but if he still refuses the women will go and tell the old men of the village. If they do not get satisfaction there, in the last resort they will take the offender to Court.

Balong women told of these events with obvious glee. The chief's sister, a youngish woman, said that she had on one occasion been 'a soldier boy', that is one of the young women chosen as messenger by the older women to do 'the fighting', and she claimed that she had helped to seize a man. The Balong also reported a case of two women who had quarrelled and had insulted each other in the standard way. The women of all Yoke village gathered and fined them £5 each, which they paid. The money was used to buy salt from a town about forty miles away. It is to be noted that this salt was divided among all the women of Yoke village, including the newly born female children. The Balong called this *titi ikoli*-like custom: *ndong*. I cannot offer a firm etymology for this, but it resembles Duala *ndon*, 'beautiful'.

THE KOM

The Kom (some 30,000 strong) live in a very different environment from the Bakweri and Balong, some 300 miles inland on the rolling mountain tops of the Grassland Plateau. The only immigrants in significant numbers are the transhumant Fulani cattle-herders who, by arrange- ment with the Kom chief, obtain permission to graze their stock on Kom lands. Descent is matrilineal, and in their traditions of migration and early history females occupy a prominent role. It is recounted that, owing to an act of trickery by an enemy, all the active male members of the community were once slaughtered. To defend the group the women decked themselves in their deceased husbands' military garb and weapons and camouflaged themselves in vines. The women kept guard and repelled enemy attacks, while the few remaining old men built the houses, hunted for food, and went and paid the required tributes.

The Kom have a female practice called *anlu* with aspects very similar to those associated with *titi ikoli* and *ndong*. *Anlu*

> traditionally referred to a disciplinary technique employed by women for particular offences. These include the beating or insulting (by uttering such obscenities as 'Your vagina is rotten') of a parent; beating of a pregnant women; incest; seizing of a person's sex organs during a fight; the pregnancy of a nursing mother within two years after the birth of the child; and the abusing of old women (Ritzen- thaler 1960: 151).

We should note here Ritzenthaler's term *disciplinary technique*. Chilver and Kaberry (1967: 141), speaking also of the Kom, say that 'when the women of a village wished to resort to disciplinary action against a man . . . they assembled as *anlu*'. *Anlu* they derive from the root *-lu* meaning 'to drive away'. The term *anlu* itself, then, is not a Kom equivalent for the expression *titi ikoli*. It appears to connote the Kom equivalent of the patterns of militant behaviour associated with *titi ikoli*.

The invoking of *anlu* is described by a Kom (Francis Nkwain) as follows:

> 'Anlu' is started off by a woman who doubles up in an awful position and gives out a high-pitched shrill, breaking it by beating on the lips with the four fingers. Any woman recognizing the sound does the same

and leaves whatever she is doing and runs in the direction of the first sound. The crowd quickly swells and soon there is a wild dance to the tune of impromptu stanzas informing the people of what offence has been committed, spelling it out in such a manner as to raise emotions and cause action. The history of the offender is brought out in a telling gossip. Appeal is made to the dead ancestors of the offender, to join in with the 'Anlu'. Then the team leaves for the bush to return at the appointed time, usually before actual dawn, donned in vines, bits of men's clothing and with painted faces, to carry out the full ritual. All wear and carry the garden-egg type of fruit which is supposed to cause 'drying up' in any person who is hit with it. The women pour into the compound of the offender singing and dancing, and, it being early in the morning, there would be enough excreta and urine to turn the compound and houses into a public latrine. No person looks human in that wild crowd, nor do their actions suggest sane thinking. Vulgar parts of the body are exhibited as the chant rises in weird depth . . .[5]

Until the offender repents, he is ostracized, a punishment said to be worse than death, which seems the more welcome because 'by it a new door is opened into a room peopled by relatives and friends and there are always sacrifices to link the living with the dead', whereas ostracism 'kills and gives no new life'. When he repents, the offender will be taken and immersed in a stream, and any of his cooking pots which had been contaminated by the garden eggs will be cleaned also. After the purification, the incident is regarded as closed, and is not to be referred to again.[6]

Thus the Kom can be seen to have a pattern of female militancy not unlike that of the Bakweri and Balong. Revenge is taken on an offender by corporate action, and typically he is disgraced by a display of vulgarity on the part of the women. The traditional picture is of such militancy being aroused by offences against women of a broadly sexual nature. Although *anlu* could involve the participation of women from more than one village, it used to be said that only very few old men could recall incidents beyond simple boycotts limited to the village where the offender lived. One might easily have been led to assume, therefore, that the practice had become enfeebled and was dying out. Experience elsewhere (for instance, among the Bakweri) has shown the unreliability of such assumptions. The concept of symbolic 'templates' which serve to generate events from time to time in unexpected ways has been set out in E. W. Ardener (1970). Something like this process took place among the Kom in 1958, when 7,000 *anlu* women rose up. It must be noted that their grievance was not, in this case, sexual insult, but the 'template' for action was that of *anlu,* and for that reason is of interest here. Events astonished everyone, including the Kom. The following account rests on Nkwain's data, although Ritzenthaler has also published a version (1960).

It may all be said to have started in 1955 when a regulation was brought in to force the women of the Grassfields to build their farm ridges horizontally along the hills instead of vertically, to prevent soil erosion. Not, you might think, a very provocative requirement. It is, however, as I can confirm from experience, much harder to ridge horizontally on a steep slope. Demonstration farms were set up to instruct the women, to no avail: they ignored the order. Some were fined. Despite the unpopularity of the measure with women, the new methods were supported by some 'progressives' (teachers and others) on the all-male Kom local government council. In 1958 a zealous Agricultural Assistant unwisely tried to force the issue by uprooting some farm crops, traditionally an offence in Kom. About this time also, a Sanitary Inspector had been trying to improve hygiene in the market by pouring away tainted liquor and destroying bad food. The Chief was also becoming unpopular with the women due to his supposed leniency with Fulani cattle-herders who allowed their stock to wander into the women's farms. Other changes at that time included the development of national politics. The Government party was then led by a Bakweri, Dr Endeley. In Kom his party was associated with the modernizing policy which had resulted in the destruction of food. The party was also unpopular on other grounds.

Matters came to a head on Friday 4 July when the Council met to consider two issues: the fining of women for farming offences, and the organizing of a welcome party for the impending visit of the Premier, Dr Endeley. A Council member, Teacher Chia, was advocating both, in the face of known opposition from the women. The atmosphere became tense. Then Mamma Abula stepped forward from out of the crowd of spectators. She performed some dance steps, and gingerly walked up to Teacher Chia and spat in his face. Suddenly,

> A woman from Tinifoinbi sprinted up to the said Chia and also spat. Then a third woman, Mamma Thecla Neng, doubled over and shrilled the 'Anlu' war cry, which was echoed and re-echoed in a widening circle beginning with the women who had been in attendance at the Council. Fright gripped Chia and he started for his bicycle only to find it covered with twines, around which a growing number of women were dancing and singing. Women started to pick up bits of stones to throw them at him cursing him as they did so. He ran to the Mission House and made for the Father's latrine. The Rev. Father bolted the door and stood with his back to it. The women gathered in dance, and vines and branches were cut and heaped in front of the latrine.

The headmaster tried to disperse the women, but they sang mocking songs about him.

The women sang and danced and, as emotions grew, told the world

38

Mr Chia belonged nowhere—'He is excreta'. And they would shrill out 'U-li-li-li-li-li' and inform the ancestors that their culprit sons were on the way to join them. Death wish! Terror! And then they turned and left the Mission and went up the Yongmbang Hill over-looking the Njinikom market, there to set up their [own] demonstration farm, with the ridges running down the hill in a challenge to the new Agricultural Department's directive. No broadcasting station could surpass the Yongmbang Hill and soon this hill was black with teeming thousands of women. When they came down that hill planning had already been fixed. 'Anlu' had started . . . The next day, Saturday, 5th July, saw the women in Bobe Andreas Ngong's compound where fighting ensued. Jerome Ngong used a cutlass on one of the women and sticks flew here and there battlewise. After ruining much property the 'Anlu' marched on the market beating and driving away such men as had dared to put up wares . . . 'The men can't have their fun while we are suffering.'

To cut a long and fascinating story short: the place was in uproar. Since the teachers and the Catholic Father had determined to send the schoolchildren out to the road to welcome the Premier, the women kept the children away from school, which therefore had to close. The prominent Catholic establishment in Kom was finally forced to concede the transfer of some unpopular teachers, but not before the notorious headmaster had died (of, it was said, high blood pressure). Disgusted with the Courts which were prepared to consider fining women, the *anlu* leaders even set up their own, and insisted on dealing with all land cases, in defiance of the Chief and the Administrative machine. '"Anlu" raged', there were 'breaches of the peace' and finally the police had to take notice, and a number of men and women were arrested. The expatriate police official in Bamenda intervened and ordered their release on condition that they report for questioning to the police station in Bamenda, about forty miles from Kom, at a later date. In the intervening weeks *anlu* operated in a hushed atmosphere that was said to be more frightening than the more overt demonstrations. The women took advice from those men who were opposed to Mr Chia and the government party of Dr Endeley. *Anlu* became highly organized.

On Thursday afternoon, 20 November, two thousand women left for Bamenda, wearing vines, and with unwashed bodies painted black. They were accompanied by two men. Another 4,000 women (the elderly, suckling mothers, and the like) settled down in the Njinikom market to await their return. The column of women were ordered not to speak to any man on the way, and to eat only Kom food and drink only Kom water which they therefore carried with them. No peel, or any remains of food, were to be left on alien soil. An exception was made of the settlement just outside Bamenda where they were to spend the night. They arrived there totally exhausted, their feet swollen, some never having travelled such a distance before. They spent the night singing special songs. The next day they marched up the escarpment to Bamenda, where the leader made a long statement to the police. In the end, however, the police decided to take no further action. The women returned to Kom in triumph—ferried part of the way in two trucks lent by the police.

For some time the opponents of *anlu* were ostracized and prevented from attending public functions and ceremonies, funerals, childbirth feasts, and cooperative farming units. They were by these means denied access to some farming lands. These were traditional *anlu* methods of forcing quick penitence. Eventually peace was made and things settled down, although to a new order. The *anlu* leader sat on the local Council. The Catholics and the *anlu* women became reconciled. Indeed they teamed up against the American Baptists who were said to have referred to the women as '*anlu*-nuts'. Mr Chia made his peace with the women too. He is now said to be happy when he recalls the day when the women 'cleansed' both him and his compound. 'I felt good after that,' he is quoted as saying. 'Be careful with our mothers.'

COMPARATIVE AFRICAN MATERIAL

The ethnographic data presented above all come from West Cameroon. The use of obscenity by women, including exposure (real or implied) of parts of the body which are normally covered, exists elsewhere. Mrs Steady kindly reviewed her material for Sierra Leone and confirmed that 'It is not unusual for signalled references to be made to the genitals or the bottom in disputes'. In what is often regarded as no more than a childish parody, she says, children 'usually accompany the gesture by the characteristic flippant remark "ax mi wes" (ask my bottom)'. 'Between adults it is far more serious. It is more commonly employed by women mainly, I think, because of the greater mobility of women's clothing.' 'Prostitutes are known to employ this form of insult whenever a client refuses to honour his credit . . .' '[At] least three cases are known where [gestures of vulgarity] were used to counter the husband's physical violence.' Mrs Steady's information all related to instances of individual action, except for one where 'this form of protest was used by a girl and her mother against a man for his breach of promise of marriage'.[7] She stresses that such vulgar behaviour would normally be considered disgusting.

Sir Edward Evans-Pritchard, in a paper about prescribed or ritualized obscenity, cites a case of female exposure which is relevant here. Among the Azande:

> the behaviour of the wives of a man when his sister's son has made a predatory raid on his belongings, for which, according to native law, there is no redress, seems from one aspect to be a custom in the same

category as those already described in this paper. These women tear off their grass covering from over the genitals and rush naked after the intruder, shouting obscene insults at him and making licentious gestures. We mention these occasions, but the obscenity, though permitted is neither a prescribed nor a collective response (Evans-Pritchard 1929: 320; 1956: 87–8).

Professor Evans-Pritchard is no doubt correct in stating that the behaviour of the women is not prescribed, but it seems to be a standardized or predictable response. Although he states that such behaviour is not collective, we may notice that he refers to 'the wives of a man', and not merely to 'a wife'.

Kikuyu women, it seems, also expose themselves in certain circumstances. In the Kikuyu data which follow we may note that the notion of 'women's secrets' once again appears in association with the technique:

It is said that in the Meru group when a girl becomes a woman, that is when her first child is born, a contingent curse is sworn on the amniotic fluid to regulate her future conduct as a woman and to preserve the secrets of the woman's social life; this oath was also used to hide the fact of second circumcisions practised on initiated girls at the time of childbirth. A form of curse employed by women and known throughout the Unit is the deliberate exhibition of the private parts towards the thing or person cursed. To do this is *guturama* in Kikuyu and *futuramira ng'ania* is to curse So-and-So in this way. Quarrelling women sometimes use it, and when co-wives dispute about a garden one of them if she gets thoroughly angry, may put it out of use entirely by uncovering her person and making sexual gestures at the garden in the presence of her rival. It is to be noticed, however, that this is not a recognized and regular form of contingent curse, and Africans, except when they are inflamed by anger, find its use disgusting. But occasions when it has been solemnly employed, even by all the women of a large community, are sometimes mentioned, as when the women of a ridge have gathered together to show their disapproval of another ridge or of some over-bearing personality who has annoyed them. The method is then to remove their undergarments, stand in line with their backs towards the offender, bend forward, and lift their skirts in unison (Lambert 1956: 99).[8]

Mary Douglas states that among the Lele of the Kasai (Congo), any married woman who ran away with a lover ran the risk of involving her relatives in a blood feud. If this happened she would be blamed, and 'The women, mothers and sisters of the dead men in the village where she had fled, would treat her with every contumely, dancing around her, singing abusive songs, stripping off their skirts, unforgivable in itself, and rubbing her face in the dirty clothes' (Douglas 1963: 137).

Some further material is also available (for the Gisu, the Bété, the

Pakao, the Igbo, the Zulu, for instance) which I will set out at more length elsewhere. The published data, while it is very useful, is by no means full, with one notable exception: that provided in a study made by Robert Edgerton and Francis Conant, published in a paper entitled 'Kilipat: the "shaming party" among the Pokot of East Africa'. We learn that:

> By means of *Kilipat*, a Pokot whose spouse has flagrantly and repeatedly misbehaved may surreptitiously collect a number of friends and neighbours to shame the erring partner into proper behaviour. Although a man may organize his friends into shaming a wife, *kilipat*, especially in its more drastic forms, is more commonly undertaken by women against husbands (p. 404).

The authors provide case reports, from which I take but a few more sentences in order to illustrate the remarkable similarities with the Cameroon material. One extreme episode concerned the seizure of a husband, and the indignities he suffered at the hands of the women while he was tied to a tree:

> The women began to sing a song which said very bad things—a very bad song. This is a standard song they sing: 'You abuse your wife. You call her names . . .' They said that he was merely an old man whose penis always pointed down, and then they laughed and laughed.
>
> While they were abusing him they danced around him and put their naked vulvas in his face. He was terribly ashamed and the smell was bad too. Some of the women also urinated on him.

He was made to undergo further tribulations.

These items of comparative material from different parts of Africa show that some elements in the patterns found in Cameroon are not unique in Africa.

MILITANT TECHNIQUES IN AFRICA AND IN THE WOMEN'S LIBERATION MOVEMENTS

Having looked at the African material, can we now see any similarities between the garden-egg-throwing women of Kom and the women who threw flour over Bob Hope during the Miss World competition in London? Are the strippers of Balong and the bra-discarders of America motivated alike? Has Germaine Greer anything in common with the Bakweri?

First let us consider the use of obscenity itself. This can best be understood through consideration of respectful, deferential, and submissive behaviour. There are a great number of symbolic systems through which degrees of deference towards a superior or the structuring of mutual attention can be manifested, and these may have positive and negative aspects. Thus not only may prescribed modes of address express relationships, but the avoidance of certain terms and phrases may also be significant; certain gestures may be exacted, while others are deliberately suppressed; parts of the body may be revealed, or they may be covered.[9] The existence of an array of signs for demonstrating respect and submission permits the generation of the oppositely marked contraries that express their antitheses: disrespect, or the denial of dominance. It is from such oppositions that the absurdities of obscenity draw their symbolic force, or derive what Mrs Steady has termed the inherent power in vulgarity. When the women of Cameroon subject a man to such a display they demonstrate that they no longer recognize his power to elicit conformity. He is further demeaned to the extent that normal social relations are denied him, and his recognition as a full member of the community may be put in jeopardy ('Mr Chia belonged nowhere'). Thus the obscenities of *anlu* mark the middle stage in the series:

respect → disrespect → no respect

(*or:* seemly behaviour → unseemly behaviour → ostracism

or: + → — → 0)

Lambert similarly explains that, when the Kikuyu women lift their skirts in unison 'they indicate that they will have no further social dealings with the people of the area concerned or that they do not recognize the authority of the man whom they have thus deliberately insulted'. In Sierra Leone, within the domestic unit, as Mrs Steady puts it, such behaviour is 'a retaliatory *threat* to the husband's position of dominance in the household'.

A full examination of why certain symbols are selected to indicate deference, rather than others, is not possible here. Each will no doubt have a different social 'etymology'. We might note, however, that the use of expressions normally taboo (e.g. swearwords) seems to be more widespread among the men of some societies (e.g. our own) than among the women. The practice is often intended to symbolize the inability of others to demand deference or exert control over the speaker or group of speakers, and it may be that women do not swear as frequently because their dependent position does not allow them this freedom. Perhaps where women do adopt the habit, they feel themselves to be in relatively independent or secure positions. How far modesty and the preserving of 'women's secrets' rests upon the need to avoid the dangers of molestation, it is difficult to say.[10] If the motive for obscuring parts of the body by women, through verbal avoidance or otherwise, is interpreted as a form of self-defence, this itself implies a position of weakness or inferiority, and the symbolic usages to indicate politeness might be an extension of this. I cannot go into such speculations now, but we can note the need for further discussion.

In moving on to examine the modern women's movements in America and Europe, I stress the distinction between 'women's rights'

43

and 'women's liberation'. Those who concern themselves with the former seek the recognition of a claim to a greater share of valued resources, both tangible and intangible, as contemporarily defined. Those concerned with 'women's liberation' believe that this cannot be achieved without changes in the stereotypes of women which have supposedly largely been determined by men. Victoria Brittain says of those representing the former movement: 'When they think in feminist terms . . . it is about actual discrimination and prejudice against women rather than a general challenge to society's stereotyping of women' (1971: 12). Germaine Greer, a liberationist, speaks of the necessity for women to question 'the most basic assumptions about feminine normality': a little more variation in the stereotype will not do (1970: 14). Betty Friedan believes that there is acknowledged evidence 'which throws into question the standards of feminine normality, feminine adjustment, feminine fulfilment, and feminine maturity by which women are trying to live' (1963: 31). The dichotomy between the 'reformists' who are interested in 'rights' and the 'revolutionaries' who are interested in 'liberation' is not, of course, rigid, and most women liberationists include 'reformist' proposals in their programmes. Nevertheless the distinction is a useful one. Perhaps the notions 'instrument' and 'expression' may be relevant here: women's rightists may be concerned with overcoming 'instrumental exploitation' (involving money, jobs, consumer goods, etc.) and women's liberationists with 'expressive exploitation' (which is 'related directly to the irrational and unconscious psychological processes and motives characteristic of man's complex mental structure' (De Vos)).[11]

Social anthropologists recognize that men and women in society organize their perceptions through 'models' of varying degrees of articulation and generality. The difficulty which men (and ethnographers) encounter in identifying the models of the world which women actually use—as opposed to those which, directly or indirectly, they admit to—has been raised by Edwin Ardener. He asked: 'if the models of a society made by most ethnographers tend to be derived from the male portion of that society, how does the symbolic weight of that other mass of persons—half or more of normal human populations . . . express itself?' (above: p. 3). His remarks are a modern formulation of the question for which Freud said he could find no answer, despite his 'thirty years of research into the feminine soul, . . . *what does a woman want?*'. E. Ardener suggests that we might abstract female models of the world by a study of symbolism, since, owing to the relative inarticulateness of women, they are less ready to speak, and ethnographers are less attuned to hear them.[12]

It seems to me that the women's liberation movements can best be understood as attempts 'to speak': their volubility is, indeed, a marked feature. Yet women, it seems, encounter many difficulties in doing so, for 'this world, always belonging to men, still retains the form they have given it' (de Beauvoir 1953: 641), and, 'one of the results of the sexual role-playing which both Freud and society as a whole encouraged, is' (according to Figes 1970: 141) [13] 'that most women, even if asked, would no longer really know what they wanted'. 'Women', writes Firestone, 'have no means of coming to an understanding of what their experience *is*, or even that it is different from male experience. The tool for representing, for objectifying one's experience in order to deal with it, culture, is so saturated with male bias that women almost never have a chance to see themselves culturally through their own eyes. So that finally, signals from their direct experience that conflict with the pre-vailing (male) culture are denied and repressed' (1972: 149). Women, then, are searching for new models of themselves and the world around them. All women, and all men belong to many different sets, for each of which we may expect there to be different models. Tiger notes that 'being human is more persuasively characteristic of a human male than being male' (1971: 56) and similarly 'being a male is part of being a person' (p. xiv). This could be rephrased: the set 'person' (and the set 'human') includes the set 'male'. In such a scheme, we might presume that it also includes the set 'female'. Ardener in his 1968 paper on Bakweri models of men and women states: 'The objective basis of the symbolic distinctions between nature and society, which Lévi-Strauss recently prematurely retreated from, is a result of the problem of accommodating the two logical sets which classify human beings by different bodily structures: "male"/"female"; with the two other sets: "human"/"non-human". It is,' he suggests, 'men who usually come to face this problem, and because their model for *mankind* is based on that for *man*, their opposites, *woman* and *non-mankind* (the wild), tend to be ambiguously placed. Hence in Douglas's terms (1966), come their sacred and polluting aspects. Women,' he continues, and he is thinking primarily of Bakweri women, 'accept the implied symbolic content, by equating *womankind* with the men's wild' (above: p. 14). While it might be true that Bakweri like other women are often prepared to play men's games, as we have seen they sometimes, like the proverbial worms, turn. We also find, implicit in recent writings of the women's liberation movement, the very complaint that while 'male' may indeed be ascribed to the set 'human', the set 'female' does not have an equal place in it.[14] Firestone explicitly states that: 'Women, biologically distinguished from men, are culturally distinguished from "human"' (1972: 192). Her answer is 'not just the elimination of male *privilege* but of sex *distinction* itself: genital differences between human beings would no longer matter culturally' (ibid: 19).

Thus among the models being sought, are many in which the criterion of sex is apparently to be regarded as not of diacritical importance, a position which may appear to point to statements that there is no difference at all between men and women. Yet in fact the differences are rarely if ever denied; indeed, the opposite is usually true: they are

45

stressed. '[T]here will always be certain differences between man and woman;' writes de Beauvoir, 'her eroticism, and therefore her sexual world, have a special sensitivity of their own and cannot fail to engender a sensuality, a sensitivity of a special nature' (1953: 686). Firestone, herself, states that 'men and women are tuned to a different cultural wave-length, that in fact there exists a wholly different reality for men and women' (1953: 151). Thus we find, beyond the search for new models for various sets which can include both men and women, a desire, conscious or not, to identify a specifically female model (of that 'special nature') in which the essential attributes, physical, spiritual and moral appear: a model of what we may perhaps term 'femineity' [15] of the deepest structural level and greatest degree of generality, which is quite distinct from the old, supposedly male-derived, 'femininity' with its load of associated 'secondary sexual characteristics'. Greer admits to 'relying upon a concept of women which cannot be found to exist' (1970: 21). Firestone seeks 'an exploration of the strictly female reality', from which will be developed an 'authentic female art', a task which, she stresses, is not to be regarded as reactionary but rather as progressive. This searching for 'femineity' may possibly have a parallel in the attempts to isolate 'negritude' by some Africans. Femineity is not merely an equivalent of femininity, since it is located at a different level of abstraction and articulation. In Edwin Ardener's terms, as outlined in the Introduction above, it more resembles a 'p-structure'.[16]

Most men and some women find it hard to understand the appeal (not necessarily totally uncritical) which the writings of the women's liberationists have had for many women (both in and without the movement) who might appear to have gained access to resources to an extent at least equal to that of their male counterparts. It is the identification of the model of 'femineity' and its relation to other models which, I suggest, such women feel, intuitively or otherwise, to be unsatisfactory. The more sets which women consider do or should include themselves, the more critical does an acceptable model of femineity become in establishing separate sexual identity and the more critical does the question of the relevance of this identity to these other sets become.

In Cameroon, the militant techniques associated with *Titi ikoli, ndong,* and *anlu* did not originally seem to have been principally used for securing 'women's rights'. The reason for this was probably that there were other sets—e.g. bisexual kin groups—which had an interest in preserving these rights, at least to an acceptable minimum degree. A woman's access to land, to food, to clothing, to medicines, to freedom from assault, and so forth, affected her role within the groupings to which she belonged and her duties as a mother and therefore her capability of maintaining the groups. Males as well as females had an interest in her well-being, and they would intervene on her behalf in certain circumstances.[17] In Kom, in 1958, when new forces brought changes affecting women which other groupings seemed unable to control, almost it seems by an act of inspiration on the part of Mamma Neng, the processes of *anlu* were redirected to the defence of 'women's rights', but this seems to have been somewhat novel.

Insults of the type associated with *titi ikoli* (although often referring to the external organs of generation) do not seem to have been regarded as reflecting upon, or as being directly concerned with, a woman's capacity, role, or 'function' as child-bearer, even though motherhood is a matter of the very greatest attention in Cameroon societies. It is interesting to note, therefore, that liberationists single out the sociological and anthropological theories of 'functionalism' for special criticism, particularly as they are applied by American educational sociologists influenced by Margaret Mead and Talcott Parsons. Functionalist description, complains Millett (1969), inevitably becomes prescriptive. 'Utility alone detains its clear and disinterested glance.' It justifies the system it perceives. Support for maintaining existing 'complementary' sex-differentiated 'roles' is derived from it. A *Times* leader-writer was near the mark when he complained: 'Perhaps the real criticism of the Miss World competition should also be applied to the Women's Liberation movement: that they both exalt an essentially function-less feminism.' Possibly that is exactly what the latter wish to do. I suspect, however, that they may not agree with *The Times* that the Miss World competition is functionless: it may seem to them to reify one of those male stereotypes of women which they find so inadequate, and which may be used to exclude them from other human sets to which they feel they should have the possibility of belonging (e.g. sets defined by 'competence' perhaps, or other criteria).

Titi ikoli, then, arose in cases where neither women's rights nor their functions as mothers was the basic issue: this was of another kind. I venture to suggest that it was the dignity of a concept which they considered valuable and beautiful—the dignity of their sexual identity of the order of that which I have called 'femineity' and of which the symbol was their unique sexual anatomy. Unaware of this long-standing preoccupation among Bakweri, Greer arrives independently at a position close to theirs when she recognizes the value of such symbolism and seeks its reinstatement. 'The vagina,' she complains, 'is obliterated from the imagery of femininity in the same way that signs of independence and vigour in the rest of her body are suppressed.' It may seem contradictory that women should suppose that vulgarity can be a means of enhancing dignity. It can be one when the obscenities are merely signals conveying a message which is not obscene.

Cameroon women particularly abhor the imputation that vaginas smell, an accusation which does not seem to have been common in America and England until recent years.[18] Suddenly women learn that 'there are some things even a girl's best boy friend won't tell her'. As Fiona McKenzie (1972) remarks, 'He doesn't need to. Media man does the job for him.' 'The problem of vaginal odour was invented by the

47

toiletries industries,' says Greer (1971: 28). Mary Douglas (1966: 142) has suggested that 'When male dominance is accepted as a central principal of social organization . . . beliefs in sex pollution are not likely to be highly developed.' [19] It is tempting to follow this by arguing that it was the weakening of the authority of the American male which led to the sudden discovery of the need for vaginal deodorants. But, however they are explained, the reaction among women has been swift. Campaigns have been mounted against their introduction. 'As anxiety-makers, vaginal deodorants are tops: not only a fear that you may smell,' writes Jane Alexander, 'but a fear that you are *sexually* offensive. They rouse terrible wrath in some people—notably sensualists and women's liberationists and people who are concerned with human dignity' (Alexander 1971: 93). *Shrew* complained that 'Most women would be too embarrassed to talk about their private sexual areas to all and sundry, yet somewhere a panel of admen and probably women, must have sat round and worked out a campaign about us. The campaigns,' the paper states, 'are in themselves an invasion of the special privacy of women . . .' ('Women's secrets' yet once again!) [20]

Greer suggests that 'efforts made to eradicate all smell from the female body are part of the . . . suppression of fancied animality' (1970: 38). Perhaps the accusation that women smell may seem to support the repudiation of their classification as human beings by placing them among the animals. This might account for the fact that the insult may become the concern, not merely of the victim, nor only of women who are sexually active, but of women of any age-group. It is interesting that Bakweri say that there is a special association of women with apes, in so far as women are sometimes said to be afraid that they might give birth to them, and their children are thought sometimes to be attracted away by them from human society into the wild of the bush. The word for ape should not be mentioned in their presence.[21] As a footnote, as it were, we should also note that the reaction against brassieres also appears to be the rejection of the implied accusation that women's unique anatomy is not acceptable in its natural state. 'What's wrong with being real?' says Midge Mackenzie. 'I never tell women that they should try to improve on nature. . . .' [22]

CONCLUSION

I suggest that the Cameroon women's movements and those of women's liberation can no longer be viewed only as isolated and independent phenomena. For instance, we should consider whether, by focusing attention as Greer would wish upon the vagina Bakweri women may be demanding respect, not merely for their sexuality in the narrowest sense, but also for a more general model of femaleness (call it 'femineity' or what you will), pride in which and acknowledgement of which is perhaps necessary for the releasing of that vigour and independence which Greer is seeking. Is this the level at which the Cameroon women and the liberationists meet? Both seem to be concerned with the 'deep structure' of human identity. 'Feminism,' says Mitchell '. . . *is about being women*' (1971: 96). To use terminology suggested elsewhere (E. Ardener 1971): perhaps *titi ikoli* is a programmatic statement for 'women's lib'. Few I think would doubt that 'Black is beautiful' is a symbolic statement of a programmatic type. The song '*titi ikoli* is not a thing for insults—beautiful beautiful' offers a remarkable coincidence.

The *realien*[23] of the traditional women's militant movements in Cameroon and women's liberation in America and England are, of course, different; may not the springs of action share a common source? We have discussed the opposition of positively and negatively marked patterns of symbolic behaviour in Africa. When stating that 'In extremities of random violence or in the breaking of cultural taboos, feminists turn femininity on its head' Mitchell exemplifies this (1971: 69).[24] Greer speaks (though not approvingly) of those in the movement who 'mock' and 'taunt' men. This she may not herself do, but does not the mode by which she presents her case itself sometimes appear to be a verbal display of vulgar parts? 'The key to the strategy of liberation,' she says, 'lies in exposing the situation, and the simplest way to do it is to outrage the pundits and the experts by sheer impudence of speech and gesture . . .' (1970: 328). *Titi ikoli* indeed!

This article has attempted to do two things. First, ethnographic material from Africa has been presented which is of independent interest. Second, an attempt has been made to set alongside this material other data on the women's liberation movements which offer parallels. From within entirely different social contexts, women of dissimilar positions in relation to their worlds and with very different experience, have produced statements and patterns of behaviour of beguiling similarity. The one element which the generators have in common apart from their humanity is their sex. If we allow ourselves to adopt, for the moment, the hypotheses that the parallels are closer than would result from chance, we are led inevitably to consider a *third* aspect: whether or not we are dealing here with phenomena of a universal kind. Whether perhaps women require a model of 'femineity' of a certain nature, the maintenance of which may, in certain circumstances, seem to some to be under stress. Perhaps Germaine Greer, by an effort of the intellect, has raised to consciousness, structures of thought of the set 'female' which the Bakweri (and possibly others) have intuitively perceived and expressed symbolically. The problem of whether or not the parallels which have been laid out in this article are coincidental or are a result of observational overdeterminism, or whether they represent universals of some kind, cannot yet be decided. The evidence so far does, however, draw me towards the last proposition.[25]

Notes

A version of this article was first read at the Institute of Social Anthropology, Oxford, on Friday 12 March 1971. The study is being further elaborated for a longer work now in preparation (*Nudity, Vulgarity, and Protest,* forthcoming).

1 Bonjongo Civil Cause Book 2/1956 (164/56).

2 Bonjongo Civil Cause Book 2/1956 (135/56).

3 Lisoka Civil Cause Book 1/1957 (112/56).

4 Muea Civil Cause Book 1956 (17/56).

5 This extract and others which follow have been taken from a very interesting paper on *anlu* by F. Nkwain (1963). Estimates of the number of women involved are his own. Another account of these events is given in Ritzenthaler (1960).

6 See Ritzenthaler (1960: 152).

7 Personal communication: 'The use of sexual gestures in disputes' (1972).

8 An illustration of Kikuyu women performing a vulgar dance may be found in Wellard.

9 For a discussion of 'meeting' and 'greeting' behaviour in animals and man see, for example, Callan (1970: ch. 7).

10 Possibly the use of terms for sexual organs as expletives primarily symbolizes the power to control the part referred to and is at some level a threat to do so. Thus the uttering of the term for female genitals might represent the threat of rape. Of course, even if such primary referents applied, they might not necessarily be in the awareness of those using the terms: speakers might only associate their use with robustness or aggressiveness of a general kind. We should not in any case over-overlook the 'social content' of rape: perhaps the component 'assertion of dominance' greatly outweighs that of 'sex'.

11 De Vos, G., 'Conflict, dominance and exploitation in human systems of social segregation . . .', quoted in Tiger (1971: 77).

12 Edwin Ardener's comment that even female ethnographers have faced difficulties in gathering and presenting effectively data on women's models of the world is borne out, not only by an examination of work done in past decades, but by looking at a recent attempt to present a female view of Hagen life by Marilyn Strathern. In her interesting book *Women in Between* (1972) she finds it necessary to write at the beginning of the crucial chapter on 'Pollution and poison': 'It is with male dogma that I have to deal in the main, for men . . . are the more articulate and coherent in their statements. Women do not make contrary assertions with the same apparent cogency; they half, although only half, agree with what men say' (1972: 159). Ioan Lewis has argued in a number of publications (e.g. in *Ecstatic Religion,* 1971) that the relative inarticulateness of women is part of the reason why women so frequently speak in tongues and get possessed.

13 In answer to Freud's question, which she quotes.

14 Hence, I suggest, the extensive coverage given by writers like Millett, Greer, Figes, O'Faolain and Marines, *et al.,* to quotations from male literature which are intended to demonstrate the low esteem in which women are held by such writers. Stress is often placed on the view of women as polluting or de-civilizing in-

fluences; and complaints are often made of the dehumanization of women by their being regarded as sex 'objects'.

15 Femineity: The quality or nature of the feminine sex; womanliness; womanishness. (First usage: Coleridge, 1820) *Oxford English Dictionary*.

16 Suppose we postulate, for the moment, that the search for 'femineity' is an attempt by some women to bring into consciousness their 'p-structure' of women; in these terms 'femineity' would be the 'p-structure' of the muted group 'women' in a given universe. Suppose that 'femininity', on the other hand, is an 's-structure' generated from a different 'p-structure' by the dominant group 'men' in this same unit. 'Femineity' and 'femininity' are not then to be envisaged as opposites or necessarily totally incompatible. They could be brought into conjunction if an appropriate transformation (or 'mode of specification') is present in the perceptual system: muted 'p' (transformation) dominant 's'. Perhaps some system like this is often adopted and some women (such as the diplomats' wives) happily endorse the model of 'femininity', while others find the required transformation uncongenial, and sense that the model is not directly compatible with their underlying perceptions of the nature of women. Hence comes the attempt by some to generate a wider range of 's-structures' of women (realizable in the world of events), and the attempt by some to bring to light the basic properties underpinning their perceptions of what is possible. See Introduction, above, for the use of some of these terms.

17 The Bakweri, for instance, have a system of double-unilineal descent (see E. W. Ardener 1956). Three different kin groups have an interest in a woman and/or her children: her patrikin, her matrikin, and, later, her husband's patrikin. There are various ways in which women can assert their 'rights'.

18 As an example of what she ironically terms his 'neo-Freudian contribution to sexual understanding', Firestone (1972: 68) quotes the following interesting affirmation by Theodor Reik (1966): 'I believe that cleanliness has a double origin: the first in the taboos of the tribes, and the second another matter coming thousands of years later, namely in women's awareness of their own odor, specifically the bad smells caused by the secretion of their genitals.'

19 One might perhaps rather say that sex pollution becomes a problem when there is a critical lack of fit between the male model (of, in the case of the Lele and the Hagen, supremacy over women) and a discrepant model which the actions of women force upon the attention of men. By operating according to their own distinctive models, women may seem, in this sense, to threaten to distort or pollute the male model (Douglas 1963: 113; 1966: 149, 150; Strathern 1972: ix, 153, 150).

20 Quoted in Alexander (1971: 94). Mrs Barbara Bond reported an incident among university students in Sierra Leone which might have a bearing on our discussion. It seems that female students resented publication of an article in a student journal which discussed the practice of abortion in the university. A special meeting was called and the women imposed a fine upon the men. Was this, I wonder, because they were guilty of getting their facts wrong, or had they committed the offence of making public women's secrets? (Bond 1972, verbal communication).

21 The complex relationship between Bakweri men and women and animals has been discussed by E. W. Ardener (above). Bakweri men boast of the power to turn themselves into elephants. Some women claim an identity associated with bush-pigs. The relationship of women to apes and water spirits (possibly originally manatees) seems to be of another more dangerous kind.

22 Quoted in Wade (1971: 20).

23 By *realien* is meant here the specific and contingent forms which different elements in a model assume in any given situation in the so-called 'real' world of events. Recalling the former analogy, given on p. xix above, the particular shape of the nose, and of the mouth, etc., revealed through a screen constitute the *realien* of that particular realization of the underlying structure of the model.

24 One way the Kom *anlu* women turn 'femininity' on its head is by referring to themselves as men and by addressing men as men would women: 'Sweet girl, is there any kola nut in your bag?' (Nkwain 1963).

25 That processes of a similar nature may be found in association with other sets defined by different criteria (not necessarily biological) I hope to demonstrate in further research now in hand. For some preliminary data and comment, see S. Ardener (1974). The study of women has its own intrinsic interest, as does any other field of inquiry, but it should not be divorced or regarded as isolated from the general study of society. Any insights gained in one field should enrich our understanding of others.

References

ALEXANDER, J. 1971. Down There. *New Society*, 21 January 1972: 93–5.
ARDENER, E. W. 1956. *Coastal Bantu of the Cameroons*. London: International African Institute.
— 1970. Witchcraft, Economics, and the Continuity of Belief. In M. Douglas (ed.), *Witchcraft Confessions and Accusations*. London: Tavistock.
— 1971. The New Anthropology and its Critics. *Man* (N.S.) **6**: 449–67.
— 1972. Belief and the Problem of Women. In J. S. La Fontaine (ed.), *The Interpretation of Ritual*. London: Tavistock; and above.
— 1973. Some Outstanding Problems in the Analysis of Events. Conference paper, Decennial Conference of the ASA (publication forthcoming).
ARDENER, S. 1974. Nudity, Vulgarity, and Protest. *New Society*.
— forthcoming. *Nudity, Vulgarity, and Protest*. London: Paladin.
BEAUVOIR, S. DE. 1953. *The Second Sex*. London: Cape.
BRITTAIN, V. 1971. A Conspiracy to belittle Women's Liberation. *The Times*, 12 January 1971: 12.
CALLAN, H. 1970. *Ethology and Society: towards an Anthropological View*. London: Oxford University Press.
CHILVER, E. M., & KABERRY, P. M. 1967. The Kingdom of Kom in West Cameroon. In D. Forde and P. M. Kaberry (eds.), *West African Kingdoms in the Nineteenth Century*. London: Oxford University Press.
DOUGLAS, M. 1963. *The Lele of the Kasai*. London: Oxford University Press.
— 1966. *Purity and Danger*. London: Routledge & Kegan Paul.
EDGERTON, R. B., & CONANT, F. P. 1964. *Kilipat*: the 'Shaming Party' among the Pokot of East Africa. *Southwestern Journal of Anthropology* **20**: 408–18.
EVANS-PRITCHARD, E. E. 1929. Some Collective Expressions of Obscenity in Africa. Reprinted in, *The Position of Women in Primitive Societies, and Other Essays*. London: Faber & Faber, 1965.
FIGES, E. 1970. *Patriarchal Attitudes*. London: Faber & Faber.
FIRESTONE, S. 1972. *The Dialectic of Sex*. London: Paladin.
FRIEDAN, B. 1968. *The Feminine Mystique*. Harmondsworth: Penguin.
GREER, G. 1970. *The Female Eunuch*. London: MacGibbon & Kee.
— 1971. The Smell Sell. *Sunday Times*, 25 July 1971: 28.

LAMBERT, H. E. 1956. *Kikuyu Social and Political Institutions.* London: Oxford University Press.

LEWIS, I. M. 1971. *Ecstatic Religion.* Harmondsworth: Penguin.

MCKENZIE, F. 1972. A Way to Sell Cleanliness. *Oxford Review,* 16 September 1972.

MILLETT, K. 1971. *Sexual Politics.* London: Hart-Davis.

MITCHELL, J. 1971. *Woman's Estate.* Harmondsworth: Penguin.

NKWAIN, F. 1963. Some Reflections on the 'anlu' organized by the Kom Women in 1958. MS. Buea Archives.

O'FAOLAIN, J., & MARINES, L. 1973. *Not in God's Image.* London: Temple Smith.

RITZENTHALER, R. E. 1960. Anlu: a Woman's Uprising in the British Cameroons. *African Studies* **19** (3): 151–6.

STRATHERN, M. 1972. *Women in Between.* London: Seminar Press.

TIGER, L. 1971. *Men in Groups.* London: Panther.

WADE, V. 1971. The Women's Women. *Sunday Times Magazine,* 12 September 1971: 20–3.

WELLARD, J. (n.d.) Kikuyu. *Man, Myth and Magic* **4**: 1561–5.

Judith Okely

Gypsy Women
Models in Conflict

In this paper I shall discuss the extraordinary contrast between the outsider's stereotype of the Gypsy woman, and the ideal behaviour expected
of her by the Gypsies themselves; the two are more closely connected
than the conventional opposition between fact and fantasy, the real
and the ideal. The relationship is reflected in the Gypsies' beliefs in
female pollution. This cannot be satisfactorily explained through the
Gypsies' internal organization alone, but can be properly understood
only when set in the context of the Gypsies' external relations and of the
more general pollution taboos between themselves and outsiders or
Gorgios (to use the name given by Gypsies to all non-Gypsies).[1] I also
examine how the Gypsy women use their special relationship with outsiders to resolve problems of formal subordination to men. The disjunc-
tion between the outsider's stereotype and the insider's ideal, expressed
in pollution taboos, is to some extent bridged by an exchange of fantasies between the women and men of opposing groups.

I

GORGIO VIEW OF GYPSY WOMEN

Throughout Europe the Gypsy woman is presented as sensual, sexually
provocative, and enticing. In England a stereotype of the Spanish
Gypsy is often thought to be typical and is so depicted in popular
paintings: a black-haired girl in low décolletage, with flounced skirts
and swaggering walk, hand on hip—every operatic Carmen walks this
way. One of the *Concise Oxford Dictionary* definitions of Gypsy is,
'(playful) mischievous or dark-complexioned woman' (1964: 517). She
is thought to be sexually available and promiscuous in her affections,
although sexual consummation and prostitution are elusive in the image.
Sometimes the suggestion is explicit: in the eighteenth century, a farmer in
the area where I did my fieldwork, referred to the local Gypsies as follows:

> These miscreants and their loose women, for no doubt all of them are
> so, as they lie and herd together in a promiscuous manner . . . a parcel
> of Rogues and Trollops (Bell 1956: 78).

55

Usually the image is more romantic. Borrow wrote:

> The Gypsy women are by far more remarkable beings than the men. It is the Chi and not the Chal who has caused the name of Gypsy to be a sound awaking wonder, awe, and curiosity in every part of the civilized world . . . upon the whole the poetry, the sorcery, the devilry, if you please to call it so, are vastly on the side of the women (Sampson 1930: 123).

Arthur Symons's poem 'To a Gitana Dancing', published at the turn of the century, carries in essence the Gorgio male view of the Gypsy female:

> *You dance, and I know the desire of all flesh, and the pain*
> *Of all longing of body for body; you beckon, repel,*
> *Entreat, and entice, and bewilder, and build up the spell*
> (Sampson 1930: 135).

Ultimately, possession of this 'witch of desire', as Symons called the Gitana, can never be achieved. Frequently we find analogies made between Gypsy women and animals or the wild;[2] Mérimée compares Carmen to a filly from a stud farm (Sampson 1930: 133) and Francis Hindes Groome wrote of a Gypsy girl that:

> Of a sudden her eyes blazed again and you were solely conscious of a beautiful wild creature (Sampson 1930: 128).

The Gypsy woman, from an alien culture, but not in a foreign land, is in dangerous and ambiguous proximity. She is placed in nature and in contradistinction to the sedentary culture. Non-Gypsies transfer to her their own suppressed desires and unvoiced fears. As Goffman has suggested in *Stigma*: 'social deviants . . . provide models of being for restless normals' (1968: 172). Nothing about her is ordinary; if pretty she is made outstandingly beautiful, if old she is considered a crone. The implication is that Gypsy women are beautiful, despite or in contrast to the projected inferiority of their Gypsy males, who are victims of more derogatory stereotypes and negative projections. Borrow revealed the same bias:

> How blank and inanimate is the countenance of the Gypsy man . . . in comparison with that of the female Romany (1874: *English Gypsies*).

Gypsy males are dubbed parasites, thieves, and unclean—menacing but belittled. One reason for the denigration is that the Gypsy male, rather than the Gypsy female, is seen as a potential 'home-breaker'. He may liberate a housedweller virgin *à la* D. H. Lawrence (1970), or abduct a woman to be his own in Gypsy society. This male fear is expressed in the popular ditty about a rich lady who goes 'off with the Raggle Taggle Gypsies O'. The Gypsy woman does not offer the same threat to housedwelling society, partly because the housedweller male is credited with an independent mind in his choice of partner, while the female is not.[3] Unmarriageable but endowed with sexual attraction, the Gypsy woman's marginality also gives credence to strange, supernatural powers: for instance, her presumed ability to foresee the future and tell of the past by the 'black' art of fortune-telling. Also, depending on the outsiders' response, she can bring either bad luck by her curse, or good luck by her blessing.

GYPSY VIEW OF THEIR WOMEN

The Gorgios' stereotype clashes with the Gypsies' own ideal for their women. The Gypsies are aware that their women are attributed a special eroticism, and a tendency towards prostitution; they have in turn a derogatory view of Gorgio women, whom they contrast with their own. A male Gypsy said to Jeremy Sandford:

> We're not like Gorgios: Gorgios just take their women as they are. But our people have always been called whores and Christ knows what. Our women, when they get married, they're scrutinized, they're examined to make sure they've stayed a virgin (1973: 81).

The Gypsy female must remain a virgin until lawful marriage. Traditionally girls were inspected by married women. More recently, another procedure has been adopted, as I discovered in my fieldwork:

> It's wrong to do it before you've married. When I was going out with a boy, my mother, as soon as she heard, sent me straight down to the doctor's for an examination . . . then I took a certificate back to my mother. She did that with all my sisters.[4]

After marriage, a wife must remain sexually faithful to her husband. To maintain her reputation she must even avoid being alone with another man or being seen in conversation with him on the camp, lest she risk the accusation of infidelity. I was present when a Gorgio man called at a Gypsy trailer for the husband, who was out. The unsuspecting visitor remained, so he was instructed to stay near the open door, as far away as possible from the wife and myself. Another Gypsy woman soon appeared: 'What's going on here?' The wife replied, 'It's all right, *she's* here,' indicating my presence—another woman to safeguard her reputation. The presence of a child old enough to relate events was also considered a protection. A woman should ideally remain with one husband for life and, although divorce or separation were not rare among those groups I knew, a woman was condemned if she initiated a separation. One such woman said: 'If a travelling woman has two men [husbands] in her life, they call her a whore.' Within marriage, a wife is supposed to be subordinate to her husband's orders. In addition, her deportment and dress are dictated by certain restrictions which go further than the tenets of 'modesty' associated with housedwellers. Far from being a flighty *séductrice*, the Gypsy woman is burdened with many domestic duties. A wife is expected to give birth to numerous children and has the main responsibility of child-care. Food purchase, cooking, and cleaning are also the woman's domain.

The Gypsy woman (perhaps more in the past than now, although the tradition is still the ideal among most families) is expected to work outside the camp earning a living from housedwellers. Such activities as hawking, fortune-telling, scrap and rag collection, and begging, come under the activity which the Gypsies refer to as Calling. In some circumstances a woman may also do casual farmwork. She is greatly valued for her ability to obtain goods and cash from the Gorgio, a process which may involve conning and trickery:

> My aunt had loads of gold rings she'd got from Gorgios. When I was with her, she'd say, 'Do you like that suit the lady's wearing? Well you'll have it.' The lady'd be talked into giving it. Some'd take their earrings off. They didn't dare tell their husbands. Auntie'd say, 'See the ring she's wearing? Well, I'll have that.' And next week I'd see her wearing it.

It seems that in the past the woman was almost wholly responsible for obtaining food and other domestic requirements.

> In the old days the women earned the money. The men sat in the camp all day and the women went out.

An old woman recalled life thirty years ago.

> I'll say this for my husband, he kept a good roof over our head, but I had to get everything else.

The man was responsible for providing shelter and transport, e.g. the wagons and horses.

> Gorgio men give money to their wives. They don't make them work. Maybe it's not like it used to be, but in the old days a Traveller's wife *had* to work. Otherwise they'd beat them.

Today, with greater industrialization and the switch to motorized transport, in many cases, the man's contribution has increased relative to that of the woman. Some of his earnings are handed over for food and domestic expenses, yet it is still considered important that a woman should be able to earn a good living, if only in crises.

> I'd take my last pegs from the line, clean 'em, and sell 'em 'fore I let my kids starve.

CONTRADICTIONS

There is a paradox embedded in the Gypsy woman's role. Within her own society she is hedged in by restrictions, expected to be subservient to her husband and cautious with other men. Yet nearly every day she is expected to go out to 'enemy' territory, knock on doors of unknown people, and establish contact with new customers, some of whom will be men. Success in obtaining money or goods will depend on her ability to be outgoing and persistent, and her readiness to take the initiative. She must be aggressive—quite the opposite to some of the behaviour required of her in the camp.

There do exist formal restrictions on the woman's activities outside the camp. Fred Wood, a Gypsy writer, has claimed that in the past, at least, when a woman knocked at a door and a man answered, she was to ask for the mistress of the house, and if she did not appear the Gypsy was expected to leave forthwith (1973: 29). Such restrictions explain the apparent inconsistency in the husbands' boasting of his wife's mechanical knowledge, 'She knows all about motors', while at the same time discouraging her from learning to drive a vehicle. The latter would give her considerable independence: 'I'm not having you running about; I want to know where you are.' Mechanical knowledge is acceptable so long as it is not used by the women for independent transportation. When out Calling, the woman is expected to travel on foot, or on the more constricting public transport.[5] Nonetheless such controls over the woman's activities outside the camp are either trivial or unenforceable. When Calling with the women, I discovered that they frequently conducted business with men alone and actually stressed the advantage of such a procedure:

> If you get the men by themselves and keep them talking, you can sell quite a few flowers. Tell them to get a present for their wives. They don't know what their wives want.

POLLUTION [6]

Clearly, external control over the women's sexual activities can only be effected by supernatural beliefs, and once fully internalized by the women. It is here that fears of ritual pollution have power. In addition to the pollution beliefs which the Gypsies use to erect and maintain boundaries between themselves and Gorgios, there are certain polluting powers attached to women which can be fully understood only in the context of Gypsy–Gorgio pollution. The general pollution beliefs are illuminated by an awareness of the special ecological niche which the Gypsies hold in the larger society.

Unlike most nomads, Gypsies are directly dependent on the economy of another society which is usually sedentary, around which they circulate supplying goods and services. By exploiting their mobility and by not restricting themselves to one occupation, they fill occasional and intermittent gaps in the system of supply and demand (Okely 1972). To ensure their economic survival and independence, they must initiate regular friendly contact with Gorgios and develop a multiplicity of roles

59

and disguises: those who sell carpets will conceal their Gypsy origins, while fortune-tellers will exploit them. The scrap and rag collector, picking through material which the Gorgio classifies as 'dirt', is prepared to adopt the posture expected of a despised scavenger. The same society that offers a wealth of economic opportunity for nomads simultaneously makes it hard for them to survive in other ways, because they have different patterns of land-usage and they resist bureaucratic control. This is temporarily resolved by a policy of persecution by Gorgios and of evasion by Gypsies. However, when confronted by Gorgio authorities, a subservient and humble posture may be necessary. All roles, whether trickster or victim, carry the risk of self-degradation and a dangerous sense of unreality unless the inner self is protected intact, or group integrity is maintained and expressed in an independent society.[7]

The problems arising from this relationship with the Gorgios are resolved and symbolized in the Gypsies' attitude to the body. My suggestion, which I shall try to document, is that they make a fundamental distinction between the inside of the body and the outside.[8] The outer skin with its discarded scales, accumulated dirt, by-products such as hair, and waste such as faeces, are all potentially polluting. The outer body symbolizes the public self or role as presented to the Gorgio. It is a protective covering for the inside, which must be kept pure and inviolate. The inner body symbolizes the secret, ethnic self (Okely 1974). Anything taken into the body for its sustenance must be ritually clean. Attention is directed not only towards food but also towards the vessels and cutlery that are placed between the lips. The outer body must be kept separate from the inner: even a person's shadow can pollute food. Washing habits are a crucial arena: food, eating utensils, and the tea-towel for drying them, must never be washed in a bowl used for washing the hands, body, or clothing.

> He's a real Gypsy. You wouldn't find him washing his hands in the same bowl as he washes his cup.

A washing-up bowl used for other activities is permanently contaminated and can never be made clean. The personal washing and laundry bowls are potentially polluting and are usually placed outside the trailer. A woman explained to me that both her washing-up and personal washing bowls were stainless steel. She sensed that others might accuse her of confusing them. So she threw away the personal washing bowl and replaced it with an old plastic bucket.

Gypsies clearly distinguish between something being dirty and something ritually unclean. The word *Chikli* (from *Chik* for dust or soil) means 'dirty' in a harmless way. But the word *mochadi* means 'ritually polluted'. Another meaning offered only by Borrow is 'unclean to eat' (1874). The Gorgio is condemned as *mochadi* for his eating and cleaning habits and because he does not distinguish between the inner and outer body; for example, Gorgios possess and use kitchen sinks for multiple purposes. Gypsies either board up their sinks or commission caravans without them and instead use a variety of bowls.

If you look at a Gypsy's trailer, you won't find a sink, that's what Gorgios use.

People say we're dirty . . . they don't see that we think they're dirty . . . Sometimes you go to houses and maybe the outside and the garden look alright but you should see what's inside.

In trying to relate pollution beliefs to other factors, Mary Douglas explains the Pygmies' absence of rules of purity and sacramental religion in terms of their social organization, which is decentralized and fluid (1973: 132-3). The Gypsies' social organization is very similar, with one major difference: their need for regular interaction with an encompassing, hostile society. The Gypsies' rules of purity fit with an obsession with an external ethnic boundary. The internal fluidity of their society vanishes when juxtaposed with the external Gorgio society. The Hadza, studied by Woodburn and cited by Douglas, have a similar organization to the Pygmies, but are notable for a strong male/female segregation with a menstrual taboo and menstrual couvade. In a divorce-ridden society with frequent husband/wife disputes, Douglas writes, 'this formal taboo' expresses 'the pressure of social relations' (ibid.). I suggest that, unlike the Hadza, the male/female pollution beliefs among Gypsies cannot be explained only in terms of the internal organization, but specifically by the organizational relationship and pollution taboo between Gypsy and Gorgio. Here the woman's dual external and domestic role is important.

In addition to the paradox in the behaviour required of Gypsy women in the encampment, compared to that outside, there is another with which they are connected. Unlike pastoral nomads or hunters and gatherers, Gypsies must obtain the bulk of their food from a host society. Gypsies may have been able to obtain more wild game in the past, but even then a large amount of food had to be purchased or obtained from the Gorgio cultivator. With greater urbanization, this dependence has increased. Thus food, which must be clean for the inner body, is acquired from the potentially dirty Gorgio. The Gypsy woman is the crucial intermediary in this transaction since she has the main responsibility for acquiring or purchasing food, as well as its preparation or cooking. She goes between the unclean, alien, and, by implication, unsocialized or 'wild' Gorgio and the clean Gypsy group: she is the link between uncontrolled 'nature' outside the Gypsy system and controlled 'culture' inside it.[9]

Women must be careful as to their method of obtaining food, the type of food acquired, as well as its preparation, which may involve cooking. One danger is that they might obtain unclean food: a fear often voiced is that Gorgios could either deliberately or inadvertently poison food.

61

Judith Okely

But another danger is that the women might trade their sex for food and thereby threaten the ethnic inheritance of the group.[10] The pollution taboos associated with Gypsy women largely reflect these problems: the woman's need to control her sexuality in certain contexts; the separation between her external, unclean Calling role and her internal, clean culinary role; and the necessity for discrimination between Gorgio and Gypsy males as sexual partners.

Figure 1

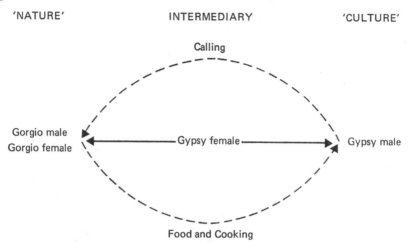

In the nineteen-twenties, T. W. Thompson, a Gypsiologist, recorded aspects of female pollution current among English and Welsh Gypsies of the time (1922, 1929). My own fieldwork revealed the continuation of some pollution taboos,[11] although it was often difficult to obtain distinctly positive or negative information on many occasions. The Gypsies are notoriously circumspect with outsiders: direct questioning, even with trusted friends, was usually greeted with silence, avoidance, or deception. If, indeed, female pollution taboos have become less important, this coincides with the relative decline in the women's external economic role, and thus my case that the two are interconnected is strengthened. The Gypsy woman's external contribution was still vital in the nineteen-twenties and the preceding years for which Thompson recorded his information. A meticulous ethnographer, he has noted the facts but he can offer no explanation. The power of the Gypsy female to pollute a Gypsy male I would summarize in these three alternative ways, using both Thompson's and my own material:

1 Female sexuality is inherently polluting if mismanaged.
2 Menstruation is associated with pollution.
3 Childbirth is polluting.

Thompson finds greater emphasis on 1 and 3, a stress which was confirmed in my own fieldwork.

1 Sexuality as inherently polluting if mismanaged

The woman must be careful not to expose certain parts of her body or to bring it into contact with a man (private sexual intercourse within marriage being the only permissible context in which this may occur). Both in the past and today this is exemplified in restrictions in the women's dress. Today shorter skirts are permitted than formerly, but not mini-skirts. I found that blouses must cover the body up to the base of the neck. Tight sweaters and hot-pants are banned. If trousers are worn by women, the hips and upper thighs have to be covered by a dress or smock. The woman has to be careful in her movements. According to Thompson, her legs must be held close together and she must not bend forward from a standing position, especially with her back turned to men. This was confirmed in my fieldwork:

> When that Gorgio woman first came on this site she didn't understand. She kept bending—in a skirt right up here . . . the men had to cover their eyes . . . and she had a low neck, that was terrible.

> Travellers don't like girls to sit with their legs apart . . . even a girl of that age [6] would be told. It wouldn't be allowed.

Thompson recorded that a woman had to take special precautions in her toilet habits. A woman's underwear had to be washed separately from the men's clothing otherwise this could be polluted. It had to be dried out of sight. I never saw women's underwear on the crowded lines, except sometimes when hidden inside other clothing. Thompson also recorded how men could be polluted by touching women's clean linen or by walking under such a clothes-line. A woman's dress could also pollute men's underwear, according to Thompson. A woman had to wash her body in complete privacy and ideally from a special bowl reserved also for washing her underwear. Any man inadvertently seeing a woman relieving herself, i.e. exposing herself, was also liable to pollution. In my fieldwork one of the major reasons given by Gypsies against unsegregated toilet blocks was that a man might catch a woman by surprise. Breast-feeding, according to Thompson, was also to be done in private. I found that the vast majority of women avoided breast-feeding altogether and opted for bottle-feeding, despite the contrary advice of midwives and health visitors.

> I breast-fed only one of mine. But I locked myself in the trailer first and drew the curtain. We wouldn't let a man see. That's filthy.[12]

Thompson records that sometimes husband and wife, if not every member of the family, had to have separate crockery. I found cases where each member, whether adult or child, retained his or her own cup. Thomson's material indicates that food preparation and Calling require distinctly separate ritual procedures, thus, I suggest, reinforcing symbolically the separation between the woman's external and internal roles. The woman risks polluting a man via his food. Thompson records that food or water was polluted if a woman stepped over it, held it too close to her, or touched it inadvertently with her skirt. Frequently it was said that a woman could pollute red meat if she touched it before cooking, and did not use an implement. Further fieldwork may reveal whether this is still the case. Traditionally, for cooking or food preparation, the woman had to wear a large white apron encompassing her lower body, front and back. Today these are smaller and patterned, but still considered the mark of a 'true Gypsy'. The apron for a Gorgio housewife has a diametrically opposed function which is to protect the dress from the 'dirt' of food and cooking. For the Gypsy, the apron is to protect the food and cooking from the 'dirt' of the dress, which is ritually contaminated by the outer body and specifically the sexual parts.

Thompson described the elaborate preparation required traditionally of a Gypsy woman going Calling:

> After removing the ample white apron she wears in camp, she fastens the money-bags in position round her waist; puts on her hawking-apron, which is of black with an embroidered hem; fixes the monging-sheet [i.e. begging sheet]—a square damask cloth—behind her so that it is accessible from either side; re-ties the kerchief she is wearing on her head, and puts on over it her long-poked, lace-trimmed bonnet (1922: 19).

Then she ties her shawl into a sling to hold her baby, puts on a red cloak, and takes up her basket. Notice how the money is placed beneath the hawking-apron which acts as the shield between the potentially polluting dress (and sexual parts) and the potentially pure monging-sheet which often contained food, and had thus to be protected from contamination. The hawking-apron (black) was never to be worn while cooking as it would in this other context be considered by some as *mochadi*. Some women still wear black embroidered pinafores for Calling or for funerals.[13] I found that black is also associated with mourning and death, which seems to be considered extremely polluting.

Although Thompson has recorded the polluting power of the female body, her clothing, her contact with food and Calling activities, he has not emphasized the more specific mismanagement of her sexuality (that is: illicit sexual intercourse, not simply the suggestion of sex): 'If a man marries an "unmarried mother", they say he's a fool because she isn't *pure*,' I was told.

Uncleanliness comes from illicit sex both before and after marriage. It is said that a husband once had the right to throw his wife on the fire for a transgression. Of one woman believed to be associating with Gorgio men, it was said: 'She's been picking up men. She should be burned, that's what she wants.' To which the speaker's husband replied:

'Time was a *moosh* [man] would put his wife in the canal or push her in the fire if she did that.' [14]

Recently it was reported that a Gypsy branded his wife 'with a red hot cleaver when she refused to answer questions about her sex life' (*The Times*, 27.2.74). Fire is considered to be the suitable purifier for *mochadi* articles (e.g. the possessions of the dead), and so presumably also for impure women. The possibility that illicit sex is more polluting for the female may be where the symbolic and biological potential of the body is used: for a man, sexual intercourse involves temporary absorption into the other, while for the female it may entail permanent absorption, by conception, of the 'other' into the inner body. Since the Gorgio is generally considered *mochadi*, there is the implication that sexual relations between a Gypsy female and a male Gorgio are especially polluting. Moreover, the offspring from a casual sexual encounter between Gypsy and Gorgio is more likely to be born into the Gypsy group, if the mother rather than the father is Gypsy. Thus sexual infidelity with Gorgios by Gypsy women is more threatening to the group than that by Gypsy men. Possibly, pollution via illicit sex may not occur between a Gypsy woman and man.

Defloration, however, even within the context of marriage, can be seen as an unclean act, a loss of purity. Both Thompson's (1927) and my own material indicate that it is usual for a young couple wishing to marry, to 'elope' or run off together, ostensibly without the knowledge of the parents. They return after a few days for formal acceptance and, in a minority of cases, for a Registry Office ceremony and feast. The act of defloration has occurred in a *liminal* place away from the camp and the Gypsy group.[15] I suggest that defloration is probably seen as polluting, and comparable with polluting events such as birth and death, *rites de passage* which should also occur outside the camp. While Thompson has discussed at length the pollution associated with birth and death, he has not examined such possibilities in marriage, although his material elsewhere hints at this (1927: 123).

2 Menstruation as polluting

Thompson's records and my fieldwork indicate a milder emphasis on this as a source of pollution. Only among some groups was the woman not supposed to cook during menses. Then, either her husband or other women took over this task. I was able to confirm this from only two such cases, but the occasional trips I noticed to fish-and-chip shops by husbands may have been to protect themselves from pollution. Sexual intercourse seems to be prohibited at this time.[16] Specific mention of menstruation is not supposed to be made in front of men, because they might risk pollution (see also Thompson 1922), so information is limited, especially for male fieldworkers. T. Acton has suggested recently that the taboo has declined because of the invention of the sanitary towel. He inadvertently reveals ethnocentric bias by his assumption that a 'neater' or seemingly more 'hygienic' containment would solve the whole symbolic problem (1970). Moreover, even the technical problem is not solved by a modern invention: one married woman who, together with her family, showed no inhibition about dispersing all manner of rubbish and uncovered faeces a short distance from their camping spot, told me: 'I never throw them [sanitary towels] out. I don't believe in that. I always burn them.' The implication was, perhaps, that these articles were especially ritually polluting.

3 Childbirth as polluting

Thompson considers that the Gypsy woman is the greatest potential source of danger to men during and following childbirth. Traditionally the woman retreated to a special tent during labour and for a time after the birth. She had her own crockery and was not allowed to prepare food for men for some weeks. Later the tent, bedding, and utensils were burnt. The new-born baby was also considered *mochadi* for a time and had to be washed in a special bowl, and so also its clothes. Today the woman and baby are still regarded as temporarily *mochadi*, and cooking must be done by other women or older children. Moreover the woman is forbidden to discuss her experience with any man or even to tell any man other than her husband (which she will do only reluctantly) the fact that she has entered labour and requires aid. A young woman was warned by the hospital to report immediately she had pains as serious complications were expected. One evening, when she was in the company of an uncle as well as her husband and aunt, labour pains began:

> I was doubled up. My uncle asked what was the matter. I couldn't tell him, he was a man. You don't tell men those things . . . They went out for a drink and I had to wait till my husband came back. I walked up and down thinking, 'If only there was a woman I could talk to.'

As in the past, men must not assist women in labour. The almost universal preference for childbirth in hospital has been misinterpreted as a conversion to Gorgio medicine and the Welfare State. Yet women I encountered in fieldwork were reluctant to attend prenatal clinics and often jettisoned any prescriptions such as iron supplements. Any attendance at clinics indicated more a desire to ensure a hospital bed. It is significant that the Romany word recorded by Smart and Crofton (1875) for doctor is *drabengro*, the same word as used for 'poisoner'. Hospital food is avoided because it has been cooked by Gorgios and in a polluted place. The women usually discharged themselves early, to the consternation of the medical authorities.

The nurses at the hospital said, 'We're sick of the Gypsies. They never come to the appointments at the clinics.' Mary wouldn't eat the food. She wouldn't let them wash her. She cried a lot.

Many Gypsies even complained of rough treatment and poor attention during the birth. Rather than being a safety measure for the women, hospitalization is a convenient way of dealing with a polluting act. The Gorgios are given the task of supervising the process and disposing of polluted articles.

From the last two sections we can see that at menstruation and childbirth the woman's ability to pollute is temporarily intensified because they are occasions for the outlet of bodily waste. The female sexual orifice is a 'natural' point of exit for polluting bodily waste, in the light of the Gypsies' distinction between the inner and outer body, where rejected matter from the inner body is especially polluting.[17] While, for some families, menstruation may not be considered especially polluting, childbirth seems always so. A certain shame is attached to pregnancy. Women must conceal their shape with coats or other very loose garments (coats are otherwise rarely worn). Pregnancy is proof that the woman has had sexual intercourse. Conception is a dangerous affair and must not be misplaced, i.e. the father must be a Gypsy. The term used by Gypsies is to have 'fallen', or 'when I fell for . . .', the added name being that of the child not the father. The baby is ambiguous matter because it has been covered by the blood and waste of birth: the inside come outside. The baby remains polluting for a while, possibly because it has not been 'made' a Gypsy until some socialization has taken place.[18]

J. S. La Fontaine, in discussing women's *rites de passage* in relation to the mode of descent in a society, has suggested that the elaboration of ritual connected with the defloration of Gisu females reflects the importance of male control in a patrilineal society, whereas the greater elaboration of ritual at first menstruation among the Bemba is consistent with a matrilineal society. She does not 'know of a cognatic society in which *rites de passage* reach the scale and elaboration' of those she discussed (1972: 184). For the Gypsies, a cognatic society, those *rites de passage* associated exclusively with one of the sexes are not 'elaborate' in La Fontaine's sense. There is little ritual attached to first menstruation as such, it is merely the point at which girls become capable of polluting men.[19] Defloration is a dangerous and private transition, not so much a demonstration of male possession. Conception and childbirth are again dangerous but made private. The problem is not one of control by a particular descent group or kinship line, with name and property to transmit, but the protection of the ethnic group as a whole from the host society.

It is notable that the women's ability to pollute men, while heightened at certain times, is also ever present, and is not merely associated with certain events or *rites de passage*. The elaboration and public aspects of precautionary ritual lie in *continuing daily* observances. Gypsy men are innately pure, almost by predestination, whereas the women have to aspire to an elusive purity by good works, whether as virgins or wives.[20] Since, in their external role, Gypsy women are always vulnerable to sexual contamination by the non-Gypsy, they must be taught that their ever-present sexuality and fertility are dangerous. The woman's dress, deportment, and behaviour are matters for constant public scrutiny. They must shield their sexual parts, control their movements and mis-placed desires. If women were distinctly polluting merely because of their unique bodily waste, then aprons would presumably be required only at childbirth and menstruation. However, women's sexuality is always potentially polluting to Gypsy men. The Gypsy women must protect all Gypsies from pollution by controlling their sexuality: if indiscriminate and casual with Gypsies, they could be so with Gorgios.

For the Gypsies, the mouth is a possibly dangerous point of entry into the inner body, and must absorb only ritually clean food. Women have an added vulnerability because of their sexual anatomy, which is some-what analogous to a mouth. The woman's sexual organ is regularly polluting as a source of waste, but is also always vulnerable to pollution by the absorption of foreign polluting matter, mainly by sexual inter-course with the Gorgio. The ambiguity of the woman's sexual orifice, as point of exit and entry, is reflected in the separation made between it and food. In both the woman's Calling and culinary roles, aprons sym-bolically protect food from contact with the lower body. Ritual control of sex is connected with control of the consumption of food.

The separation between food and female sexuality manifests itself further in a way which is distinctly related to the Gypsy woman's exter-nal role. In *Figure 1*, the Gypsy woman's roles were shown as a circular process: Calling on the Gorgio, followed by the importation of food and its cooking for the Gypsy. Calling and cooking are *activities*, the only apparent *object* is food. The missing commodity or 'object' in the first stage of the cycle is sex, which must never be exchanged for food. Hence ritual observances separate objects as well as actions. It is precisely because of their identity as members of the female sex that women are singled out for their roles. Therefore sex in some form, if only as gender, is ever present in the exchange, although sexuality is not released. In the second part I shall demonstrate how gender and latent sexuality are used.

II

WOMEN'S PERSPECTIVES

Here a standard male-oriented inquiry might end. However, I am interested in the women's perspective: something which has aroused greater interest since Feminism took new confidence in the Women's

Liberation Movement. Frequently in anthropological inquiries women have been seen as separated from major political and economic decision-making, and the extent to which they may participate informally or influence indirectly is not often fully explored. Emphasis has been placed on the male interpretation of events. Anthropologists have often been in closer contact with the menfolk of particular societies and they have found them most articulate. The fieldworkers, whether male or female, have also imported a male bias which has filtered their observation of the alien society at every level (London Women's Anthropology Workshop 1973; E. W. Ardener 1972 and above).

There are some basic problems which women in nearly every society have to resolve. These were present long before the Women's Liberation Movement and therefore have universal, historical significance. But my mode of presentation arises specifically from the position of women recently in industrialized society.

1 Women have been formally assigned a single economic role rather than a choice from the multiple alternatives open to men. While women have the main responsibility of child-care, food preparation, and domestic work, their economic contribution outside the home has been denied or belittled and underrewarded relative to that of men.

2 Women have rarely been given or achieved formal or actual political power. Their political activity has been largely by influence and usually through a male intermediary.

3 The biological difference between male and female has been the basis for a dichotomization of social quality. The female has been deemed subordinate. The animal, irrational, or supernatural charms associated with her are merely another way of describing and reaffirming that inferiority.

4 Women have been subject to greater controls on their sexual needs and desires than men. Virginity, sexual fidelity, and abstinence have been demanded more of women than of men.

If we assume that these imbalances have to be culturally imposed without much assistance from innate qualities, some conflicts may have to be resolved. Women from birth are confronted with an alternative, superior model reserved exclusively for males. These conflicts are of a different order from those in a society where some members, both male and female, are subject to restrictions which do not apply to other men and women from a different family, race, or class, for whom alternatives exist. Sexual discrimination is built right into the natal family and may therefore be the most provocative or most powerful restriction. Even if carefully socialized, women may not automatically be prepared to accept the major domestic role, minimum external economic and political participation, implied inferiority, and greater restrictions on their libido.

69

They will find ways of avoiding them.[21] I am not suggesting crudely that men alone have necessarily imposed these restrictions; women have assisted by some complicity, consciously and unconsciously (Okely 1963). Men as well as women may need to find ways of circumventing the same restrictions.

Edwin Ardener has suggested that a closer examination of aspects such as ritual may reveal that women have their own conflicting cosmology which may be observable at the level of belief rather than the verbal (see above). This could be further extended: women's alternative view may be observable in almost all nonverbalized activities or behaviour, not simply ritual, and also within the crevices of verbalized activities. The observer may be able to reveal new connections, alternative statuses implicit in the women's situation, sometimes by logical analysis or by association, especially where there are paradoxes or inconsistencies with the male model. The women's implicit situation may never be made explicit, never voiced (even if a sympathetic female anthropologist were to encourage the women to talk in confidence). The resolution of certain problems may occur only at an unconscious level. (This analysis of social positions acted out but not articulated by a group of persons within a specific society, may be compared to the method of psychoanalysis where conflicting or dangerous phenomena may be repressed by the individual and only articulated with the assistance of an analyst.)

So far, the material on Gypsy women has implied that she is little more than an intermediary between the Gypsy male-dominated society and Gorgio society—slightly more active than in the view that women are passive objects exchanged in marriage between two male-dominated groups (Lévi-Strauss 1969: 65). The Gypsy women are overtly subordinate to the men in the internal Gypsy society. However, the Gypsy society cannot be seen in isolation from Gorgio society. It is my contention that Gypsy women resolve some of their problem of subordination to Gypsy men in their external relation with Gorgio society. They liberate themselves in devious, unspoken ways.

ECONOMIC ROLE

Although Gypsy women within their own society have the major responsibility for child-care, food preparation, and domestic work, as we have seen they are expected to go Calling at Gorgio houses. At one level they are 'forced to' by their men, and allegedly beaten if they don't earn enough.

> She has to go out with a thin woollie and her pinny, with a basket selling lace in all weathers. Her husband doesn't give her any choice.

However, this duty should also be seen as an escape from a domestic role. The same woman who gave me the statement above was described as follows:

> Mum does love to be out. She's happiest then . . . She's had to earn her living since she was twelve. Her dad made her.

I found that many women gradually being settled on local authority sites complained of boredom. Sedentarization restricted their external activities and intensified their domestic role. One women who had ceased to go Calling said:

> When you think of a woman's job, all it is, is pots and pans, cleaning and children. It's all right for some women whose husbands let them drive off in the day. My husband won't let me. There's not much to a woman's life.

When Calling, the woman makes contact with people outside her domestic sphere, beyond even her own society. Her identity is not simply as a wife and mother or member of a kin group, but that of an independent worker. In contrast to the lot of most 'working wives' in the larger industrial society, Gypsy women avoid monotonous wage-labour: for example, low-grade factory jobs which are often reserved exclusively for females. One woman who did take a factory job for a few weeks said: 'I hate factories: the same thing every day and you have to come in at the same time, otherwise they knock some money off your wages.'

She also compared Calling with farm labouring: 'I like Calling for scrap. It's much better than picking potatoes all day. I'd rather work for myself than a farmer or someone else.'

Calling involves self-employment as opposed to wage-labour. The work offers an opportunity for decision-making, independent of men. It requires a multiplicity of skills acquired through a long process of participatory education from childhood. Also, in contrast to many female occupations in the host society, the Gypsy woman's work is not simply an extension of a woman's supportive and domestic role, as is often the case with cleaners, primary school teachers, nurses, and secretaries.

Given the dangers of sexual infidelity and contamination of the race, it might seem odd that men expose their women to such risks and do not monopolize the external economic activities themselves. Crude explanations might be that this is due to laziness or exploitation. A more satisfactory one is that they do so because women are more successful at Calling than men would be. Here the Gypsies can exploit the housedwellers' ideal or stereotyped woman, whether Gypsy or Gorgio. In the host society, economic support is usually considered primarily the male's duty, so the Gypsy woman out Calling conceals her role as major breadwinner and often poses as an abandoned, near-destitute wife and mother. By eliciting the pity of the Gorgio, she can extract a greater economic return.

PHYSICAL COMBAT

Gypsy women are considered by Gorgios to be physically less threatening than their men, since they are not credited with abilities to attack or defend, and they are thus able to make closer contact with Gorgios than their men can. The Gypsies are aware that, by many housedwellers, women are expected to be nonviolent. When a Gorgio woman, who was married to a Gypsy, was involved in a fight with a Gypsy woman, she was complimented: 'You're not a Gorgio. You hit back.' While exploiting their presumed vulnerability, the Gypsy women actually cultivate fighting abilities. I heard a mother repeatedly chant the following maxim to her seven-year-old daughter, after the girl had been hurt by another:

> Don't throw stones, stripe 'em up then they won't come back no more. If you can't hit 'em, kick 'em; if you can't kick 'em, pull their hair; if you can't pull their hair, pinch 'em; if you can't pinch 'em, bite 'em; if you can't do that, you're bloody useless. You'd better lay down and take your punishment.

She said her own mother used to tell her that. The woman's reputation as a fighter is important for her self-esteem. One woman who lost a fight which I witnessed, tried to convince her neighbours that her misfortune was merely an accident:

> You know this morning, I went to hit her like that. [She crooks her elbow.] But she leant that way. She moved a different way than I was expecting. And you know how I fell down? That was 'cos I had my arm up. With all her weight on me. She's a big woman, well I couldn't stay up . . . I'm not *trashed* [scared]. That woman could come up here. I can look after myself.

Fighting prowess is useful in external relations and with other Gypsies. It follows that unlike the ideal in bourgeois society, the Gypsy woman is not especially valued for 'femininity'. Physical frailty and the use of cosmetics leading to obsessive narcissism and mirror self-consciousness are not generally encouraged, although smart fashionable clothing and elaborate hair-styles may be worn on special occasions, such as fairs or weddings. Jewellery (such as gold earrings for pierced ears and sovereign brooches), however, is more important. Large rings are highly valued as weapons in a fight.

POLITICAL ROLE

In the decentralized, nonliterate Gypsy society, which has neither chiefs nor fixed leadership even within the competing flexible groups linked by kin ties, in so far as it is possible to talk of a political–jural sphere, women's rights and roles are usually subordinate to those of men. Within marriage the husband has formal power over his wife in decision-making. It is frequently said that in a domestic quarrel the husband has the right to beat the wife. Her kin rarely intervene, and the woman has little defence:

> If I come up against my husband, I don't fight with him 'cos I know it's no use. I can't win and if I go on at him too much, he starts smashing up the things in the trailer [which she has to replace]. So you know what I do? I scratch myself, dig my nails into my hands and my skin and I pull my hair. That's the only thing I can do.

Apart from this inverted aggression, the wife has a formal right of retaliation:

> The woman's one right is to leave her husband. But he must come and fetch her. She mustn't eat humble pie and return by herself. Otherwise she loses face with the other Travellers . . . The husband does a lot, maybe he beats her, but it's her one way out to leave him for a while.

It is still said that the husband even has the power of life or death over his wife for major transgressions.[22]

In inter-family and inter-group relations the women sometimes act as important negotiators or representatives. I am uncertain, however, how far they can initiate strategies, perhaps they merely communicate and discuss issues decided by the men. Older women are certainly sought specifically for advice in crises. In some disputes, the women are expected to fight. This does not occur simply in a situation of hysterical loss of control and not for purely 'subjective' reasons as in the male-oriented description of women fighting. Frequently 'sexual jealousy', a psychological explanation, is given for female combat, while 'social status', a sociological explanation, is given for male combat. Neither explanation should exclude the other. It does happen that women, in defending their social status acquired via a spouse, may have to fight a sexual rival. But Gypsy women also assume more blatantly political roles. One woman may take on the equivalent representative from another family in order to defend the interests of her husband and family, for example in a dispute over camping land. In one such case the husband, whose wife had challenged another woman, said: 'We're gonna beat up Annie before she goes on that site. I tell you she's not going on that site.' While not participating, her husband identified himself with his wife's action. In another case, a wife threatened to fight the man of a rival family:

> It's gonna be a case for hospital. I don't mind if I go to Holloway. I'll beat him. I'll take his neck and screw it . . . I'll make him drink his blood. There's gonna be blood running down that site . . . I weren't interested in the place 'till he came shit-stirring. He wants to be over everyone.

On other occasions the men may assume the fighting role.

As in her external economic role, so in her political relations with the Gorgio society, as already suggested, the Gypsy woman is able to exploit the Gorgio ideal of women being the weaker sex. Regarded by Gorgios as nonviolent and incapable of independent decision-making, the women are left by their men to cope with visiting Gorgio authorities. The women can be suitably evasive and indecisive. When Gypsies are threatened with eviction the men usually disappear from early morning to night. The women have to offer excuses and plead with the police, public health inspectors, security agents, and social workers. Safety for the family from prosecution or permission for a prolonged stay on the camping site will depend partly on the women's success. The women deal with unwanted journalists and cameramen:

> Once they came with those things that go round [ciné-cameras] and Elsie and I went for them, threw them up in the air . . . smashed them. They didn't come back.

Men more than women are vulnerable to the superior force of Gorgio authority: husbands not wives are arrested, prosecuted, fined, imprisoned, and taken for military service. At least one Gypsy man spent the whole of the war in women's clothing, thus eluding Gorgio control. His simple transformation assured him the near-magical safety with which females are endowed. The female's apparent vulnerability to rape is her very protection. As already indicated, the Gypsy woman is well prepared for possible attack. 'I always keep some hot water boiling. All I need do is sling it at any man that tries anything.'
Sometimes the women will act to defend their husbands:

> One day the *gavvers* [police] turned up. John had just come back from work and I was making his tea, he was tired. They said they'd have to take him to the station. I asked if he could have his tea first and they said no. This *gavver* was standing in the doorway and I said, 'You can have your tea', and I picked up the kettle and threw the water in his face . . . At the station the same *gavver* said, 'Oh no, not her.' He thought I was mad.

Few Gypsy women are charged with assault.

RITUAL EQUALITY AND SEXUAL RIGHTS

Edwin Ardener has suggested that men are usually more aware of other cultures than women through greater contact, and so are more 'likely to develop metalevels of categorization' which distinguish themselves plus their women from other men plus their women (E. W. Ardener above, page 6, and 1972). Gypsy women are not lacking contact with the outsider. Although 'culture contact' by itself may not necessarily bring articulated independence of the male model, it is important to remember that the women may make different use of this experience to their *covert* advantage, and manipulate the male models of *both* societies.

Whether or not Gypsy men see Gorgios and Gypsy women alike in certain contexts, as part of non-mankind, they do classify their women as ritually unclean. Whereas both Gypsy men and women are equal in their need to protect themselves from pollution from the outer body in their eating and washing habits, women are additionally and inherently impure by reason of their sex, and Gypsy men are vulnerable to such pollution. The opposite is not the case. The Gypsy male is superior and inherently pure, in opposition to his inherently impure and inferior female. However the Gypsy female, when placed in opposition to the dirty Gorgio, acquires some compensatory superiority. (Both Gypsy men and Gypsy women are belittled and may be regarded as polluting by the wider society; Okely 1973c.) This sense of superiority is observable, but not consciously articulated, in two encounters between Gypsy women and Gorgio men: one where the woman acts out a sodomite role; the other with an implicit fantasy of castration:

> A Gorgio man, visiting a Gypsy on business, stood with his back to the wife who sat on her trailer step, in the company of women and children. She grabbed a hand brush and kept pushing it towards the man's buttocks: 'Stick it up his arse . . . right up!' The women shrieked with laughter.

When out Calling in a van, we drove towards a workman to ask directions. Rose thought I was going to hit the pink conical road markers: 'Mind the tinkerbells!' Her mother retorted contemptuously: 'I thought you meant the tinkerbells between 'is legs. We wouldn't want to damage those!'

The various ritual restrictions demanded of the Gypsy woman will appear somewhat humiliating in the context of her own society. But when seen in terms of her relation with Gorgios they may be voluntarily acceptable reminders of her own power: her decision whether or not to enter sexual relations with a Gorgio determines the ethnic purity of her people.

We have seen that the Gypsy woman is subject to greater restrictions on her libido than are Gypsy men. Loss of male virginity and extra-marital relations with Gorgio women were not greatly disapproved of among Gypsy men, and might even be a matter for boasting. Women seemed to resign themselves to this. One wife ignored what her husband did outside the camp. Another said:

> Men are born hunters. They'll always be looking out for a woman . . .
> My husband's father is still good-looking. His wife's been beaten up.
> She looks old. He's had loads of women and he talks about them in

front of her. Sometimes she talks about the women as well. She's got to put up with it.

Joking behaviour of a sexual nature was the accepted form between Gypsy men and any Gorgio women visiting the camp. It was positively encouraged by their wives, perhaps as a defence measure. 'My husband would like to take you out in his motor. He'll take you to the pictures.' However, no such joking was permissible between a Gypsy woman and a Gorgio male on the camp. Extramarital sex brought ostracism if not punishment for a Gypsy woman. Extramarital relations between two Gypsies within the society were more restricted than between a Gypsy male and a female Gorgio, although when adultery happened between Gypsies, it usually preceded or accompanied a permanent realignment in marriage, often without great upheaval.

Given these restrictions on their sexual behaviour, how do the women evade them? First, when women talk among themselves, they are able to express their sexuality without inhibition in what they refer to as 'a sex talk':

It's all right us having a laugh and joke together—just us women having a sex talk, but not when the men are there.

You know X, she was standing above me on the step and she had no drawers on. I definitely had my photo took! [23]

A: (to visiting Gorgio girl): 'We'll ask you proper.'

B: 'Have you ever had intercourse? A p— . . . have you ever had it up you?'

A: 'Nuts! that's what we mean, nuts!'

C: (brandishes large horn-shaped, cut-glass vase): 'Have you ever had that? What do you think of that?' (Roars of laughter.)

Confronted with greater tolerance towards male infidelity, among themselves the women indulge in fantasies of revenge, even if rarely implemented:

If my husband went with another woman, I wouldn't have him back, but I'd beat him. I'd beat that thing up till his legs were broke, till there was no life in him.

(Notice that in contrast to the case of adulterous wives, no symbol of purification, e.g. by burning with fire, appears in the fantasy.)

Perhaps more satisfactorily than in mere fantasies, the women also resolve the problem of restriction by manipulating their actual relations with the external society. Here we return to the Gorgios' stereotype of Gypsy women, which cannot be explained solely as a transference of repression. It reflects also the paradoxical behaviour required of Gypsy women among Gorgios. Gypsy women are aware of their ambiguous role whereby aggressive salesmanship can be mistaken for sexual aggression. So, I suggest, despite the effectiveness of ritual safeguards, they exploit the stereotype, not only for economic ends, but for another purpose, concealed from their men. By acting a provocative and erotic part, they are vicariously escaping the constraints of the sexual role in their own society, while ensuring that no union is consummated. Subtly, the Gypsy woman is flouting a role imposed by her fellow Gypsies. Aggressive and alluring behaviour is tolerated by the Gypsy male because the woman pretends that nothing is really going on inside her, beyond the desire to titillate for money. It is seen by the men as a performance which is done only for economic gain and is not regarded as a real expression of Gypsy women's sexuality.

Borrow, in his book *The Romany Rye* (1969 edn: 65), is assured by Ursula that if, when in a pub with her menfolk, a handsome young officer were to wink and invite her outside, her men would be 'under no apprehension'. She would go out and merely 'make a fool' of the Gorgio. Borrow is understandably sceptical but considers only the obvious possibilities, not the woman's hidden mental experience. Then as in modern times, the women reject consummation because of their belief that the Gorgio is unclean. Their reputation is intact and they are pollution-free. But meanwhile they have enjoyed their power. Clébert, writing of French Gypsy women, describes how they have no taboo about exposing the breasts and wash at public fountains with 'no consciousness of the slightest lasciviousness' (1967: 218). However normal this may seem to Gypsy men, it seems unlikely that the women are unaware of the outsiders, for whom the breast is forbidden fruit. Even Clébert admits to admiring the sight. He also writes that Gorgio observers have misinterpreted Spanish Gypsy women's dances: 'they are not erotic. At least they are not so intentionally.' Again I doubt whether the dancers are oblivious to their observers' response.

I give two cases from my own fieldwork: On one occasion, when we were alone, a young wife described to me her acquaintance with the farmer for whom she and her family were fruit-picking. He asked her to 'come away' with him. 'He showed me all the week's wages. He said he'd give me that and more, and a nice house.' She made use of his home and telephone, but only when his wife was present. She recalled his remarks with obvious pleasure: 'He said "I can't go to sleep at night, you know why?—you women are much more lively than our kind. Our women are dead."' She revealed only part of the story to her husband when the farmer became too demanding. On another occasion I went out one evening with three women whose husbands believed we were going for a quiet chat at the local. We drove some distance to a more exotic pub. We got talking to several men, one of whom secretly offered one woman whom I will call '*X*' some 'hot' (stolen) copper. The women were friendly, *X* flirtatious, but avoided any intimacy. As we drove back:

> *Y:* 'That man was trying to ask me out. He asked why we'd all come here. I said, "We're only here for the beer!"' (Laughter)

Z: 'We can't tell them [husbands] about it.'
Y: 'No, my husband mustn't know. If he knew we'd been talking to those men there'd be murders!'
X: 'We'll say we just went down the road.'
Z: 'Yes, you mustn't tell them, understand.'

Ursula admits to Borrow that she will steal and lie to obtain things from Gorgios, but is extremely insulted when he suggests she might also play the *lubbeny* ('prostitute'). The very word *lubbeny* is unutterable by her. 'A person may be a liar and thief, and yet a very honest woman' (1969: 63). I also found the words 'prostitute' or 'whore' virtually unspeakable; they were communicated to me in a whisper, in contrast to 'cunt' which was used frequently and indiscriminately even to young babies. The idea of prostitution crops up in strange ways. There is a repeated mythical tale of a grandmother:

> Grandmother used to drink like a man. She ran a brothel. Wicked woman. At the end she owned two houses . . . When grandmother was in the pub one night, a man with a long beard came in. He goes up to her and says, 'Have you got a light, my pretty?' meaning to ask her if she was willing. My grandmother gets some paper, rolls it up, pushes it in the fire, and says, 'Here's a light, my pretty,' and she puts the paper to his beard and it goes up in flames!

Here again is an example of a Gypsy woman expressing ritual superiority over a Gorgio male. The beard, a common psychoanalytic symbol of genitals, is purified by a burning phallus. One young woman with whom I went Calling, jokingly suggested we should manage a brothel. Neither the grandmother nor my friend were prostitutes themselves. Instead they favoured exploiting prostitutes, or rather *exploiting prostitution*, without tainting themselves. The possibility of selling sex for food is formally suppressed but thus pushes its way into stories and jokes.

Prostitution appears more blatantly by projection in the Gypsies' stereotype of the Gorgio woman, which is comparable to the stereotype held by Gorgios of Gypsy women. Gypsies attribute to Gorgio women the inverse of behaviour expected of Gypsy women. Gorgio women do not control their sexuality: they 'show their arse', wear no knickers, strip-wash in front of men, and put on provocative make-up and revealing dress. For Gypsy men Gorgio women are fair game, if not actual prostitutes. During the early part of my fieldwork three men joked with me. My naïve response was repeated amidst uproarious laughter around the camp:

Male Gypsy: 'If I gave you two hot pennies out of the fire, what would you do then?'
Female Gorgio: 'I'd drop them.'

78

The joke partly said that the Gorgio girl would drop her knickers for the price of two pennies: a cheap prostitute indeed. (The pennies could also be seen as purifying sexual organs.) I doubt whether this joke would ever be played on a Gypsy woman.

The boundary erected by both Gypsy and Gorgio between the two societies becomes a useful device for resolving powerful areas of conflict by compartmentalization. Different role potentialities in a single individual are split between two societies. Lévi-Strauss expresses these potentialities in marital terms: 'This deep polygamous tendency, which exists among all men' (1969: 38); Freud would state the problem more explicitly as a sexual drive. Lévi-Strauss reserves such tendencies exclusively for men. It is more credible that just as men may be dissatisfied by the ideal woman and ideal role they have created for themselves, so may women be troubled by alternative images and tendencies within themselves. Both men and women protect themselves by giving these tendencies, oversimplified, to an alien people. Thus (as in *Figure 2*) virginity, monogamy, and sexual abstinence, the ideals, are placed on ego's side of the ethnic boundary, while prostitution, promiscuity, and passive availability are placed on the other. A woman who does not conform to any of the first set will be automatically classified under the other pejorative set. Although possibly originally articulated by men, these divisions are usually accepted by women. Within the larger Gorgio society, an ethnic boundary may not always be used.

Figure 2

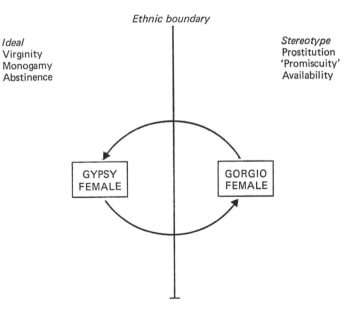

There appears to be no ready Gypsy category in which to place Gypsy women resorting to prostitution and remaining in their own society. Also, empirically, prostitution is extremely rare. I encountered only one example. Deserted by her husband, the young mother wished to keep her children with her. Until her eventual re-marriage she temporarily offered sexual favours for money. Her sense of duty made her behaviour excusable to the Gypsies. But she was likened to a Gorgio. She was told: 'You shouldn't do that. You're like the land girls.' For Gypsy women the separation between the ideal and the fallen woman is reinforced by pollution beliefs, on a par with the separation they must make between sex and food. The few Gorgio women drifting into Gypsy society as real or honorary prostitutes and conforming to the stereotype, were treated as polluting. Their apparent ability to pollute other *women* was derived from their uncontrolled sexuality, not simply from their eating and washing habits.

> She was eating a meat pie and picking some of it out; 'I don't like that jelly,' she said. I told her 'I reckon you like the jelly . . . you're dirty. I wouldn't have you drink tea with me, not let you touch my cups.'

Even the few Gorgio women who enter the society with the respectable status of wife are at first held in contempt and ostracized, until they have demonstrated meticulously their desire to conform to a Gypsy identity.

As a counterpart to their sense of ritual superiority towards Gorgio men, which I have already indicated, Gypsy women assumed an aggressive and dominating attitude towards Gorgio women. Gorgio women, thought to show uncontrolled and polluting sexuality, were described in the following ways: 'Just a big hole with lots of hairs in it'; 'red' or 'cranky cunt'. The Gypsy women's response to this image was frequently: 'I'll put my boot up her cunt.' Gorgio women, ever open and available, were thought to want the crudest of sexual satisfaction, if not rape.

When prostitution is resorted to deliberately as a way of life, by either the Gypsy or the Gorgio, then the ethnic stereotypes assume new significance. The few 'regular' prostitutes of Gypsy origin had moved into Gorgio society and become housedwellers. They concealed their origins and dressed and behaved not as Gypsies, but as they pictured Gorgio prostitutes to be. For them, being a prostitute may initially be the enactment of a fantasy. As the traditional control of their sexuality breaks down, they act out the opposite stereotype. In order to consummate an illicit relationship, they cross the ethnic line. An eighteen-year-old girl who had left her family and moved into lodgings, visited her cousin on an encampment (while recovering from an operation). She wore hot-pants, tight sweater, and lots of make-up:

> I might move to London, you could earn £15 a day at striptease, or you could stay in a flat and have a photographer visit you and take

pictures. No one else would see you. If I got money, I'd buy a motor bike and all leather gear.

Her attempts at prostitution were still fairly amateur.

Like Gypsy women acting in real or make-believe fashion in Gorgio society, some Gorgio women also appear to use man-made stereotypes to meet their needs. Escaping certain roles within their own society, they go off with the 'raggle-taggle' Gypsies. I am referring specifically to women in transit, not those who assume the role of permanent wife with all its restrictions. I encountered two such drifters who, in breaking all the rules of dress and behaviour, invited anger and scorn from the Gypsy women. It is only retrospectively that I understand their deliberate tactlessness and apparent irrationality. They were fully aware of the correct code for Gypsy women and occasionally conformed to it. Generally they were not aiming for honourable acceptance but were instead enacting their own fantasies. They seemed to like the idea of the Gypsy male as exotic seducer and images of themselves as peculiarly seductive, either as outsiders or as stereotyped Gypsy women. Although in their case not fictitious, their form of prostitution was freer and more amenable to fantasy than in Gorgio society, where prostitution is more routinized and supervised by men.[24]

This use of the Gypsies to soften and romanticize the prostitute's harsh role and image reappears within Gorgio society. For example, there is the curious phenomenon of the Gorgio stripteaser without any Gypsy connections, who assumed the name of 'Gypsy Rose Lee', later celebrated in the film and musical, *Gypsy*. The stripteaser expressed most blatantly the Gorgio stereotype of the Gypsy woman who is sexually arousing but untouchable. This masquerade takes another more satisfactory form: Clébert, in affirming the absence of prostitution by or among Gypsies, notes the existence of Gorgio prostitutes in Pigalle dressed up as Gypsies (1967: 208). Here the unobtainable is made obtainable through living fantasy.

The ideal, stereotyped, and illicit relations between female and male Gypsies and Gorgios are represented in *Figure 3*.

Each of the two social groups idealizes and marries its own kind. The women, if not the men, of the opposing group are attributed stereotyped qualities which are the inverse of the ideal. Since both sexual and marital relations between the two groups are disapproved of, if not prohibited, no real exchange of sexual or marital partners should take place. On a statistical level such exchange is indeed rare. There is, however, an illicit, unorganized exchange of fantasies between the male and female of opposing groups. These fantasies are the unconscious link between the ideal and the taboo. Men have fantasies about the 'other' women and women have fantasies about the 'other' men. Both have fantasies about themselves in this rapport.[25] At the level of fantasy, Gypsy women, confronted with greater sexual control than men, equalize their situation.

Nothing is actually given, but the possibility is admitted. Perhaps the Gypsies may be more aware of the stereotypes which Gorgios attach to them than is the case in reverse, and exploit these.

Figure 3

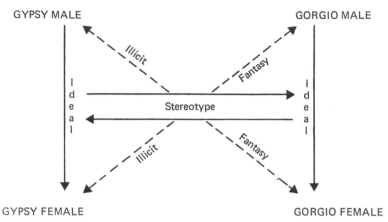

Key

The vertical line from male to female represents the public Ideal woman within the group.

The horizontal double lines of exchange represent the public stereotype of the women, if not the men, of the opposing group. This is the inverse of the Ideal.

The diagonal broken lines represent the illicit fantasies exchanged between individual women and men of opposing groups.

The Ideal man for either group is 'missing' because, from the male point of view, at least, and unlike the Ideal woman, it is not the inverse of the stereotype of the men in the opposing group.

To conclude: I hope to have shown that the ideal of Gypsy women held by Gypsies, and the pollution taboos associated with women, are interdependent with the relationship between Gypsies and Gorgios, and also with the stereotype which Gorgios have of Gypsy women. Further, while conforming to the ideal, and conscious of the Gorgio stereotype, Gypsy women seek expression, on less recognized levels,[26] for their conflicts with men of both groups.

Notes

1 *Gorgio* is the Romany word for 'stranger' or 'outsider', and has similar pejorative associations to those that the title 'Gypsy' has for some housedwellers. Although many English Gypsies may refer to themselves as 'Travellers', especially to outsiders, I have chosen to use the title 'Gypsy'. The definition of a Gypsy or Traveller, where descent is a necessary condition, I have discussed in another paper (Okely 1973a). That paper, 'Gypsy Identity', is to be published as part of a research project organized by Barbara Adams at the Centre for

Environmental Studies, and sponsored by the Rowntree Trust, to all of whom I am indebted. An earlier version of the present paper on Gypsy women was first read at the Women's Anthropology Group, Oxford, and I am grateful to Shirley Ardener for her original encouragement. My own data are based on 12 months' fieldwork between late 1970 and early 1972 among Gypsies with whom I lived mainly in Southern England, and more especially near the larger industrial centres.

2 For the placing of other women in the wild, see Edwin Ardener above, p. 5 ff. In this case housedwellers may associate Gypsy women, more than their own women, with the wild.

3 This sexual discrimination is comparable to that embedded in the racialist's frequent fear that a black man might marry a white man's daughter. There is less preoccupation with the fear of a black woman marrying a white man, because the latter is considered less vulnerable to seduction without reasoned choice.

4 All unacknowledged quotations are from my field notes; they are reconstructions of conversations which were written up as soon as practicable after the event. Direct recording would have been inhibiting and in most circumstances extremely provocative to this non-literate people who have learnt to associate note-taking with police harassment.

5 Before motorization, women were permitted to go out Calling with a pony and open trap, which were presumably more inhibiting to sexual activities than is the privacy of a motor vehicle.

6 It will be obvious to the reader that in my discussion on pollution, boundaries, and the symbolism of the body, I have been greatly influenced by the work of Mary Douglas, and more specifically her *Purity and Danger* (1966). So implicit are her ideas that I can no longer give page references.

7 This schizoid situation can be compared with that portrayed by Laing in *The Divided Self* (1965), where the public role and the personality projected for outsiders are separated from the private, inner self. Increasing separation may endanger the inner self and its sense of reality. (I am grateful to Martin Thom for drawing my attention to this and for our discussions on aspects of this paper.) In contrast to the isolated individual, the Gypsy can display and nourish his 'inner self' with all members of his ethnic group, who are all in a similar predicament.

8 Anne Sutherland in her study of Gypsies in California (1972) places greater emphasis on the upper and lower part of the body. I am grateful to her for the stimulus of her paper which raised questions I then had to answer in my own fieldwork.

9 I follow here Edwin Ardener's use of 'nature' and his amplification of Lévi-Strauss (1972, and above, pp. 5–6, 14). The Gypsies, like the Bakweri, have also the 'men's wild', associated with hunting and 'real' nature.

10 The Gypsies have an ideology of 'pure blood' although in fact those with one Gorgio and one Gypsy parent can be assimilated.

11 Thomas Acton (1970) claims that the emphasis on the uncleanliness of women has virtually disappeared. However, his own material sometimes contradicts this. Moreover he does not discuss the pollution associated with childbirth.

12 The restriction on public exposure of the breasts is in marked contrast to the Gypsies in California studied by A. Sutherland (1972) and Gypsies in France (Clébert 1967: 218). However, Sutherland recorded that a woman could pollute

83

a man by lifting her skirt and exposing the lower part of her body (cf. the paper by Shirley Ardener above).

13 These pinafores, sometimes specially commissioned from local dressmakers, have no sleeves and cover the upper and lower body, front and back.

14 Personal communication, B. Adams, 1972.

15 Victor Turner (1970: Ch. 4) in discussing the *liminal* period in *rites de passage* emphasizes its temporal and ceremonial aspects. Although both Turner (1970: 98) and Douglas (1966: 96) mention the possibility of a *liminal* person being removed elsewhere, neither fully explores the idea of a *liminal place*. For the Gypsies, the choice of *location* unaccompanied by elaborate ritual and public ceremony, may, in some instances, demonstrate a marginal state.

16 One man jokingly made me repeat some words which sounded like *Rattvalo Kauri*. These he refused to translate. The other witnesses appeared tense. I discovered later, via Smart and Crofton (1875: 128, 92), that the words meant 'bloody penis'. Presumably this had a special horror because it implied tabooed sexual intercourse during menstruation. It had been engineered so that the words were uttered appropriately by a Gorgio woman.

17 Presumably semen is clean because of its fertilizing qualities. It is not waste by definition, although it may be wasted.

18 Despite the Gypsies' ideology of purity of blood, they sometimes adopt Gorgio babies and, provided these are socialized as Gypsies, their genetic origins become irrelevant. See Okely (1973b).

19 It appears (although further fieldwork is necessary to clarify this) that women past the menopause are still capable of polluting men.

20 This distinction was clarified for me after noticing a similar theme in Julie du Boulay's paper on Greek women (1974), read at the Women's Anthropology Group, Oxford, and later published.

21 Simone de Beauvoir has emphasized the evasions made by women: 'Il est donc nécessaire d'étudier avec soin le destin traditionnel de la femme. Comment la femme fait-elle l'apprentissage de sa condition, comment l'éprouve-t-elle, dans quel univers se trouve-t-elle, enfermée, quelles évasions lui sont permises' (1949: II, Introduction).

22 See also Borrow (1969: 76), recording customs in the nineteenth century: 'A man by Gypsy law, brother, is allowed to kick and beat his wife, and to bury her alive if he thinks proper.'

23 Here the woman's vagina is wittily compared to a camera. I have excluded other examples for reasons of discretion.

24 The ex-prostitute 'J' in Millett's essay (1971: 120) recalls: 'It's very hard to find a prostitute who hasn't got a pimp.' Nevertheless, prostitutes may have the ideal of independence: 'If you have a lot of men . . . then you're not dependent on any *one* of them' (op. cit.: 86). See also de Beauvoir on prostitutes (1949, Volume II).

25 This relationship between two ethnic groups can be compared to the asymmetrical relationship between black and white races. In cases where sexual and even marital relations occur, each partner may continue to live out his or her fantasies in the concrete situation. See Bastide, 'Dusky Venus, Black Apollo' (1972), for an examination of the continuing inner conflicts in mixed marriages.

26 Men, also at an unarticulated level, may have another view of their situation.

References

ACTON, T. A. 1970. The Functions of the Avoidance of Mochadi Kovels amongst Gypsies in South Essex. Part of thesis, Nuffield College, Oxford. Shortened version published in 1971 in *Journal of the Gypsy Lore Society*.

ARDENER, E. W. 1972. Belief and the Problem of Women. In J. S. La Fontaine (ed.), *The Interpretation of Ritual*. London: Tavistock; and above.

ARDENER, S. G. 1973. Sexual Insult and Female Militancy. *Man* 8: 422–40; and above.

BASTIDE, R. 1972. Dusky Venus, Black Apollo. In P. Baxter and B. Sansom (eds.), *Race and Social Difference*. Harmondsworth: Penguin.

BEAUVOIR, S. DE. 1949. *Le deuxième sexe*. Paris: Gallimard.

BORROW, G. 1874. *Romano-Lavo-Lil*. London: J. Murray.

— 1969. *The Romany Rye*. London: Dent, Everyman edn.

CLÉBERT, J. P. 1967 *The Gypsies*. Trans. C. Duff, Harmondsworth: Penguin.

DOUGLAS, M. 1966. *Purity and Danger*. London: Routledge & Kegan Paul.

— 1973. *Natural Symbols*. Harmondsworth: Penguin.

DU BOULAY, J. 1974. The Woman in Greek Village Society. To be published in part.

ELLIS, W. 1956. The Nuisance and Prejudice of the Gypsy Vagrant to the Farmer. Cited in V. Bell, *To Meet Mr Ellis*. London: Faber & Faber.

GOFFMAN, E. 1968. *Stigma*. Harmondsworth: Penguin.

HINDES GROOME, F. 1930. Kriesgspiel. Cited in J. Sampson (ed.), *The Wind on the Heath*. London: Chatto & Windus.

LA FONTAINE, J. E. 1972. Ritualization of Women's Life-crises in Bugisu. In J. S. La Fontaine (ed.), *The Interpretation of Ritual*. London: Tavistock.

LAING, R. D. 1965. *The Divided Self*. Harmondsworth: Penguin.

LONDON WOMEN'S ANTHROPOLOGY WORKSHOP. 1973. Collected papers.

LAWRENCE, D. H. 1970. *The Virgin and the Gypsy*. Harmondsworth: Penguin.

LÉVI-STRAUSS, C. 1969. *The Elementary Structures of Kinship*. Trans. J. H. Bell, J. R. von Sturmer, and R. Needham. London: Eyre & Spottiswoode.

MÉRIMÉE, P. 1930. *Carmen*. Excerpt from Ch. III cited in J. Sampson (ed.), *The Wind on the Heath*. London: Chatto & Windus.

MILLETT, K. 1972. Prostitution: a Quartet for Female Voices. In V. Gornick and B. K. Moran (eds.), *Woman in Sexist Society*. New York: Signet.

OKELY, J. M. 1963. The Spectre of Feminism. *The Messenger* (4): 4–5.

— 1972. Work and Travel. Paper presented at the Centre for Environmental Studies.

— 1973a. Gypsy Identity. Paper presented at the Centre for Environmental Studies.

— 1973b. Family, Marriage and Kinship Groups. With Okely 1972 and 1973a in *Gypsies and Government Policy in England*. London: Heinemann, 1975.

— 1973c. No Fixed Abode. Talk given on BBC Radio Three, 9 September 1973.

— 1974. Gorgios and Gypsies: Public Health and Inner Purity. Paper read at the Institute of Social Anthropology, Oxford. To be published in revised version.

SANDFORD, J. 1973. *Gypsies*. London: Secker & Warburg.

SMART, B. C., & CROFTON, H. T. 1875. *The Dialect of the English Gypsies*. London: Asher & Co.

SUTHERLAND, A. 1972. The Romany in America. Paper read at the Institute of Social Anthropology, Oxford. To be published in a fuller version by Tavistock, London.

SYMONS, A. 1930. To a Gitana Dancing. In J. Sampson (ed.), *The Wind on the Heath*. London: Chatto & Windus.

THOMPSON, T. W. 1922. The Uncleanness of Women among English Gypsies. *Journal of the Gypsy Lore Society*, third series 1: 16–43.

— 1927. Gypsy Marriage in England. *Journal of the Gypsy Lore Society*, third series 6: 101–29.

85

— 1929. Additional Notes on English Gypsy Women Taboos. *Journal of the Gypsy Lore Society*, third series **8**: 33–9.

THE TIMES 27 February 1974.

TURNER, V. W. 1970. *The Forest of Symbols*. Ithaca and London: Cornell University Press.

WOOD, M. F. 1973. *In the Life of a Romany Gypsy*. London and Boston: Routledge & Kegan Paul.

Hilary Callan

The Premiss of Dedication
Notes towards an Ethnography of Diplomats' Wives

PRELIMINARY METHODOLOGICAL REMARKS

This preliminary paper is based on a year's fieldwork among members of a large British diplomatic mission in a Middle Eastern capital. I shall call this, for brevity, the British Mission. I do not know how far my remarks apply to other British missions, nor their foreign counterparts; my own material, apart from written sources, is drawn predominantly from this one environment. So far as any special technique is being employed it is that of 'participant observation'; but since the term has slightly unusual implications here, one or two comments are in order.

'Studying one's own people' is a well-established tradition within anthropology, and the special opportunities and problems of the field-worker on home ground have been widely enough discussed. It is generally true, however, that in these cases (of which Kenyatta is perhaps the most distinguished example), the fieldworker is born into his culture and absorbs it in the ordinary way before acquiring the specialized techniques which he then takes back home. It must be relatively rare that (as in my own case) exposure to training precedes membership of the society under investigation—a membership acquired through marriage rather than birth. Of course the latter is true of diplomats' wives generally, not just those who are also anthropologists.[1] Diplomatic society is importantly different from a 'total culture' in that one joins it—in the capacity of a wife—late in life.[2] What this adds up to is that this study is the work of one who in the perspective of general anthropology if not of diplomatic society wields an unusual combination of insider and outsider status.

Related to this is another slightly odd feature of my own position. Participation in diplomatic life presupposes some degree of conformity to a role-model whose nature is of course at issue here. There thus arises the problem of judging how far to conform: and it arises in both 'deep' and 'superficial' versions. Superficially, the greater the conformity the fuller the acceptance and access to perhaps vital information but the greater the loss, probably, of scientific objectivity as well as sheer working-time. More deeply, the collective self-image of diplomats' wives (whatever structure it finally turns out to have) leans very heavily on a

87

sense of the Embassy community as focus for the individual's primary or only commitment beyond her immediate family. This part of the model is highly conscious and endlessly talked about. 'Be loyal to the chaps in the team.' 'Official duties come first.' [3] Hence any involvement not in accord with this—and certainly any suggestion of an objective personal stance towards Embassy life—leads at its mildest to one's being perceived as deviant: and this not for surface reasons, although these are often put forward. 'Don't get too involved in your job, or you won't have enough time for bazaars and entertaining.' Thus any kind of 'alternative' commitment on my part, even that implied in a would-be objective set of attitudes, is in direct violation of my definition as an Embassy wife—a definition which I cannot but have since the system furnishes no other. Compare the 'sympathetic outsider' identity available to the traditional fieldworker. Confrontations of a major or minor kind are always a possibility, and to have confrontations with 'one's people' is, no doubt, bad fieldwork: although I have found them mitigatingly useful in the sense that prodding a thing can help one to discover its shape. The problem of participation exists, I am sure, for every fieldworker; in cases like this it exists in a slightly peculiar form, both existentially and politically.

A final methodological difficulty—obvious no doubt, but here spelled out for completeness—is the unknown extent to which perception and objectivity are themselves distorted by personal involvement in the issues under study. I can only say I am aware that the path I am trying to tread is a precarious one for any social scientist. I must leave the reader to judge whether the effort is worth it. I shall be satisfied if he decides to regard what follows as an attempt to make anthropological sense out of essentially personal experience.

THE QUESTIONS POSED

The purpose of this paper is to explore a fundamental ambiguity in the situation of the diplomat's wife, and to look at some of the causes and consequences of this ambiguity. To be more precise, I am speaking here of the situation when the family is *en poste* (during a home posting there is nothing specially interesting about the wives' position) and I am concerned mainly with those whose husbands have representational responsibilities—i.e. belong to the more 'senior' branches of the Diplomatic Service. For the present, the problem can be roughly stated thus: What are the reciprocal claims and duties binding the diplomat's wife to her husband's employers, here taken to include the organization as locally embodied? To what extent can she be considered a ratified member of the organization? What are the areas where her status is undefined, and why? Since we are not dealing with a straight-forward employer–employee relationship, what is the basis of the authority which the organization frequently exerts over wives? Wherein lies its claim to legitimacy? No immediate answer to these questions can be elicited either from the literature or through questioning of individuals; and the fact that they are not perceived internally as problems, itself calls for explanation.

It should perhaps be said that this is not a feminist issue in any simple sense. The language of 'discrimination' and 'liberation' is inappropriate for this study, of which one purpose is to document the dependence of a formal institution on a series of unstated—and perhaps unstatable— assumptions about the family and the man–woman relationship. As it happens, the British Civil Service was one of the earliest employers to deal equitably between its male and female employees: the point at issue here is the equivocal position of the formers' wives. (The converse problem does not exist on any scale in the British Foreign Service.) Further, many of the apparent constraints on individual freedom are not confined to wives and may come about for purely practical reasons (geographical mobility, etc.) which are not of particular interest here. The diffuseness of the diplomat's role—i.e. the lack of sharp definition of 'public' and 'private' identities—spills over onto his wife, and is fully and consciously recognized. The literature of internal guidance makes much use—as does informal personal advice—of the adjective 'representational' and its cognates. These point to the fact that while at post neither a diplomat nor his wife is ever, in theory, 'off duty'. They are expected to live their lives on the assumption that their behaviour may at any time be made grounds for some sort of judgement on their country. Hence, ironically perhaps, a diplomatic mission has some of the characteristics of Goffman's 'total institutions'. Of course, feminist issues are implicit in this subject, but they are beyond the scope of the present paper.

PROTOCOL AND RANK

The behaviour expected of diplomats' wives divides up fairly neatly into the demands of protocol, formally stated in the various textbooks and other literature on the conduct of diplomacy, and those built into traditional ways of doing things. In general, the principle that the wife of a diplomat is absorbed in her husband's role, sharing his rank and immunities, is built into protocol; and this is not surprising in a set of conventions going back to the Congress of Vienna (1815) and beyond. Thus Satow, in what is perhaps the standard British textbook (first published in 1917 but revised in 1957) writes:

> Wives of diplomatists enjoy the same privileges, honours, precedence and title as their husbands. The wife of an envoy consequently is entitled to:
> 1 A higher degree of protection than what is assured to her in virtue of her birth and sex.

2 The same personal exemptions as belong to her husband. She accords to ladies of position at the court equality in matters of ceremony, only if her own husband accords equal rank to the husbands of those ladies.

She claims precedence and preference in respect of presentation, reception at court, visits and return visits, over other ladies, only if her husband enjoys preference over the husbands of those other ladies (p. 257).

The principle is reiterated in a very recent work:

The Vienna Convention was drafted to cover in broad terms the social and family customs of all states. It is generally admitted that all persons over whom the diplomat, as head of the family, exercises legal authority, should participate in the immunities granted to diplomats.

. . . The diplomatic list mentions the names of all members of the family of a foreign diplomat required to conform to the obligations of etiquette. This list always includes the wife and the daughters who have already been presented in society.

Precedence for ladies is regulated largely by the rank of the father or the husband (Wood & Serres 1970: 35, 102).

The existence of a formal ranking principle among wives, then, is clearly established. Of course, in day-to-day events one deals with a complex interplay of formal with informal factors. The significance of formal rank or precedence is not so much that it is always reflected in daily contact as that it is the only general structural principle relating the individual wives to one another, given that they are related at all solely in virtue of their links with an institution which is itself hier-archically organized. Hence rank among the wives can be disclaimed, felt uncomfortable about, made a joke of—and invoked, with varying degrees of forcefulness, in any social crisis. An extract from a circular issued in March 1970 by the Diplomatic Service Wives' Association will illustrate the way in which an awareness of rank can be combined with a well-meaning desire to minimize some of its effects:

As the Committee feel that it is most important to have a properly balanced Committee representing all grades in the Service, they have decided this year to divide the ballot into sections because in the past it was generally the more senior and better-known wives who were elected. It had been hoped to divide candidates into three sections and for members to vote for one from each section. However as there have been no offers to stand for election from Grade 9 or 10 wives, this year there will be two sections only. [The candidates are then listed, each with her husband's grade.]

From a structural point of view, to incorporate the married woman in her husband's 'slot' is probably the simplest of a number of ways of defining her relationship to the hierarchy. An interesting question arises here, whether rank-ordered relationships can exist cross-sexually, or whether male and female hierarchies are kept separate. Either pattern is logically feasible, but in the British Mission the former is certainly followed, at least in the higher reaches where the gradient of authority is perhaps sharper. Thus an Ambassador will frequently issue instructions to his staff and their wives; and his wife, in matters that concern the social life of the Embassy, is fully entitled to do the same. Wives have told me that considerable unease can be generated when the wife of a senior diplomat works as secretary or assistant to someone junior to her husband. 'It doesn't always work. You are always your husband's wife.' The principle is clearly laid down in the literature of internal guidance; and it often happens that I am asked to do something by another wife, in the tone of one giving friendly instructions, where no formal relationship exists between us beyond the fact that her husband is a senior colleague of my husband.

With reference to the interpretation of rank in general, the point has been made to me by Goffman (personal communication) that human hierarchical relations are often best viewed not in terms of simple domination but rather as a neat device whereby the social system makes use of easily available *procedures* of behaviour ('deference', etc.) to serve quite sophisticated ends, such as what he terms 'public order'. The fact that a diplomatic mission is strongly hierarchical does not indicate that the Foreign Office is full of authoritarian personalities (although it may be) but reflects the fact that rank in diplomacy is a communication device of prime importance. It is well known that in international relations the 'level' at which something happens constitutes an additional code for the interpretation of whatever is said or done. How far, if at all, this peculiarity in the operation of rank extends to wives, I have not yet begun to investigate.

However one accounts for the importance of hierarchy among officers in a Mission (and here it is useful to distinguish between 'rank' and 'authority', and between the two senses of the latter term) it is not really surprising to find this structure reflected in some way among the wives. I suggest, however, that the existence of this 'wives' hierarchy' is not quite a sociological truism; and further that, given its existence, it calls for a separate analysis and treatment. While not yet being in a position to carry out such an analysis, I can offer some preliminary suggestions.

One of the mythologies about women in general says that they, being dependent on men for their place in society, are more concerned about rank and status than are men. This may often be true, for all I know. But as far as diplomatic society is concerned, the following would be a more accurate picture. Among officers, male and female,[4] rank-consciousness exists for good job-related reasons, as I have indicated.

Rank relationships are normally subsumed within instrumental ones. Among the wives rank also has an instrumental aspect. 'Senior' wives really are likely to be the more experienced in diplomatic life, and are useful people to go to for advice about correct dress, entertainment, and so forth. But instrumentality is not, as with the officers, pushed to the forefront of the relationship; perhaps because, unlike their husbands, the wives are not involved in daily collaboration over intellectually taxing matters. For this reason it is possible that, paradoxically, rank presents itself to the wives and is experienced by them in a more 'naked' form than by the officers to whom belongs the formal status. However, there exists another, conflicting ideology among the wives: that of playing down rank and maintaining democratic relationships within the Mission. One part of the wives' self-image defines them as people who do not take too seriously the rank differentials existing among their husbands—and who, indeed, by their warm, feminine qualities can do much to soften up the social structure of the Mission. This is consciously felt and also reflected indirectly in, for example, the cosy literary style of the circulars and notices that go round the various wives' groups, spattered with chummy exclamation marks. The official Diplomatic Service Wives' Association prides itself on being, in some sense, 'non-rank'; although as I have shown it finds itself obliged to use the formal rank structure on occasion in order to create an equitable distribution of office.

In seeing themselves in this way as tender-minded with respect to rank, the wives are of course drawing on another bit of the mythology of and about women. There does not yet exist, so far as I know, an adequate account of this mythology as it holds in our society in general. When such an account is written it may enable us to see the wives' ambivalent self-image with respect to rank as a consequence of broader confusions in the mythology of women; felt more keenly than usual, perhaps, in diplomatic life because some of the issues are here presented with special sharpness. Whether this be true or not, I suggest also that the ambivalence in the wives' feelings and behaviour about rank is related to their ambiguous position *vis-à-vis* the organization which dominates so many areas of their lives. I want to consider this position in the second part of my paper.

OFFICIAL STATUS

Rank does not present the only—or necessarily the main—problem of self-definition for the diplomat's wife. I should like to move on now to the more general issue that I mentioned at the beginning: the position of wives as a category *vis-à-vis* the official structure and work of a diplomatic mission. This, of course, is to phrase the problem over-simply, and to beg the question 'whose model?' The only adequate way to approach a fieldwork problem of this kind would be to piece together the ideas held by the several categories of people involved and at different levels of analysis; as formally and quotably laid down, consciously and unconsciously believed, taught, manifested in behaviour, perceived, and perceived to be perceived. This would be a large undertaking, even for a society as small-scale, in a sense, as the British Mission. I here attempt no more than a level-one sketch.

The formal literature on diplomatic procedure is unclear about the exact status of wives in a Mission—surprisingly so for a field where precise definition normally counts for so much. We have seen that diplomatic privileges are extended, by international agreement, to the officer's family. What is thoroughly obscure is the capacity in which wives are entitled to these privileges; whether they, like an Ambassador's staff, are considered to be members of his official suite. Nowhere have I found this formally stated; one has to read between the lines even of the text-books. Satow writes that inviolability 'implies a higher degree of protection to the person of the diplomatic agent and his belongings than is accorded to a private person. It extends to his family, suite, servants . . .' (p. 176). The implication seems to be that family are not diplomatic agents. Again, in connection with immunity (pp. 192–3), he enumerates the official suite of an Ambassador, then adds, 'Also to the wives and families of the above'. This too seems to say that wives and families are not members of the official suite. The Pan-American Convention of 1928 has the same implication (ibid.): for purposes of inviolability 'the members of the respective families living under the same roof' come under a different heading from 'the entire official personnel of the diplomatic mission' (Article 14). Wood and Serres do not raise the issue. But Satow states elsewhere:

> At many capitals a list of the diplomatic body is . . . published from time to time. This generally includes the wives and adult daughters of the members of the mission (p. 254).

At least two thoroughly official slots exist for wives of the diplomatic corps, with clearly designated duties and functions: those of Ambassadress and Doyenne.

> If [a newly accredited Ambassador] is married, the ambassadress must call on, and receive, respectively, the wives of [other ambassadors; envoys, ministers resident, chargés d'affaires] (Satow: 149).

> The wife of the Dean (Doyen) of the Diplomatic Corps has her particular obligations as regards the wives of the heads of mission, namely their presentation to the wife of the Head of State. When the Dean is a bachelor, the wife of the head of mission next on the Diplomatic List after the Dean assumes these obligations (Wood & Serres: 30).

93

OFFICIAL DUTIES AND INFORMAL OBLIGATIONS

Since no clear and consistent picture emerges from the rules, we have to look at what happens in practice, and search for principles underlying wives' behaviour and idea of themselves. I rephrase my problem in the form of a set of naïve questions. In a diplomatic mission, what do people think the wives are there for? What do the wives think they are there for? Who do they think they are? I offer the following assortment of remarks and extracts from conversations, not as carefully garnered 'texts' but as indications of some sort of conscious model.

'Never forget that you are not doing the job. Your husband is' (senior wife, giving advice).

'Not many careers would give you such an opportunity to be involved in your husband's work' (senior wife).

'I should expect my wives to . . .' (former Ambassadress).

'My job? Helping Tom (Dick, Harry . . .) with his work, and looking after my family' (diplomat's wife).

'I'm no good at committee work. However, if I have to do it I have to do it. After all, I'm not here for the good of my health' (diplomat's wife).

'Will you help write invitations for the Queen's Birthday Party? Well you see it's something the wives always do, otherwise the secretaries are landed with a beastly job' (senior wife).

'As you get more senior you'll find you have to give up University work because you'll get more and more involved in the charity work the wives do—and they have to do it, even if it's a terrible bore' (senior diplomat).

'Your position with respect to me in the hierarchy is exactly the same as your husband's' (senior diplomat, in course of argument).

'Whatever happens, we don't want to get involved in anything controversial; we must be completely passive listeners' (senior wife, commenting on proposal to organize panel discussions with prominent local ladies).

'My dear, the problem with going out to work is that in the tropics you can't trust servants with the children!' (diplomat's wife).

One could pick up a number of points here, but I want to focus on the issue of work; on the pronounced job-mindedness which characterizes the wives of the British Mission. One can generalize here, and despite the occasional grumble they do feel that they have a job to do and a contribution to make to the Mission. ('I do think you could manage the Spring Flower Show. After all, you'll have to do something for the Embassy some time.') In this they are supported by the internal literature, which stresses the importance of the wife's role and says, for example, that her attendance at parties (especially those of the Head of Mission) is, except in cases of domestic emergency, compulsory.

What then does the wife's work amount to, and in what respects can it be considered a job? Entertaining and being entertained officially are an important part of a diplomat's work, and it is taken for granted that if he is married his wife will share this work with him and on occasion assume the major part of the load. These 'official duties' performed by wives are formally recognized to the extent of an additional element in the officer's foreign allowance if his wife is with him *en poste*. People will say, when pressed in argument, that this element constitutes payment for the wife's performance of her 'official duties', but it has a number of un-salary-like features: (*a*) it is paid to the husband not the wife, (*b*) to decline the 'job' and the money is not a realistic option, (*c*) as one wife wrote to an internal publication, 'If this is pay, I want more!'

It is important to make the obvious distinction here between mechanism and function: between the obligations which wives and others feel they have towards the Mission and the end-product of their efforts. I spoke earlier of 'instrumentality' in connection with the wives' experience of rank, and showed that the instrumental aspect of rank among the wives, while less prominent and of a different sort from that among the husbands, could not be discounted. Similarly it would be naïve to regard the wives as non-functional decoration at scenes of official entertainment. Their functionality is not that of their husbands, it is true. For all sorts of obvious reasons, they are in theory largely excluded from the information-handling which is the core of the diplomat's work. It is not easy, either, to say how far the conduct of international relations genuinely depends on the social contribution of Embassy wives, and how far 'official duties', like housework, have expanded over the years to fill the time available. Bachelor diplomats of either sex are mildly inconvenienced by their station but not noticeably hampered in their careers. This of course does not rule out the possibility that the machinery cannot function unless there are *some* wives to perform 'official duties'. The interesting point, however, is that the indispensability of the wives' social contribution is an article of faith—reflecting, of course, a series of traditional assumptions about the domestic and social accomplishments of women.

A functional account of the role of wives at the level of face-to-face interaction has not yet been attempted, but might take the following form. At social gatherings whose purposes are understood to be instrumental, the presence of wives with whom one can behave in restricted code affords the ratified participants opportunities to intersperse instrumental with non-instrumental contacts, and this presumably has some effect on the characteristics of such gatherings. It is of course possible (though rarer I think than commonly supposed) for business to be straightforwardly transacted through or between wives. More interestingly, the presence of wives also affords a means for people to phase in, phase out, and set up boundaries around instrumental contacts. Hence we might say that the role of wives is instrumental at some meta-level of analysis. These observations lead towards a 'bricks-and-mortar' type of model of such gatherings, in which significance attaches to a relative interchangeability among the wives as restricted code operators. Such a model might furnish an explanation for something I have frequently observed. Within such gatherings any forgetful lapse into non-restricted code tends to generate embarrassment, *anomie*, and, characteristically, an attempt at protective isolation of the offending episode; 'How intellectual you are for such a charming young lady!' The model would also, one hopes, account for the apparent existence of a rule against over-intense conversational involvement at parties on the part of wives. What is needed here is something I am not qualified to attempt: a sociolinguistic analysis of female, male, and mixed interaction at official gatherings—including the functions of pseudosexual behaviour ('gallantry').

'Official duties' shade off, without sharp dividing lines, into the rest of what wives consider to be their work: in the main, corporate activities directed towards fund-raising for charity. Here again there is an emphasis on traditional women's skills: cooking, flower-arrangement, handicrafts. I make no comment here on the benefits accruing from these activities materially to the recipients, politically to the Mission, and internally to group solidarity. I am interested purely in the senses in which those engaging in them regard themselves, and are regarded, as being 'at work'.[5] A point of ethnographic interest here is the way in which commitment to voluntary work of this kind, together with 'official duties', is perceived as an intrinsic part of the wife's identity; the role of Embassy wife possesses, as it were, an *ex officio* moral content.[6] Voluntary work performed by middle/upper-class married women is not, of course, confined to diplomatic environments. The only unusual feature of the latter (unusual, that is, in modern times and Western society) is this intrinsic bondedness of the moral stance with the occupational-at-one-remove identity.

INDEPENDENT INTERESTS

It is in this context that we can best view the question of wives taking paid employment outside the Mission. The regulations of the Service state that the wife of a diplomat may not, in the country where her husband is serving, accept paid employment without the permission of the Head of Mission. It is common for wives to be employed within a Mission as secretaries and occasionally at higher levels, as where two officers marry *en poste* and the wife retains her job until her husband is re-posted. Outside employment for wives is a burning issue which has generated lengthy discussion over the past few years and led to a change of policy on the part of the Administration which is considered enormously liberal. The position now is that Heads of Mission are encouraged to—and do—look favourably on a wife's request for permission to work, provided this does not conflict with immunity, with local practice, or with her or her husband's representational duties. It is felt in official circles that by taking an outside job a wife can often widen her contacts and hence enlarge her social contribution to the Mission. Nevertheless, this change of policy has left untouched the underlying principle: that in this area the Administration claims an uncompromising authority over its employees' wives, which it expresses in a quasi-statutory language.[7] Now the Diplomatic Service Regulations are the nearest thing the Foreign and Commonwealth Office has to a contract of employment with its staff; and in it the presence of a rule such as this one is a juridical paradox, given the contractual obscurities which I have documented in the position of the wives. The paradox disappears only if we make explicit the submerged assumption about the pattern of jural relationships within the family: namely that a husband occupies the kind of position in his family where he can be held accountable to his employers for his wife's activities; and conversely that a married woman, unlike a man, can be answerable for her actions not only to private conscience, her own undertakings, and the law of the land, but also to an organization with which she has accidental but no contractual links. To say this, however, is to put the matter very brutally, and in a way which (although it follows from the data) would be disowned with indignation by many of the very individuals who operate the system. Therefore to spell out assumptions of this kind, or at least to be content with having done so, is to miss the sociological point. If I may anticipate my conclusions a little, one of the suggestions I want to make is that many of these assumptions cannot be stated, and that for precisely this reason, an interesting mechanism exists for preventing them from becoming apparent.

Returning to the specific issue of wives' independent employment and its relation to 'work', I want to suggest that both the authority claimed by officialdom in relation to the former, and the uneasy feelings expressed about it by individuals, cannot be fully explained by the practical and political problems attendant on having an 'outside' job. I mentioned earlier the unusually diffuse character of the diplomat's role; this may partly account for the fact that the system demands or (more accurately) takes for granted an unbounded commitment on the part of its employees and also of their wives. In the case of wives, as we have seen, the expected commitment is as much moral as it is occupational. ('Let's not be selfish. Let's think what we can give to the Embassy, not vice versa.'—former Ambassador's wife.) This assumed commitment runs throughout the internal and external literature and the core of commonly held attitudes. It shows up particularly well in the 'working wives' debate, where those who wish to allow wives to work rely to a man on the argument that a wife's usefulness to the mission is likely to be enhanced by her having a job—provided, everyone agrees, that she does not neglect her official duties. Given this expectation—rarely formally stated—of a generalized commitment on the part of wives to the aims and functions of the Mission, it is not hard to see that the competing set of responsibilities created by independent employment presents a threat which in turn generates ambivalent feelings within individuals and—at the official level—an attempt to maximize control.[8]

PARADOXES

The case of diplomats' wives is not the only one where marital status is deemed of itself to accord a woman an all-encompassing role. The 'traditional housewife', as an alternative example, springs most readily to mind. The interest of the present case lies in the fact that unlike the housewife (which she often is as well) the diplomat's wife experiences the presumption that she is committed to an institution from whose central operations she is necessarily excluded. We have here a close parallel with a point I made earlier in connection with rank. Despite its diffuseness, a diplomat's commitment to his work, like that of any worker, is seen as fundamentally objective, instrumental, firmly tied to the attainment of perceived ('though often indefinite') ends by rational means. This is not and cannot be true of his wife in her capacity of diplomat's wife. Hence, perhaps, the moral—even ritual—colouring to the collective image of 'the wives' work'.

The task of accounting causally for the existence of this presumption would require the combined talents of the social historian and the ethnographer of expatriate communities, and is beyond the scope of this study. What I want to show here is that the presumption—itself paradoxical—is closely bound up with a further series of paradoxes in the situation of diplomats' wives; and further that the paradoxes are to some extent resolved, or at least fudged, through a psycho-social transformation of the presumption into what I call the 'premiss of dedication'.

The diplomat's wife, as we saw, is assumed to have a primary commitment ('loyalty') to a set of activities in which she is not instrumentally involved or at best peripherally so. Her expected contribution to these activities is based on a traditional definition of the feminine sphere which is essentially typological (social duties and charity work) and to which her individual talents and interests are likely to be largely irrelevant. Her pursuit of these talents and interests tends in any case to be severely restricted. Naturally, some wives are known to be better than others at 'wives' work'. But such work is necessarily defined as the kind of thing any woman can do competently. Hence there is an interchangeability at the root of the wives' self-image which is not shared by 'full' employees, whose jobs (while less individualized than some) are at least mutually differentiated. This interchangeability is modified to some extent by the reflections of the hierarchy among the wives; but again this is not straightforward, given the aforementioned oddities in the wives' experience of rank, and given also their awareness that their relative 'rank' is based on their husbands' achievements rather than their own.[9] The wife's precise status with respect to the organization is impossible to establish, either in theory or in practice. For some purposes she is treated as if she were an employee of the organization, especially as regards behaviour expected of her and control claimed over her.[10] But the basis of such control—normally to be looked for in rewards, sanctions, and the social contract generally—is not at all clear, and is certainly not typical of the employer–employee relationship in Western society.

Now, in what sense can we accurately say that the above summary represents a set of paradoxes at the root of the wives' situation? We can clarify the matter by asking, what would it take for this situation not to be paradoxical? Something like the following, surely, would have to be the case. For women who become the wives of diplomats marriage of itself would generate an exclusive, primary identification with the husband's rank and activities, together with a personal orientation to 'wives' work'. The marital relationship would be such that wives would be *de facto* bound by their husbands' obligations, and husbands correspondingly answerable for their wives' actions. Ideally, these things would be true because men and women would be 'built' in such a way as to guarantee their truth; and it is interesting that in argument people often produce pieces of folk-biology to defend the naturalness of the system. ('Feminism or no, the facts of life are that women have to raise children and are dependent on men.' 'You can't escape from the umbilical cord.') I would label these 'charter myths' except that we do not know, scientifically, how true they may be.

Now, I want to maintain that, irrespective of the fact that these 'conditions' may have been met at other times and places, to the extent that they are not met here and now the situation of diplomats' wives (as indeed of their husbands) is paradoxical. This, of course, is only one source of paradox for wives—the other is the sheer structural ambiguity of their position which I have described. I concentrate on the former here because I want to suggest, further, that in this sense and for this reason the above 'conditions', among others, are assumptions of the system.

My thesis is that these belong to the peculiar class of assumptions which, within the terms of a given socio-intellectual system, cannot be stated. I make two points in this connection. First (and fairly obviously) this range of assumptions cannot normally be articulated by those individuals who are morally and professionally committed to the system. The assumptions are unacceptable because they conflict with other aspects of received present-day Western ideology. I do not distinguish here between psychological and social phases of this argument; a

theory of cognitive dissonance might well be relevant on a psychological plane. The second point is much more difficult to express. It is
possible, as I have indicated, to hold fierce arguments with people and
in this context to force from them statements—some more logical than
others—about principles underlying the system. It would, however, be
rash to relate these admissions too straightforwardly to the normal,
smooth functioning of the Embassy machine. To state the assumptions
is already to distort them—whether in any consistent direction I am not
sure. But it seems to be true that 'embeddedness' is the nature of these
assumptions. Parallel to the principle in nuclear physics and in anthropology that to observe something is to alter its nature, we can say here
that to state an assumption is to distort it; to affect, in some obscure
manner, its truth-value. (It follows of course that what I have said myself
is inaccurate. I accept this.)

If I am right about the unavailability of these assumptions to the
conscious model, then we are entitled to look for some counterpart to
them within this model. Putting the matter differently and a little more
broadly, we can ask, what serves within the conscious model to prevent
the paradoxical features in the situation of diplomats' wives from being
perceived and defined as such? Here, I suggest, the 'premiss of dedication' slots in. This is, as I said earlier, a psycho-social transformation,
and internalization, of the organization's implicit presumption of moral
commitment to itself on the part of its employees' wives. I make no
comment on the mechanics of such a transformation, beyond admitting
that the term 'psycho-social' papers over much ignorance. We have
what looks like a more grown-up, less coerced version of childhood's
successful manœuvre: 'I'll do it because I want to and not because you
tell me to.' Within the British Mission, wives' dedication to diplomatic
aims and activities is taken for granted in the logic of the system and then
again in the wives' own conscious ideology; it is the most prominent
single feature of their collective self-image. I would go so far as to
suggest that the premiss of dedication is the logical anchor of the complex of claims and obligations linking diplomats' wives to their husbands' employers [11]—a function variously fulfilled in different societies,
but in a Western context most commonly achieved through formal
contractual relationships. Whether or not I am right on this last point,
it is clear that so long as the premiss of dedication remains unques-
tioned, the various paradoxes and ambiguities in the position of wives
which I have been discussing throughout this paper, cannot become an
issue.

Behind this truth, as I see it, lies a glimpse of another. There are a
number of ways of organizing a society or a subgroup within a society;
and the hierarchical principle is one of them. For one reason and
another, this principle is prominent in the structuring of professional/
social relationships within an Embassy. I suggested several years ago
(Callan 1970) that in any society—not necessarily human—where a

concentration of political roles within one sex coincides with individualized, long-term relationships between the sexes, a structural problem
exists over the 'placing' of members of this second sex *vis-à-vis* the
political organization. I outlined several possible solutions to this
problem; one of which was to have an ambiguity or looseness in the
position of females 'deliberately' built into the social system. I also
suggested that for reasons connected with primate evolution, this
solution may be one which human societies are predisposed to adopt.
Here, it seems to me a real possibility that the ambiguities in the
position of diplomats' wives are no historical accident, but rather an
ethnographic realization of the above option. This idea awaits further
study.

CONCLUSION

Throughout this paper I have not been primarily concerned with women
per se in relation to men in the Diplomatic Service, but rather with the
husband-wife axis and those women who stand in a certain categorical
relationship to the men who participate in the social/professional
structure of a Mission. Models about wives, however, quite obviously
cannot be disjoined from models about women; and I should like to
conclude by indicating how my ethnographic material could be brought
into line with recent writings on the 'problem' of women in anthropology. Attention is being drawn—notably by Edwin and Shirley
Ardener and other students—to the articulateness or lack of it of
women, and the reasons why they often figure in distorted fashion
in ethnographies, even those written by women. In addition to all
that has been said above, it is possible to view the situation of diplomats' wives in terms of semantic field and structural level. The terms
'diplomat' and 'diplomat's wife' are a pair of designations referring
initially, I suggest, to a surface structure of social classification and
possessing, at that level, a measure of symmetry. At a level of deep
structure, however, they are no longer symmetrical. The label 'diplomat' affords its owner a model (conscious or not) for all manner of deep-
structure self-definition, and similarly for others describing and defining
him (or her). The label 'diplomat's wife', to the extent that it affords
such a model at all, does so only imperfectly, contingently, and de-
pendently.

Now, if we want to say that diplomats' wives are in any sense inarticulate, we must be extremely careful. The wives are intensely self-aware in
the sense that they talk and think a great deal—and very intelligently
and sensitively—about their own role. What I think is happening here
is that in logical terms this form of self-awareness represents an attempt
to stretch the surface-level designation 'diplomat's wife' further than it
will really go; to use it as a kind of hook on which to hang more deep-
structure self-definitions than it can really carry. Viewing the matter in

101

this way, one would say that the premiss of dedication has as an important function the provision of a relatively content-free deep-structural prop for this quasi-logical operation.

If this analysis were pursued, I think it would demonstrate that the collective uneasiness generated by the whole working-wives issue goes far deeper than any of the interpretations I put forward earlier. The working wife, by asserting in her style of life a deep-structural personal identity independently arrived at, threatens to undermine the fundamental logic of the categories through which the Mission as a whole perceives and orders its social world.

The above discussion does not specify the point on the consciousness/ unconsciousness dimension at which these logical or semantic operations might be thought to occur. I want to suggest, however, that if the situation of diplomats' wives is one in which no alternative model is available, then the premiss of dedication has also to do with the processes whereby alternative models are ruled out *ab initio*—and with them all possibility of realizing awareness of any form of 'femineity' in S. Ardener's sense. This in turn might have much to do with the prominence in the wives' self-conception of 'femininity': another essentially surface-structure attribute.[12] The diplomats' wives whom I have been studying, even if they do not like 'Dames in an order of chivalry or girls at Roedean' quite 'perform a male scenario' (cf. E. Ardener, p. 15 above), overwhelmingly see themselves as anchored to life, work, and the social order through the medium of their husbands and the latters' work-generated network of relationships. In this limited sense they are women who do not and cannot 'speak'.

The picture I have given of diplomats' wives is based, as I said at the beginning, on rather specific fieldwork experience; and I have tried to indicate the probable limits of its generality. These limits exist, of course, in time as well as in space. On the other hand, parts of my analysis probably apply in contexts other than the diplomatic; the limiting issues are not yet clear. Some features of the situation I have described seem unlikely to persist indefinitely; a fact which the anthropologist, with his own brand of conservationist fervour, will doubtless be tempted to deplore.

Among the things I have tried to do in this paper is to document the fact that the position of wives in a British Mission has elements of ambiguity, paradox, and, for some, stress. If this is accepted, one could look in more than one direction for an explanation. The common-denominator effect of the need to preserve international conventions is clearly a factor; and a theory of social change on the lines of the Wilsons' (unevenness of scale) might be useful. I have chosen to focus here on the situational and semantic oddities of the wives' position because this, for me, is the direction in which a preliminary study such as this one should develop, in order to contribute maximally to our efforts towards a satisfactory anthropological account of women.

Acknowledgement

For advice and comment while this paper was being written I wish to thank Shirley Ardener and the Oxford Women's seminar group, especially Drid Williams; and also Gerald Obermeyer. Any mistakes are of course my own. Finally, lest any should doubt my sympathy towards my 'subjects', I pay my respects to my good friends, too many to name, of H.M. Diplomatic Service.

Notes

1 Indeed, the question arises whether what I am studying is a society at all, rather than a collection of individuals randomly drawn together by a common definition, location, and life-style. But since the wives themselves think they are a society and try to behave as one, I take them at their (implicit) word.

2 But I suspect—I have no figures—that a small degree of endogamy exists through the life-cycle daughter-secretary-wife.

3 All quotations used in this paper are real ones; i.e. either they come from internal and external literature, or they were said to me or in my presence.

4 I have not yet had the chance to include any woman diplomat in my study, nor a husband of one, but clearly ought to do so.

5 Goffman (1961) has noticed that total institutions and their like characteristically hold some sort of end-of-term party with some degree of role-reversal, skits on authority, witty songs, and other forms of in-joking. For the British Mission's Christmas Staff Party (significantly nicknamed the Servants' Ball) a funny song was written which contained a verse contrasting the wives' charity work with 'real' work. This verse was considered to be in bad taste and was not performed.

6 This fact may be remotely connected to the myth of women as the compassionate, nurturant half of the human race, as in the case of official entertainment there may be some half-buried idea that women are the ones with charm and social skill, which they put at the disposal of the Mission. 'It's enormously helpful to my husband if I happen to get on well with someone he needs to cultivate.'

7 The argument here is not affected by the fact that diplomatic status, as well as curtailing her opportunities, can often present insuperable obstacles to a wife's working—as where the local authorities refuse work permits to foreign Embassy wives, or where immunity conflicts with the legal responsibilities of, say, a doctor or barrister.

8 The ultimate sanction against breach of the regulations is, of course, dismissal. I am told that it would take a test case to establish whether in English law an employee can be rightfully dismissed on grounds of disobedience by his/her spouse—in other words, whether an individual can make contracts binding on the marriage partner.

9 Even this requires modification. For some purposes wives can be presumed to have capacities commensurate with their husbands' rank, and a folk-theory of marriage can—under pressure—be produced in rationale. 'If you were a security guard's wife, we wouldn't expect you to show political judgement.'

10 Every officer is subject to an annual report by his superiors. This report includes provision for comment on the wife's performance. A belief exists among some wives (denied by others but in my opinion quite well-founded) that their nonconformity to what is expected can lead to negative sanctions—diminished

career prospects—for their husbands. It would be extremely difficult to determine exactly how much of this goes on. Much depends here on the idiosyncrasies of individual reporting officers. I have been assured by senior diplomats that it can and does happen; but I am uncertain what analytic status to assign to such assurances. What seems most significant is that the belief exists among the wives and hence is likely to influence their behaviour. Incidentally in the U.S. Foreign Service, the principle has now been laid down that a wife who accompanies her husband to a post does so 'as a private citizen'. She cannot be required to engage in 'wives' work', nor can her husband's efficiency report include any comment on her performance. Friends in the State Department tell me that the position is more 'progressive' on paper than in practice.

11 I except, of course, those aspects of the wife's relationship to the Foreign and Commonwealth Office which are contractually laid down: entitlement to travel and medical expenses, widows' gratuities, etc.

12 The pair 'masculinity/femininity', like 'diplomat/diplomat's wife' and most generally 'man/wife', is symmetrical on the surface: in the depths no longer so.

References

ARDENER, E. W. 1972. Belief and the Problem of Women. In J. S. La Fontaine (ed.), *The Interpretation of Ritual*. London: Tavistock; and above.

ARDENER, S. 1973. Sexual Insult and Female Militancy. *Man* (N.S.) **8** (3): 1–19; and above.

CALLAN, H. 1970. *Ethology and Society*. London: O.U.P.

GOFFMAN, E. 1961. *Asylums*. New York: Doubleday; Harmondsworth: Penguin.

SATOW, SIR ERNEST, 1917. *A Guide to Diplomatic Practice*. (4th edn, Sir Nevile Bland ed. 1957.)

WOOD, J. R., and SERRES, J. 1970. *Diplomatic Ceremonial and Protocol*. London: Macmillan.

Drid Williams

The Brides of Christ

INTRODUCTION

This paper is about a community of sisters who have chosen to spend their lives within the enclosure of Warnley Fen Monastery in England.[1] They belong to one of the contemplative monastic orders of the Roman Catholic Church—the Carmelite Order—which originated with hermits living on the slopes of Mount Carmel in North Palestine in the twelfth century.

The particular Order we are concerned with is one of Discalced Carmelites (literally: 'unshod') so called to distinguish them from their parent order of the Calced Carmelites, also still in existence. After the Council of Trent (1545–63) the condition of being 'barefoot' indicated an acceptance of the need for reform. Being 'unshod' is thus a condition associated with penitential orders. The discalced Order was founded by Teresa of Avila, also called Teresa of Jesus, who was born at Avila in Spain in 1515.[2] She entered the Carmelite Convent of the Incarnation there as a novice in 1536, and founded the first convent of the new or reformed Order, St Joseph's, also at Avila, in 1562. In addition, she was the foundress of the order of Discalced Carmelite Friars, one of whose first two members was St John of the Cross. The discalced Province was given recognition by Pope Gregory XIII in 1580, and Teresa, who died in 1582, was canonized by Gregory XV forty years later.

Now, nearly four hundred years after Teresa's death, the Discalced Carmelite Order has a total world membership of 13,643 women (including 12,238 professional nuns, 432 novices, 813 externals and comprising approximately 783 Carmels or monasteries). The sisters of Warnley Fen form one of the thirty-seven Carmels in Great Britain, which include 578 professed nuns, 14 novices, and 34 externals, 646 women altogether. These figures were taken from statistical tables for the year 1971.

It is well known in social anthropology that one of the crucial problems facing anyone trying to understand another culture is that of language. Even among speakers of the same language, where 'translation' would not appear to be a problem, different individual or group usages of the common tongue are a source of perplexity. This is some-

105

thing that should be kept in mind here, for the language the nuns use, English as it is, is really as unfamiliar to our own 'secular' society as are the values and concepts according to which they live.

As will be described, our very use of the term 'secular' is indicative of an outlook on life quite different from that of the Carmelite sisters. So, too, is the very important idea of anonymity which they share and which involves a voluntary renunciation of many of our common categories connected with 'personality', 'ego', and the like. Self-denial, for example, is a prerequisite for their understanding of what they term 'transformation', which is inner evolution towards 'personhood' and 'selfhood'. There are some further linguistic details to be noted: the sisters live in a 'monastery', whereas we might expect their dwelling to be a 'convent', but it is only in English-speaking countries that these two words are considered to give any indication of the sex of the community ('monastery' is derived from the Greek *monos* meaning 'solitary' or 'alone', and 'convent' from the Latin *conventus*, 'living together'). The sisters describe their way of life by the hyphenated term: 'cenobitic-eremitical' (from the Greek words for 'common life' (*koinos bios*) and 'hermit' as used of Christian mystics since the second and third centuries). The term indicates two aspects of the contemplative way of life which the sisters practise, some of whose forms I describe below.

SOME THEORETICAL CONSIDERATIONS

The main section of this paper is based on two questions: First, how do a contemporary group of Discalced nuns see themselves in their cosmology? Second, how do they see themselves in relation to women in secular life? The paper focuses on a synchronic, largely present-day description of how the sisters at Warnley Fen live, what they think and what they do from day to day. I shall not be able to plunge straight into that description, however, as I shall explain.

There are several difficulties connected with describing a group of nuns, whether of an active or a contemplative Order. These are intimately bound up with understanding human actions or ways of life which are defined as 'religious', 'liturgical', or 'ritualistic'. Faced with a group of people like the Carmelites who permanently isolate themselves, and who distinguish themselves from us and from other Orders in particular ways, we fall into the trap of assuming that the difference between their modes of thought and action and our own is merely one of degree. We may recall that Dumont (1972) pointed this out with reference to our Western egalitarian view of the caste system in India. We might, for example, wrongly consider our passing desires for privacy and for being alone to be of the same nature as the conviction of the contemplative nun seeking a constitutional, Rule-based condition of solitude. A similar example would be the false assumption that a whim to excel physically is the same as the dedication necessary to follow the way of life exemplified by Dame Margot Fonteyn. For 'us', the occasional needs for privacy or to excel at some physical skill are thought of as 'impulses' which in the context of an 'average' life have their proper places, but which are subordinated to what many think of as larger biological, economic, or secular-professional imperatives. For 'them'—that is the groups of 'dedicated' people such as nuns—these impulses seem to override everything else. Their lives assume, sometimes literally, a cloistered, closed-off character, juxtaposed in our minds to other social groups, just as our moods and feelings, of which one may be for solitude, are juxtaposed to all the other thoughts and wishes we may have. Such a view is obviously wide of the mark. Religious Orders isolate themselves in virtue of a submission to a cosmology, to a whole view of the world, to a conceptual structure which involves notions of mankind's and womankind's relation to nature, to time, to ultimate questions about life and death, and last, but by no means least, to God.

Against our background of Western, secularized, and individualistic thinking, it is difficult to comprehend *a group of anything*—far less people—other than as separate elements, as separate 'things', acting and reacting in accordance with their separate, individual natures. But seeing groups in this way means that we separate the individual from the relations involved, so how can we possibly comprehend a group of women whose reference point is *not* the individual, but the whole? In religious Orders, individualistic elements, as we commonly understand them, are mainly disregarded. Individuals are seen as more or less successful expressions of the whole, and as having resulted from the whole. There is, in other words, a typological, not an individual perfection involved. Seclusion for the nuns is a social imperative for the group not merely a response to individual psychological impulses.

The defining characteristic of any Christian and many other religious Orders lies in the notion of hierarchy. Terms which the nuns use freely in their universe of discourse (which we will examine more fully later) such as obedience, humility, poverty, self-transcendence, etc., are impossible of understanding without reference to the principle of hierarchy, which Dumont defined as

the principle by which the elements of a whole are ranked in relation to the whole (1972: 104),

it being understood that in the caste system and, according to Dumont's view, in the majority of societies in the world, it is religion which provides the view of the whole, and that the ranking will be religious in nature. A note on the Carmelite usage of this word in a religious context will be helpful here, for it is often misunderstood. The etymology of the word 'hierarchy' is complex, but the nuns render it as follows: the Greek *hieros* means 'holy', while *archo* means, in general, 'come first',

107

as *archomai* means 'begin'; hence, to the nuns, 'hierarchy', in its simplest definition, denotes 'what comes first' in a religious ordering. If it is applied to orders of angels, it does not mean that one order of angels has power over another or that they are in any sort of superior/inferior relation to one another. On the contrary, even in Scholastic theology, it was not possible to speak of the concept in such superordinate/subordinate terms. Rather, the ordering connoted a proximity/distance relation to God.

An archangel might be thought to have greater responsibility perhaps, or more important functions to perform in relation to God, but it does not follow that the relations are more important or more 'powerful' in relation to each other. The ordering was not 'pyramidal', or based on exercise of power. In any case, in Christian theology, an angel is a 'messenger' or a 'refraction' of God (in Muslim terms, an angel is a 'thought' of God). Dumont's concept of hierarchy is often misconstrued merely as a superior/inferior secular ranking system, for example, on a political level, rather than taken in its cosmological meaning. The result is a confusion of the conceptual with the material level and, from this, we may safely assume that, in recent radio discussions of the use of the term in anthropology, Michael Lane was wrong and Peter Rivière (1972) was right in his interpretation of Dumont's use of the concept of hierarchy. The nuns easily fit into the category 'homo hierarchicus', but they do not fit so easily into other categories of general anthropological or sociological explanation.

The doctrine that human actions, events, and ideas can never be assessed in isolation, but only as part of a total system is certainly not peculiar to Dumont or to any one school of sociology or anthropology. As an idea, it has been present in the writings of Marx, Comte, Durkheim, Radcliffe-Brown, Malinowski, and many others. According to Edmund Leach it was even present in Sigmund Freud's view of the human personality, but, the second of our problems of understanding arises just here. Leach says that earlier varieties of functionalism have assumed that the purpose or need served by the interconnectedness of cultural phenomena is of an economic or political kind. Marx thought that the interconnectedness preserved the system in its struggle against the natural environment, Durkheim and Radcliffe-Brown thought that it preserved the system 'as such' in good health, and Malinowski thought the whole system was for the purpose of satisfying the biological needs of the individual members of society.

If we start from any of these types of explanation about the general interconnectedness of human cultural phenomena, then the Carmelite nuns, or any basically religious, liturgical, or ritualistic social facts are regarded as 'disfunctional', 'aberrant', and 'irrational'; that is, if we accept the narrow definition of 'rationality' as actions or thoughts which serve purely technological or economic ends (cf. Wilson 1970). But so much eludes purely economic or political or physiological generalization of this kind. We may be sure that the populations of monasteries have eluded such explanations. If we consider only the female part of the Carmelite Order, this involves nearly 14,000 women, so might we not justifiably ask if the theory really fits the facts?

A group of nuns is not 'simply' a collection of females. I find it impossible to define them as a group of self-sufficient individuals, though to some extent they are that. I also find it impossible to define them in classical sociological terms as 'economic individuals' or 'political individuals', or the like. In order to define them, one is necessarily projected into a structural universe, that is (following Dumont) into

the whole which governs the parts, and this whole is very rigorously conceived as based on opposition (1972: 81).

At every turn, during the period of research, I was faced with the non-substantiality—and by that I mean the *formal* character—of their way of life—hence the need for structural analysis.

Before going into the ethnographic detail of the lives of the sisters, one or two more general comments should be made about their Order and their Foundress. Women who founded congregations did so, perhaps, for many reasons, including the desire to present a 'witness' of the values of a contemplative life to their contemporaries. The notion of 'witness' should not be confused either with 'use' or with 'utility'. The Carmelites see themselves as 'useful' to the wider society metaphorically, as breath is of use to the body, but they have rejected any notion of economic, political, or biological 'use'—or, more accurately, these aspects of life are, to them, of secondary or tertiary importance. Thus, they can be seen as living, though hidden, symbols of a way of life, a conceptual way of perfection which dominates any interconnectedness of empirically observable actions in relation to them. But then, the God they serve is a 'hidden God' as well; the technical theological term being *deus absconditus*.

The structures of their existence are nevertheless tied to empirically observable circumstances in their daily Offices, to the liturgy in which they participate. Their existence turns around certain of their fundamental conceptual distinctions. The first and most important of these is that of 'above/below', or 'higher/lower', or, empirically, 'up/down'. The secondary fundamental opposition is that of 'internal/external', 'intrinsic/extrinsic', or, empirically, 'inside/outside'. The first term of the primary opposition, e.g. 'above', 'higher', or 'up' is closely related to the first term of the secondary opposition, e.g. 'internal', 'intrinsic', or 'inside'. The terms 'Bride' and 'Spouse' are used in relation to the figure of Christ, who was human. The 'Bride' is the human soul, the 'Spouse' is Christ, obviously in his divine, not his human aspect (cf. John of the Cross, *Spiritual Canticle*, Peers, Vol. II: 23–397). Their aim is union with God. To achieve this life aim, a condition necessary to their way of life as contemplatives, is solitude. Solitude is related to the concept of 'the desert'.[3] While the activities of all Orders are put into the service of such guiding ideas, even if the Order is 'active', the aim is the same and the principle is similar.

The popular misconception of the prototypes distinguishing the active from the contemplative Orders are the Biblical figures of Mary and Martha. Teresa insisted that the Carmelite way of life included both types of characteristics commonly associated with these women. Teresa held that internally, in every woman, 'Mary and Martha toil together'. Whatever mode of outward expression a nun may choose with regard to an Order, the key notion is that of a partnership. The nuns' rejection of human male partnership, is not, in my view, merely negative since they conceive a partnership with God to be an expression of a greater love. The love they serve is not connected with male physical companionship and comfort, but with an interior life.

Historically, Teresa's 'Way' was, and is, called the 'Way of Perfection' and her method involves reaching the innermost mansion of the Interior Castle. In a Papal Brief dated 7 February 1562, issued when the first Discalced Convent of St Joseph's at Avila was established, Teresa was authorized to draw up statutes and ordinances, 'lawful, honest and not contrary to Canon Law, and after making and ordering them, wholly or partially to improve, remodel, change, revoke or entirely abrogate them, according to the character of the times, and in the same way to draw up new ones'. This is important because it shows that (1) Teresa had complete freedom, and (2) though we may not wish to admit it, the only 'origin' we could show anthropologically for the phenomena under discussion would be structures of human minds, specifically, those of Teresa and John of the Cross.

Teresa's *Constitutions* were, in fact, endorsed in advance: they were given apostolic authority, their observance was prescribed, and any other authority was forbidden to issue judgements, interpretations, or definitions which would contradict them. Thus armed with authority, confirmed by another Papal Brief issued in 1565, Teresa drew up her Constitutions, in the spirit of which, subsequently, all communities of Discalced nuns were to be governed. She was the only woman to have established an Order of Friars, of which John of the Cross was one of the first two members. John helped to form the spirituality of the nuns in his role of confessor, director, and adviser. It is as well to say here that it is to Teresa's confessors that we owe her extensive writing. She would never have written a word had she not been under a vow of obedience. She considered it an unwelcome, tiresome, and troublesome task.

Regrettably, there is space for only a few comments about Teresa herself, who by anyone's standards was a remarkable woman. She had a vivid and forceful personality, she hated pretentiousness. With combined shrewdness and irony laced with considerable humour, Teresa

110

writes, for example, about a certain lady who mixed devoutness with self-importance, that she and others like her

> were saints in their own opinion, but, when I got to know them, they frightened me more than all the sinners I have ever met (Peers 1946, Volume III: 66).

She was wont to deliver such aphorisms as

> From foolish devotions may God deliver me!

Allison Peers, a recent translator of her works, remarks that

> many have supposed the *Interior Castle* to be concerned solely with raptures, ecstasies and visions, with Illumination and Union, or to be a work created by the imagination, instead of *the record of a life* [my italics].

But, he says

> There is no life more real than the interior life of the soul; there is no writer who has a firmer hold on reality than Teresa (1946, Volume II: 193).

These remarks are important, for they reflect the down-to-earth character of the saint, and her most often quoted statement that 'Our Lord is also to be found among the pots and pans' is appropriate to lead into a consideration of the daily life of the sisters at Warnley Fen.

THE DAILY LIFE OF THE NUNS

The monastery is astir at half-past five in the morning as the nuns rise and hasten to the choir for Lauds: the morning song of praise. After this act of public, liturgical prayer, each nun returns to her own room or 'cell' or she stays in the choir for an hour of private prayer. True to the spirit of their Order, the nuns remain in solitude except when engaged in liturgical prayer, common work, or recreation. Solitary converse with God is at the core of the Carmelite vocation: at least two hours a day are solely devoted to it. The cloister bell rings at 7.50 a.m. calling the community to Mass. After a brief preparation in the ante-choir, they enter the choir in procession wearing the traditional white mantle over their brown habits. Silent thanksgiving and the Office of Terce follow the Mass.

Their ordinary work begins at nine o'clock when visitors to the monastery are having breakfast. Some of the community engage in the necessary tasks of any large, self-supporting family; housework, cooking, laundry, sewing, and gardening. Many are employed in the printing trade, involving designing, typesetting, photography, printing, and colour work as well as accountancy. Although this is common work, as far as possible the sisters remain alone in silence, speaking only

111

when necessary. Exterior silence is thought to aid the inner silence and calm which is necessary for attentiveness to God. The Carmelite life follows a rhythm of work and prayer, in common with all monastic life; the Carmelites understand work to be another form or way of praying.

The morning period of work ends at 11.15 a.m. The nuns then assemble in choir for the Office of Sext. The rather early mid-day meal follows Sext, and, having had only a breakfast of coffee, bread and butter following Lauds, the sisters are ready to eat. Their diet is simple, but wholesome and adequate. It consists mainly of produce from their own small garden and farm, for they have dairy cows, chickens, vegetable gardens, and fruit trees. They make cheese, some of which is occasionally sold to visitors. The nuns all lend a hand with washing up after the meal and with the preparation of vegetables. They then separate to continue their various occupations until two o'clock. Three-quarters of an hour each day are devoted to serious reading and they spend this time in their cells or, in fine weather in their cloister garden. Just before three o'clock, they assemble in the choir for the Office of None.

There are several hermitages inside the enclosure and, once a month, each nun enjoys a day of complete solitude, free from all duties. Perhaps twice a year those who wish may spend three or four days in complete solitude. There is a strong orientation towards eremiticism in the Order. In contrast to the general cenobitic-eremetical life of the Carmelites, is the case of a nun who lives in one of the hermitages near the monastery. This nun provides a limiting case with regard to Carmelites, for, although she is a consecrated virgin like them, and like them attends Offices and Mass, sitting across from their choir, the only persons she ever converses with are her confessor, and once a month with the Prioress. She also says a few words to the sister charged with her provisions and to a caretaker who looks after necessary affairs in nearby villages for her. She speaks to no others and represents, therefore, a more absolute expression of the eremetical spirit.

Vespers, the evening Office of praise and thanksgiving, is sung at 4.30 p.m., and an hour of silent prayer follows this Office, as in the morning. Supper is at six o'clock. From September until Easter the evening meal is restricted. The community feels that abstinence from meat, the Unmitigated Rule, and a measure of fasting, is a small way of sharing in world poverty. The nuns also manage to live so that they give something to the needy of the world. After the supper things are tidied up, they gather for an hour of recreation together. Sometimes they just chat and share ideas, sometimes they dance or sing, or put on their own 'theatricals'. In the long history of the Teresan Carmel, this time of shared recreation has played an important role, contributing a warm, loving, and relaxed atmosphere to an otherwise austere, spiritually very intense, life. The hour of recreation fosters intimacy and a strong bond of love among the community.

After recreation, the nuns go to the choir for the Office of Readings. From then on until the time of the Great Silence after Compline, which will last until Lauds the next morning, they retire to their own cells to pray, read, write, or to do creative or artistic work, each according to her own taste, for this last period of the day is free time. At 9.30 p.m. they gather in the choir for the short prayer of Compline. The chapel bells ring out their call to prayer regularly across quiet fields and woods. Sun and moonlight touch the steeple of the chapel which points steadily skywards, clearly visible above clustering oaks, beeches, and cedars. This image of the landscape and church steeple, suggestive of a horizontal line crossed with a vertical, forms a remarkably good point of departure into essential structural and conceptual aspects of the cosmology of the nuns.

SPACE–TIME IN THE CARMELITE ORDER

We must consider two structures fundamental to the space–time of the Carmelites. In reality they are one, but the homology will emerge later. The first structure is based on a cross of two lines, as shown in *Figure 1*.

Figure 1

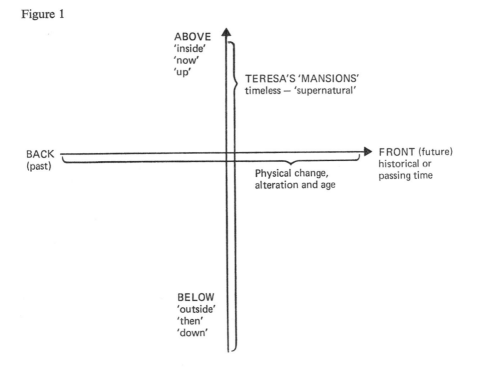

The horizontal line represents chronological, 'historical' time; the past and the future, the temporal, seasonal changes and cycles with which we are all familiar. This (in their terminology) is 'natural' or physical space–time, the line on which we might express physical birth and death, on which we might count the passage of years or reckon age. In Evans-Pritchard's terminology, this line represents ecological space–time. The vertical line represents what I shall call 'liturgical space–time', the moving present, or 'now'. We will recall that the first two terms of the primary and secondary conceptual oppositions of the nuns, i.e. 'above' and 'inside', were linked. In the Carmelite cosmology, the vertical line of space–time is connected with higher and lower states of being, which are in turn connected with devotion to God and with constant inner efforts towards greater self-awareness. It is as if the Carmelite has two 'maps': one which locates her in ordinary geographical space–time, and another consisting of an interior 'territory' of a spiritual and psychological nature in which she is located at the same time.

Our attention is drawn to three essential features of this interior territory, i.e. self-understanding, and how one might think of the soul and where the 'castle' is located, through these statements of Teresa herself:

(i) It is no small pity, and should cause us no little shame, that through our own fault, we do not understand ourselves or know who we are (Peers 1946, Vol. II: 201).

(ii) I began to think of the soul as if it were a castle made of a single diamond or of very clear crystal in which there are many rooms, just as in heaven there are many mansions (ibid.).

(iii) Let us return to our beautiful and delightful castle and see how we may enter it . . . for, if this castle is the soul, there can clearly be no question of our entering it. For *we ourselves are the castle* [my italics]; and it would be absurd to tell someone to enter a room when he was in it already! But, you must understand that there are many ways of 'being' in a place (op. cit.: 203).

The Carmelite is always at some 'place' in physical or natural space–time—on the horizontal line, as it were, and at the same time is somewhere, i.e. in a higher or lower state internally, on the vertical space–time line. Thus we arrive at an intermediate stage towards the second of the space–time structures of Carmelite life. The next diagram is based on the notion of the nun's life as a continuum.

In the earlier ethnographic section, it was pointed out how the nuns' daily lives are arranged. They arise at 5.30 a.m. and the Great Silence ends twenty-four hours later at 5.30 a.m. when they arise again. It is perhaps helpful, in approaching the second structure, to think of an ordinary clock with a twenty-four hour 'continuum' arranged around it (*see Figure 2*).[4]

The heavy line on the diagram opposite represents the time of the Great Silence. There, we see the 'life-track' of the nuns as it unfolds through historical or 'passing' time. It is fairly easy to visualize how a

Figure 2 (The time-track has no beginning and no end, but the hands of the clock indicate the time when the nuns rise. Only death ends the individual motion of a nun on this time continuum. Collectively the motion is perpetual.)

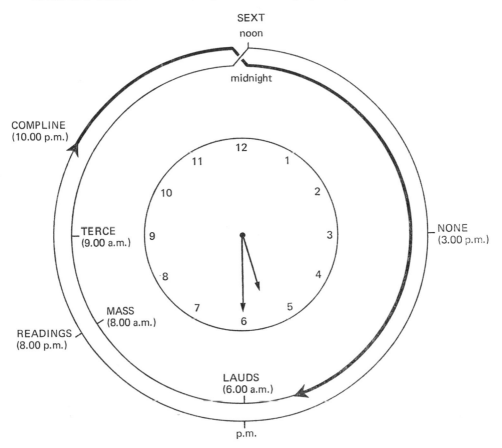

group of these diagrams stacked one on top of the other, or thought of as a movement around an ascending spiral, as in *Figure 3* overleaf, would correspond to the structure previously examined.

It is perhaps important to consider that a nun who spends sixty years in a Carmelite enclosure, if she is in the chapel choir for Mass and Readings at 8 a.m. and 8 p.m. every day, is in the same place at the same time exactly 42,800 times during those years. It is not very puzzling as to why this represents a rather different notion of space and time from that which a 'secular' person might have. While on the one hand the nuns' lives appear, syntagmatically, to 'unfold' through time, on the other, the canonical, liturgical hours form another conceptual axis of space–time which is paradigmatic to the 'life-track' in physical space–time. It is the 'p-structural' axis, of course, which makes sense out of statements such as 'I die daily' (St Paul).

The first structure, that in the iconic form of a crucifix, is used in

Figure 3 The 'life-track' of the nuns (or parts of the 'edges' of the clock) corresponds to the *horizontal* space–time line of the first static structure. The *vertical* liturgical space–time axis would be calibrated through any of the liturgical hours of the Divine Office.

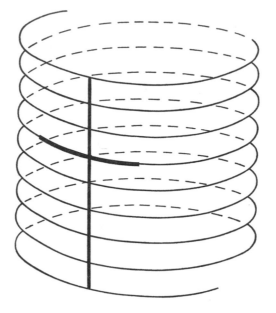

contemplation by some of the nuns. The elements of that structure, together with the diagram of the 'life-track' are included in the following more comprehensive structural picture of the nuns' lives. I am aware that this diagram goes a bit beyond the needs of the present article; however, it is a concise, theoretical model of relevant facts which in a later publication will be fully explained. As it is, the diagram is set up for group theory analysis.[5] It is based on the notion of two superimposed clock faces. This structure is based on the nuns' own notion, that of one day being equal to a life-time (*see Figure 4*).

In *Figure 4* the canonical, 'p-structural' 'shape' of the liturgical hours can be seen in two dimensions. An hour of private prayer begins each cycle of twelve hours. These are the pivotal points of the sisters' lives at Warnley Fen—the 'entrances' into the interior castle. The public prayer, or liturgy (used in the sense of 'leitourgia', i.e. public worship), begins with Lauds and the cycle finishes at about 5 p.m. The liturgy picks up again in the second cycle of twelve hours at 8 p.m. where the Office of Readings is mapped onto the earlier Mass, and the last liturgical hour of Compline is followed by the Great Silence which ends at 5.30 a.m. when the nuns arise again.

I suggest that any of the actions, or other aspects of the lives of the nuns, including fasting, penances, mortifications, obedience, humility— the lot—will be completely misunderstood unless the deep structures of the nuns' lives, only briefly outlined below, are taken into consideration.

Figure 4

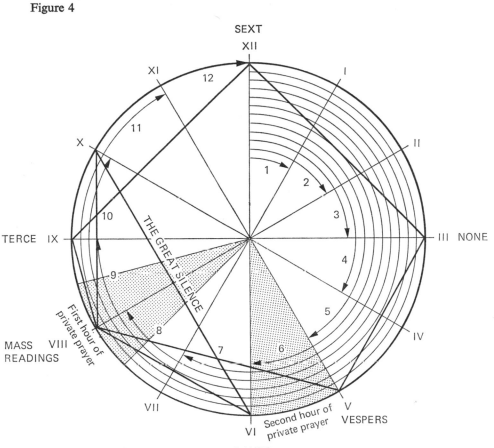

CARMELITE SEMANTICS

The structures indicated above lead us into the fields of meaning, and consideration will be given to four basic Carmelite oppositions. According to my informants, these four oppositions subsume all the major concepts of their belief. I can only give the briefest of expositions here:

Above/Below: the 'mansions', 'self-transcendence', 'eternity'

As we have seen, everything in Carmelite life is directed towards creating the conditions necessary for prayer, which is what the nuns are there for. Their commitment to ceaseless prayer involves both public and private prayer. They must constantly strive upwards, for that which is 'above', in modern psychological terms, for self-transcendence. This aim touches every part of their lives, every act they perform, every thought, every decision in the here and now. In the words of one of the sisters:

I feel really that we are already in eternity, living in eternity. I mean

117

everything counts—everything, even the least detail of our life, if you like, counts, and also we are here and now determining our own eternity, as it were 'in the Mansions'. Therefore, each day is tremendously important, because of the decisions we're making—the whole time, and those decisions are determining our—eternity.

In practical terms, this is expressed in relation to ordinary 'work', for example, as follows:

As regards work, I think that everything depends on the dispositions in which you work. It is the interior motive or intention that is the most important. It is the interior that will give the value to the most menial task. St Teresa brought this out very much in her own life. So, it isn't the work in itself, it's the intention—the motive behind it. What counts is *where you are* in relation to it.

Inside/Outside: esoteric/exoteric, invisible/visible
Teresa's words express this opposition most clearly:
Each of us in an Interior Castle . . . the innermost Mansion, the central point is 'indwelt' by God. Let us imagine that there are many rooms in this castle, of which some are above, some below, others at the side. In the centre, in the very midst of them all is the principal chamber in which God and the soul hold their most secret exchanges.

The Castle is, of course, invisible—not visible, for it refers to the esoteric, or inner facts of Carmelite belief and practice. Philosophically, the word 'esoteric' has been interpreted to mean, not only 'inner' (the definition we use) but 'only for the initiated'. This notion has nothing to do with Carmelite belief, for they do not consider themselves to be 'initiates' in the sense of being cultically initiated into some sort of ideas which can be held or understood by them alone.

Birth/Death: metanoia; detachment, non-identification, 'poverty'
'Metanoia' is a Greek word and has had long usage in monastic traditions; it literally means change or transformation of mind. It can as well be interpreted as change of attitude. The 'birth' of a new attitude, idea, or view means the 'death' of an old one. The change-over from an old habit of thought, for example, means that the old habit must 'die' before the new one can be 'born' or have full force in the individual's life. A seed must 'die' so that a plant can appear, to be 'born'. Spiritual 'birth' must be preceded by 'death' of such things as greed, avarice, envy, etc.; in general of egoistic or false aims; in the words of St Paul 'I die daily. . . .' This kind of 'death' requires poverty of heart, mind, and spirit, which is based on detachment.

Male/Female: God/Creation; Logos/Incarnation, Eros/Agape—Love
Basically, the male/female relation can be expressed in the relation between God and creation in Carmelite thought, the creation being

'feminine' or 'receptive' in relation to God. In Carmelite thought, *all* creation is female to God, thus the soul is described by both Teresa and John of the Cross as 'the bride'. 'Anima' and 'animus'; words which are to be found in the sisters' universe of discourse, in so far as they represent the female and male parts of the individual human psyche are words that suggest that, of all the schools of modern psychology, Jung was nearest the mark with regard to his concepts of wholeness and of expressing one aspect of this opposition as seen by some of the sisters. And I quote one:

> We must be both, mustn't we? A man, unless he develops certain feminine qualities is deficient, isn't he? He must have, at least what we call 'feminine' qualities; our Lord had them—tenderness, gentleness, intuition. He needs them, doesn't he? And a woman likewise needs to cultivate her objectivity, her intellect, yes—most certainly I would say so.

A concept of wholeness requires both. Equality of males and females either in an 'outer' or social sense or in an 'inner' or psychological sense does not mean 'being the same as' in Carmelite thought. It is in the very complementation that so much of the beauty lies. It would be an enormous loss if either sex lost the *essential* character of its being, which starts with its expression in the biological.

Clearly, whole books could be written about any one of these oppositions or any combination of them. The important point is that, in the previously mentioned structures of time and space and the semantic field which maps them, we see something of the cosmology of the nuns, and we have answered our first question. It is in accordance with these ideas that the nuns live their lives from day to day. As one of them said to me, 'Our lives have no natural explanation. Our lives make no sense and they have no meaning outside of the context of an interior life', which also, incidentally, makes sense of their notion of 'faith'. In simple scriptural terms this is defined as in Hebrews 11:1:

> faith is the substance of things hoped for, the evidence of *things not seen* (my italics).

CARMELITE VOWS

Connected with the semantic field of the nuns is their interpretation of the vows they take. Some mention must be made of these, for it is here that we most obviously encounter the problem of translation. Basically, the vows are three: poverty, chastity, and obedience. Often, these are linked in various ways in the minds of the sisters, but we will try to deal with them separately. On a level of material poverty, it is thought that 'to have enough is sufficient', so that full attention, in so far as that is possible, can be given to prayer, which is what they are there for. The 'poverty' of Carmel is, to them, however, evident in other, more subtle

119

ways. Nuns are, for example, always short of 'free' time, for their time is taken up, aside from daily tasks, by prayer. They are committed to eat and drink what another has chosen and prepared, and to sleep when another says they can. Often, they cannot indulge in doing anything really well, in the sense of spending hours on a dance rehearsal or some form of work, for example, or becoming 'totally involved' in the way people might do on the outside. This would take too much time and unnecessary interest. Things are never arranged and organized with a view towards individual convenience, or even with an aim of greater efficiency (although paradoxically, they seem very efficient indeed) because tasks must be left to the one who has been chosen for it. This is not always the best person for the job, for charity will inevitably take precedence over efficiency.

Poverty on a spiritual level is often linked with chastity. It is not looked on wholly or even most importantly as on a sexual level, but as a kind of chastity of the senses and the mind—and this is the interpretation of poverty which, as one nun put it, 'really costs'. The foregoing of eating, sleeping, and the like can be 'got used to' by anybody; it might be found in one form or another in various human communities. The real poverty which matters in Carmelite life is poverty of the heart which involves a subtle separation from friends and relatives. This is a temporary stage—the aim is to get beyond it. The nuns are perhaps, above all, loving people but there is nevertheless a sense of estrangement from family and friends. The concepts the nuns are after are often more deep, and the sisters become acutely aware that words come to have a totally different import and impact to persons whom they knew before.

They have committed themselves to having love of self and false aspects of the personality 'smashed', as it were, to be replaced by what they conceive to be a right love of self. To them, much self-love is really self-conceit and imagination, forms of idolatry, in fact. Their slow process of transformation—of *metanoia*—occurs, I am told, almost imperceptibly. No one compels them to do these things, no one does them for them, and no one tries to destroy another in any way—it simply 'happens' as a result of the way of life which they have chosen, and as one sister said, 'I would not want to choose a life which did not cost.' They try to expose themselves to truth, to 'loving truth' continually. In the beginning stages, truth is often deeply painful. Eventually, one aspect of the process they go through involves, as one nun said, 'a most crucifying loneliness'. It is an inner void which will be filled, in His own good time, by God; but when subtle severances begin to occur with one's former loved ones, it can seem a doubtful privilege, it is part of the 'dark night of the soul'.

The third vow, obedience, is looked on as an important, if not the supreme, gift of self. Clearly, the other vows precede this one, because one cannot give what one does not possess. It is the vow that is, perhaps, seen with most suspicion by novices, and is the one which is, we might imagine, the most difficult. An integral part of the spiritual 'exercises' (though they might be called spiritual acrobatics or gymnastics!) is precisely to develop the capacity to willingly submit to the judgement of another person; to give another the benefit of the doubt, as it were, to unconditionally accept that another has the same aims, purity of heart, goodwill, good intentions, and quality of love as one has (or would like to have) oneself. Obedience in any form is thus connected with the notion of self-denial and can only be achieved through the greater love they profess to serve. The nuns interpret the injunction that one should 'deny himself' literally, not as it is sometimes interpreted as to deny himself *something* (cf. Matthew 16: 24, 'If any man will come after me, let him *deny himself* and take up his cross, and follow me').

In a religious house, of course, there is little danger of a conflict of judgement on a deeply moral level such as might occur on the outside, because all the sisters have the same ideals and aims; the only differences are the interior routes towards them. Obedience in a Carmelite, or any other, monastery could be said to be 'safer' than it might be outside. There are important differences between inside and outside in this respect. Obedience in a monastery is characterized, first by the fact that it is wholly, completely, and absolutely voluntary. We might usefully contrast any monastic community with a prison community as examples at the extreme poles, because in the latter case, obedience is *compelled*; it is connected with conceptual structures of reward and punishment, viewing humans as if they were animals, not humans. Commands in a prison are issued and rules are kept through fear of punishment. We all know that no one can be compelled to love, no one can be coerced into spirituality or into believing anything, and no one can be forced or made to understand. The sisters' voluntary vows of obedience can therefore be seen to stem from a different set of ideas—from love, not fear. Final vows simply cannot be taken for quite some time anyway, by which time mutual confidence has been established. The average length of time from initial postulancy to final vows in the Carmelite tradition is five years. The danger for the would-be nun lies in obeying unconsciously, in constructing some 'image of a holy nun' which is based, ultimately, on self-love; on the desire, perhaps, to be a 'star-pupil', which can tend to produce a 'sanctimony syndrome' which, in Carmelite terms, is simply another form of escape from reality.

Although much more could be said about these and related concepts, we must press on towards the conclusions of this paper. Before concluding, however, we must answer the second question originally asked. I can do no better than to quote some of the sisters directly. These are direct transcriptions from taped interviews:

One of the questions was, how do we see our relationship to secular women. Well, my first reaction is, who on earth are secular women? One doesn't think in terms like this. One thinks of people. The world

121

is occupied by people—men and women—and one comes to the parlour or one is writing to, or thinking about or praying for, men and women, not 'secular' men and women. This is a division, and to my mind, Christ came to break down divisions to say, look, we're one human mankind and (He was saying) I have a message for every one of you and some will follow out the message in one way and some in another way. So far as I personally am concerned, to talk about secular women would be something completely foreign to my way of thinking. I talk to people.

Another sister said,

I would never make the distinction, either in the abstract—you know —thinking of women in general, or otherwise. I think I feel so much a woman myself, with the same problems basically, the same struggles and difficulties that I know women have, that I don't think of myself in any way different from them. When I meet them 'in the flesh' I'm so conscious that we're alike that I don't have the image that I'm a nun, I'm different. I just think we meet, first of all as women. They have their own areas of experience and I have mine, but basically they are women—they are women's experiences and I'm always struck by how similar, how basically the same they are. [When asked to be more specific, she continued:] Something along these lines: usually such things as vulnerability, loneliness, need for love, to belong—all the things we know characterize a woman's make-up. I never feel any strangeness with them. I always feel a great empathy.

And a third,

Well, of course, I feel that all roads lead to God. Every one of them is hard. Every one of them has its own problems and difficulties. Obviously, I prefer this life and feel that it suits my personality most in my search for God or I'd return to the world and get on with my own career. Perhaps I see myself as a weaker soul who needs support of disciplined structures, as I would tend to dissipate my energies, my attention and interest in too many directions all at once. So, I welcome the reminders that turn my whole being back to God continually. And I need them. I'm honest enough to admit that I jolly well need them.

In addition to the two main questions about the nuns' cosmology and how they envisage themselves in relation to other women, I also asked some questions on how they defined their relationship to the masculine figure of Christ. There was, as I expected, considerable reluctance to discuss this matter, as the following quotes show:

You can ask any woman about her household, how she manages her affairs, does her accounts, the ideas and concepts she lives by, what she hopes for, how she came to meet her husband, perhaps, even their courtship, and there's nothing wrong in all this, but I don't think she is expected to try to describe her most intimate personal life and emotions and it seems to me that is what is being asked.

Another said,

> The question on relation to Christ, well, I think to most of us He's just everything and all, but in a way it's such a personal thing—I don't think one can really say—it goes too deep, I think, if you don't mind.

And another,

> Quite honestly, I'm not a bit happy about what I said to you earlier on. You must see that it is such a personal matter—and so very interior that it really defies analysis. And in any case, somehow it doesn't seem quite fitting to even try to do so . . . at least it doesn't to me at present, and for this, I think one must risk seeming uncooperative.

On the relationship between the Bride, the human soul, and the Spouse, Christ, it was suggested to me that the Spiritual Canticle of John of the Cross, or Solomon's Song of Songs in the Bible, give some idea of the nature and level of that kind of love.

CONCLUSION

Having considered the original questions, how might we conclude? These women carry on an ancient tradition of contemplation: the searching of the human heart for the infinite God. As Carmelites they are one of several widely different groups of contemporary English 'mystics'. Can they really be explained adequately under the rubric of generalizations about social phenomena such as struggle against the natural environment, or individual biological survival, economic deprivation, frustration, repression, and so on? I think not, and I think we miss the mark anthropologically in studies of religious phenomena if we proceed from *a priori* assumptions that human life, in the end, comes down to such things.

Some interesting problems remain. It seems, for instance, that biologically, these women are a 'closed' group, in the sense that they are genetic terminal points, and thus it becomes clear that I cannot give any sort of genetic explanation for factors of change or continuity in the nuns' customs and institutions. This is despite the fact that they have existed in an unbroken chain for four centuries. Nor can I assume that clear-cut genetic factors can be used to define them, or their 14,000 or so counterparts throughout the world, as 'a population'.[6] If, as scientists, we seek rational explanations for continuity and change in human social institutions, perhaps we need other more objective implements, perhaps from the armoury of topology, field theory, and group theory to help us find a basis for explanations. In any case, I hope to explore this possibility at length in due course.

On a somewhat simpler level—the social division of labour—what implications for an 'explanation' of the nuns can be drawn from a consideration of their economic activities? Unlike many working individuals, they do not engage in wage-labour, nor does their community, as a corporate body, operate on the lines of a conventional business enterprise. Whereas the 'economic function' of sellers in the 'free market' of Western capitalism is taken to be the maximization (or the optimization) of profit, the nuns donate to world charitable organizations all earnings not required for essential goods and services they cannot produce within the community.

Taking still another point of view, a scientific anthropological interest lies in the fact that such groups of contemplatives form a perfect, or nearly perfect, complementary group to a prison population of women, and could be usefully compared in terms of diametrically opposed characteristics.

Finally, I hope this paper has contributed something towards perceiving and understanding women. In connection with Shirley Ardener's paper, I submit that here are a group of women who, like the Kom and the Bakweri, successfully act as a corporate body and who underline the validity of her concept of 'femineity' in contrast to femininity. The nuns' aims, thoughts, and actions are surely not in line with any of the common received images of what a woman is 'supposed' to be. Just like any women who have not—for whatever reason—had children or chosen the companionship and comfort of a married state, they too have been castigated as 'unnatural' and as not recognizing their proper place in a male 'natural order' of things. While the group of women I have discussed are not overtly militant, they share with other groups of women, such as those described by fellow contributors here, a tenacious adherence to their own 'female model', which differs from the 'received' model of women located in the dominant structure.

Notes

1 Warnley Fen is not the name of any Carmelite Monastery in England, nor, to my knowledge, does the name designate any real place in England. In accordance with their tradition of anonymity, my informants have asked that if this ethnography were published, their real identity should remain private. We have respected this desire on the nuns' part to remain anonymous, hence the fictitious name.

2 Strictly speaking, Teresa would not have considered herself a 'foundress'. She only wished to return to the Unmitigated Rule and to a strict adherence to it; however, after her death, the Discalced became a separate Order.

3 This is a central concept in Carmelite thought and life which is only mentioned here, for it would require lengthy explanation. Similarly, space has prevented a full treatment of the Carmelite view of sexuality and has made only the briefest of explanations of the semantic fields of the nuns possible. This material is being dealt with in forthcoming publications.

4 I am grateful to Shirley Ardener for suggesting this way of formulating the continuum of the nuns' lives, making their time concepts and the following two structures clearer.

5 For those interested in group theory generally, I suggest that good beginning texts are *The New Mathematics* (Adler 1964) and *The New Mathematics Made Easy* (Murphy and Kempf 1968), with special reference to the chapters on finite arithmetics. These books do not explain how the group structure (*Figure 4*) is set up, but they do give some insights into the general notion of non-metric mathematical models. It is perhaps important to mention that the genetic code is based on a group of the order twelve, and that the code itself can be simply described as a three-handed 'clock' of four codons per 'hand'.

6 For a discussion of the defining of 'populations', see E. Ardener (1973).

References

ADLER, T. 1964. *The New Mathematics*. London: Dobson.
ARDENER, E. 1973. Social Anthropology and Population. In H. B. Parry (ed.), *Population and its Problems*. Oxford: Clarendon Press, 1974.
DUMONT, L. 1972. *Homo Hierarchicus*. London: Paladin.
MURPHY, P. J., & KEMPF, A. F. 1968. *The New Mathematics Made Easy*. London: Allen.
PEERS, A. 1943. (Editor and Translator) *The Complete Works of Saint John of the Cross*. Vol. II: The Canticle, pp. 23–395. London: Burns Oates.
— 1946. (Editor and Translator) *The Complete Works of Saint Teresa of Jesus*. Three vols. London: Sheed and Ward.
RIVIÈRE, P. 1972. Tribes without Chiefs. *The Listener* **88** (2269): 365–6, 21 September 1972. Originally broadcast in a series 'Are Hierarchies Necessary?', BBC Radio Three, 31 July 1972.
WILSON, B. 1970 (Editor) *Rationality*. Oxford: Basil Blackwell.

Caroline Ifeka-Moller

Female Militancy and Colonial Revolt
The Women's War of 1929, Eastern Nigeria

INTRODUCTION

This essay is about an African case of feminism. It concerns a women's war of which memories are undimmed, although it took place a long time ago, and in parts of Nigeria is still a potent element in the culture of today.

In writing about the women's war I suggest that the nature of male domination is critical to our understanding of the formation of male/female relations at the time of the riots. I have applied the fruitful ideas of Shirley and Edwin Ardener about the meaning of militant symbolism, and the thought-content of female belief, to a set of historical data. However, I have taken my analysis in a rather different direction, in an attempt to relate the belief system to the roles Igbo men and women played as 'producers' and 'reproducers' before and after 1880. I contend that women rebelled in eastern Nigeria in 1929 because local, short-term events (in particular the introduction of taxation for women) exacerbated a long-term and general contradiction that had developed between the way women saw themselves as producers and as reproducers. Shirley Ardener has argued that when militant women adopt bodily symbolism to 'insult' offending men, they may be using genital differentiation to defend the honour of and express their pride in the essence of women's identity. She points out that sexual insult may communicate a non-obscene message. Hidden from sight behind the genitalia is the womb, which, I suggest, as the operator of female reproduction, was the source of the Igbo woman's pride in herself as a woman. In this paper we have to ask ourselves: why did a biological process, fertility, hold the key to the Igbo woman's self-image? Why should Igbo women have been so concerned about losing their powers of fertility? The answer, I argue, lies in the importance of male control of power, prestige, and authority.

A major problem faces anthropologists attempting to reconstruct female belief in Africa during the colonial or earlier eras from ethnographic and archival materials. In addition to methodological difficulties concerning the assessment of the quality and the reliability of the evidence available, the anthropologist has to remain aware at all times of two sets of values. One set comprises the premisses of colonial administrators, the other the cultural assumptions of the dominant (male) population that prescribe indigenous masculine-feminine values. In the eastern Nigerian case, students of the 1929 riots have to rely on the opinions of witnesses (principally male) to a Commission of Inquiry. Here, statements by witnesses were translated into English by male interpreters, and selected for final recording by the all-male Commission (of the four attached personnel, namely secretaries and reporters, one was a woman). The same kind of problem concerning the channels through which information that we call 'evidence' is filtered, crops up in connection with the anthropologist's use of ethnographic materials about belief, behaviour and social relations. Most of the data on eastern Nigerian peoples were collected by men who were concerned to put on record for posterity the 'facts' about African peoples before the pre-Christian, pre-colonial order passed away, and to supply the colonial administration with a collection of 'facts' about African custom. These ethnographers were not therefore worried about whether they could indeed record 'reality': to them, it was there in front of their eyes. All we can do is to bear in mind this important problem, recognizing that a feminist interpretation of such literature may overreact to a masculine-filtered body of information, in trying to compensate for the virtual absence of records explicitly describing indigenous female belief.

Since the anthropologist has to operate at several removes from the female experience of life in early colonial societies, a large part of this essay is a reconstruction of the female world from 1880 to 1929, which is based on indirect evidence. My picture of the woman's world is put together on the basis of an hypothesis which yields certain conclusions on being applied to the data. To the extent that there are no substantive studies on female belief with the exception of D. A. Talbot (1915) and, possibly, M. M. Green (1964), I am guilty of speculation and interpretation. However, the risk of such a charge does not invalidate the sociological utility of this analysis if due regard is paid to the above problems of the way values filter information, and to data which do not 'fit' the hypothesis. I have therefore indicated my sources of evidence throughout, and have mentioned in the footnotes ethnographic materials which do not appear to support my interpretation of female militancy in 1929. With this in mind, let us now proceed to consider the evidence on the rioting which took place during the women's war.

THE WOMEN'S WAR

In late 1929, women of the Igbo- and Ibibio-speaking ethnic groups in eastern Nigeria, angered at the rumour that they were about to be made to pay tax, attacked the Native Courts and District Offices of the colonial administration, freed prisoners, and looted European trading

128

factories. According to historians [1] and ethnographers,[2] women assembled in crowds ranging from a few hundred to more than ten thousand. The Kingdon Commission of Inquiry, which subsequently was set up (and which heard evidence from 485 persons) was told by a male witness that: [3]

> Many women were dressed in sack cloths and wore *nkpatat* (green creeper) in their hair, carried sticks and appeared to have been seized by some evil spirit (*Report of the Commission of Inquiry appointed to Inquire into the Disturbances in the Calabar and Owerri Provinces, December 1929*, 1930: 63).

Male informants reported that at Itu, a trading centre in Ibibio country on the Cross river:

> ... the women were led by an old and nude woman of great bulk. They acted in a strange manner, some lying on the ground and kicking their legs in the air, and others making obscene gestures (*Report:* 91).

And an English lieutenant, who led a platoon of thirty Hausa (northern Nigerian) soldiers into Opobo, an important entrepôt on the Niger delta, said of the women there:

> Some were nearly naked wearing only wreaths of grass round their heads, waist and knees and some were wearing tails made of grass. The District Officer then began to talk to the crowd. Only a few could hear him owing to the noise the others were making. During all this time reinforcements of women were continuing to arrive both by river and land. Some of these were carrying machetes ... During this time when I was not standing with the District Officer I moved up and down the fence (which marked off the administrative offices) telling the women not to make a noise. They took no notice and told me that I was the son of a pig and not of a woman ... The Court clerk and policeman were interpreting for me and told me the women, speaking in native language, were calling the soldiers pigs and were telling the soldiers that they knew they wouldn't fire but they didn't care whether the soldiers cut their throats (*Minutes of Evidence by a Commission of Inquiry Appointed to Inquire into Certain Incidents at Opobo, Abak and Utu-Etim-Ekpo in December 1929*, 1930: 7).

Those involved in the women's war, as it became known among the Igbo and Ibibio peoples, hailed from villages and towns in the oil-palm belt of the then Owerri and Calabar provinces. Here, people obtained the major part of their cash incomes from producing palm oil and kernels for sale in overseas markets. Protest meetings, organized by women who believed that they were going to be taxed, turned most often into riots in communities where trading in oil and kernels was a particularly lucrative and specialized activity,[4] where the native administration was unreformed and known to be especially corrupt (*Memorandum:*

129

The Disturbed Areas (derived from *Report*, facing page 159)

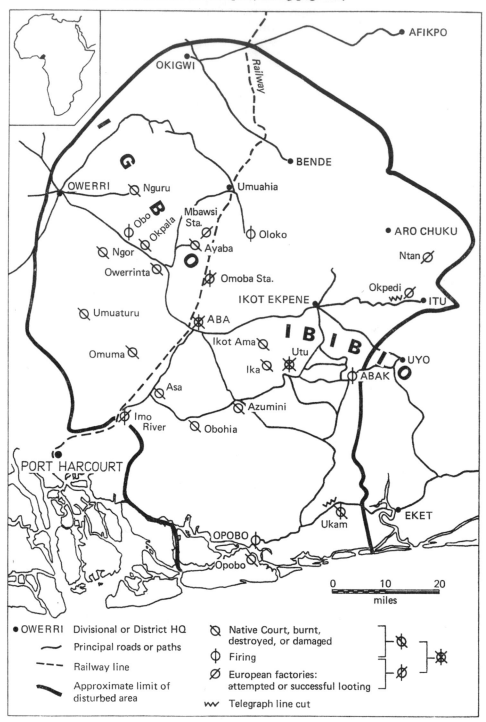

AFIKPO

OKIGWI

Railway

BENDE

I
G
B
O

OWERRI   Ø Nguru   Ø Umuahia

              Obo   Mbawsi   ● ARO CHUKU
              Ø   Ø Okpala Sta.
                          Ø   Ntan Ø
         Ø Ngor   Ø Ayaba
    Owerrinta Ø   Okpedi Ø
                     Ø Omoba Sta.   ⌇⌇ Ø ● ITU
                          IKOT EKPENE ●
    Ø Umuaturu
                    ⊛ ABA   I B I B I O
    Omuma Ø   Ikot Ama Ø
                              Utu   ● UYO
                     Ika Ø ⊛
                                        Ø ABAK
              Ø Asa
                     Ø Azumini
    Ø Imo
      River   Ø Obohia

● PORT HARCOURT
                                    Ukam ⌇ Ø   ● EKET

              OPOBO Ø
                                    0   10   20
              Ø Opobo   miles

● OWERRI   Divisional or District HQ   Ø Native Court, burnt,
                                            destroyed, or damaged
   ⌒   Principal roads or paths   Ø Firing
                                        Ø European factories:
   - - -   Railway line   attempted or successful looting
   ▬   Approximate limit of   ⌇⌇ Telegraph line cut
       disturbed area

9–10), and where earlier counts of the population for taxation assessment had been conducted even less tactfully than usual (*Report:* 93–8). Head-counting had been intensively employed in the disturbed areas since 1926 when forced labour was abolished by the administration (*Memorandum:* 43). In that year adult males were counted, but not told that it was for purposes of taxation. A tax of 7s a head was levied in 1928, to a background of smouldering discontent (*Report:* 94–5). The administration started to reassess some communities in Owerri and Calabar provinces in September 1929; officials insisted on counting not just the men, but also their women and children. Attempts to enumerate female property such as sheep, goats, and hens, as well as the women themselves, led them to believe that, since male counting in 1926 had resulted in the men being taxed, so would they be taxed.

Women therefore started to get together to discuss their fears. These meetings were held from mid-October of 1929. In the view of the Kingdon Commission of Inquiry, rumours that women were to be taxed were fanned by economic and political grievances (ibid.: 93–105). During that year prices for palm produce fell sharply, with the onset of an international economic depression. At the same time, middlemen and middlewomen had to pay more for some imported manufactured commodities which they sold in local markets, because the administration had raised the excise duty on alcohol, tobacco, and cloth in 1928 (ibid.: 103). Women were also much aggrieved by what they considered to be the extortionate practices of many of the government-appointed warrant chiefs, who had some administrative and judicial powers. It was alleged that these chiefs obtained wives without paying full bride-wealth; they were also accused of taking women's personal property against their will (ibid.: 99).

An over-zealous census enumerator, acting on behalf of one warrant chief, Okugo, of Oloko village in Owerri province, became involved in an incident with a woman. This woman, Nwanyeruwa, who became the heroine of the women's war, alleged that on 23 November the enumerator:

> came to her house whilst she was squeezing oil and asked her to count her goats, sheep and people. She replied angrily, concluding with the pointed question: 'Was your mother counted?' Thereupon Emeruwa [the enumerator] seized her by the throat and she, with her hands covered with oil, held him also by the throat, and raised the alarm (*Report:* 13).

Matters then escalated. Chief Okugo unwittingly transformed protest into revolt when he abused and assaulted women who had come to his house in order to protest about their supposed impending taxation. Three riots occurred in Owerri province between 1 and 9 December.[5] Widespread rebellion began on 11 December, lasting until the 20th of that month, after a European doctor had driven his car through massed crowds of protesting women in Aba and crushed two women to death.

131

Angered, believing that the troops would not fire on them, Igbo and some Ibibio women traders took the message of rebellion into Calabar province (*Report:* 35–8, 119; *Minutes:* 43, 45–6). Here, Ibibio women had already heard about the troubles at Oloko and Aba through marketing networks (*Report:* 35, 118–19). Events came to a head at Opobo when, on 16 December, militant women rushed the Hausa (northern Nigerian) troops while their men, armed with machetes, brought up the rear. Hemmed in, the troops fired on the mob killing thirty-two and wounding thirty-one women. In all, fifty-three women were killed in riots in the predominantly Ibibio-speaking Calabar province.[6]

THE 'WHY' AND THE 'HOW' OF THE WOMEN'S WAR

Most accounts of the riots emphasize that economic anxieties played an important part in arousing women's consciousness to a militant pitch. These anxieties were supported by general political discontent among women because of the way in which the government-appointed (warrant) chiefs carried out their duties (ibid.: 98–102). It is apparent that for many colonial administrators the riots were a totally unexpected event. The administration was particularly perturbed by the fact that the sole widespread rebellion against colonial rule between 1914 and 1930 was led by women.[7] Men, Nigerian and European alike, perceived the women to have behaved in a shocking manner. The epithets 'obscene', 'hostile', and 'disrespectful' were among those used by male witnesses to describe their women's behaviour (*Report:* 79; *Minutes:* 7, 20–6, 34).

Only two writers have approached the riots from a feminist perspective. Some years ago Jack Harris [8] argued that only women could have achieved the kind of large-scale mobilization required to launch such a movement, because they had ramifying marketing networks which they used to recruit supporters throughout the region, and because they had exercised sufficient economic influence to sustain continuous demonstrations. More recently, Judith Van Allen has emphasized that women used a traditional sanction against offending men, 'sitting upon a man', as a blueprint for methods employed when protesting in favour of women's rights in 1929 (1972: 175–6). M. M. Green and Jack Harris describe this Igbo custom as follows: [9] if a woman, or several women, think that their customary rights or economic interests are being subverted by careless men (or women) they get together outside the offender's hut, shouting scurrilous gossip, abusing the man, who cowers in his hut, and dancing in sexually loaded, obscene fashion. In *some* but not all known instances of this custom, women don palm leaves on their heads,[10] and daub their faces and trunks with clay or vegetable dye or charcoal. In my opinion, dressing in this wise expresses the seriousness with which women regard a threat to their interests, and the importance of obtaining female solidarity. Van Allen says that the women's war was an extension of this Igbo custom of

132

'sitting on a man'. To burn Native Courts, attack warrant chiefs, and loot factories was analagous to the destroying of an offender's hut and movable property, and to the barracking of victims by women (1972: 178).

It is important to note, because the literature on the riots is silent on this point, that Ibibio women are not known to have such a discrete traditional disciplinary technique. In Ibibio country, women were organized into secret societies such as the *ebere*, 'women of the land'. Missionaries and the administration had tried to eradicate men's and women's secret societies [11] by removing their customary juridico-political functions, which, in the words of an ethnographers, were: '. . . the only safeguard of Ibibio women against the tyranny of their men-folk'.[12] And so, in Ibibio communities, female protest was modelled on beliefs and rituals which were attached to once active, but still influential, secret societies.

Although the contributions of Van Allen and Jack Harris on the women's war are helpful, several issues remain unresolved and require examination. Shirley Ardener's study of female militancy in western Cameroon suggests that these issues may be an important element in women's protest movements elsewhere.[13] We may ask the following questions: What is the structural connection between women's economic grievances and their application of the disciplinary technique, 'sitting on a man' (or its Ibibio equivalent), which prescribes bodily movements defined by men as obscene, and on occasions the adoption of palm leaves, ferns, and creepers symbolic of the 'wild'? [14] What do these phenomena tell us about women's perception of themselves as women, and their relationship to men? Why should women have reacted to a deterioration in their trading position by launching a revolt in which they tried to secure political goals in remarkably ritualistic style? And in what way did the dominant sex, men, influence the events which led to the death of fifty-three women?

Although the literature on the riots affirms that the disturbances were an all-female affair, there is evidence that men did actually take part on occasions, ceasing to be merely 'passive onlookers'.[15] On 4 December 1929, for instance, men and women living in Ukam in Calabar province attacked Native Courts and assaulted the District Officer (*Report:* 24–34). The Kingdon Commission stated that men led this particular revolt (ibid.: 30–4). On 14 December the warrant chief of Utu Etim Ekpo in Calabar province urged the women to riot, with the result that twenty-one women died from soldiers' bullets.[16] In a number of other places men helped to loot factories.[17] Van Allen and others refute the suggestion of some colonial officers made to the Kingdon Commission that women were used as a 'catspaw' by men, and that men gave women the green light to revolt in the belief that soldiers would not fire on them.[18] However, the European trader Gore-Clough writes that people he knew at the time in the trading towns of the Niger delta believed that some priests and 'big men' had urged their women on.[19] Thus the evidence

133

available does not indicate unambiguously whether or not men were trying to run the movement from behind the scenes. Clearly, there would have been much variation from one community to the next in the kind of reaction among men to women's mobilization. There is, however, no doubt that the revolt was primarily a women's affair, and that it was initiated by them in the first place.

The second part of this problem, the extent of male *influence* on, as distinct from direct *participation* in, the riots, is much more significant sociologically. Men's dominance in society, that is, their control over religious beliefs and political institutions, had significant structural consequences for women. Control over land and the bulk of its most lucrative resources, for instance oil-palm trees, assured men of long-term power. In eastern Nigerian societies, what is ethnographically known as the 'formal' political system was by custom allocated to men. Any political influence exerted by women was, by definition, 'informal' power. Some may raise the objection that because women in Igbo and Ibibio country traditionally held some offices,[20] and because Igbo women were well known for their marketing associations,[21] women too wielded some 'formal' political power.[22] They also had their own relatively independent sphere of all-female activities. I would argue, however, that such instances of apparent female autonomy are probably nominal. When we look at these examples more closely we can see something rather different—evidence of the pervasive power of men. In some cases women's offices seem to resemble some recent versions of European 'tokenism'.[23] If women evolved their own hierarchy of offices on the basis of their commercial power,[24] they did so in a supernumerary capacity. The formal political system, which was under male management, did not shift towards integrating women as chiefs or priests as their economic influence grew. Women's associations simulated the values and goals which legitimated male interest groupings and societies. They also adopted the dominant ranking system of men when creating their own hierarchies of officials.[25]

Since male control was based on production, it is not surprising that such sexual antagonism as women allowed themselves to feel was articulated through economic grievances. With one exception, all the recorded cases of women's protest movements in the nineteen-twenties testify to the catalytic effect of economic discontent.[26] But, although women launched a rebellion as a result of economic anxieties, they did not achieve solidarity on the basis of common material interests. Instead, they got together in their capacity as the procreators and mothers of men. Women did not enforce such economic sanctions as refusing to cook for husbands, or boycotting markets—sanctions which Igbo women are said to have practised at other times.[27] Neither did women possess the military equipment and skills of men. Rather, they used their unarmed bodies to destroy buildings, loot factories, and assault chiefs and administrative officials.

134

Women (like men) have a specific biological role in reproduction. It is this which forms the basis of a woman's pride in herself as a woman and is at the heart of the Igbo conception of the 'spirit of womanhood' (*Report:* 20). At the same time, female specialization for reproduction and motherhood is played up in the value-set 'femininity', in a way that men's biological function is not in the linked value-set 'masculinity'. Women were therefore directed by their own 'inner' beliefs, and by the sexual values of their culture, to focus on the reproductive significance of their bodies when uniting in 1929 to protest against wrongs done.

The sexual values associated with the analytical categories, 'masculine' and 'feminine', which prescribe the behaviour appropriate to men and women, are yet another indication of male control over the cultures of these societies. Briefly (for I will return to this point later), 'feminine' norms stress the domestic, pacific and dependent relationship of women to men.[28] Values associated with the analytical category 'masculine' connote public activity and aggression, and control and defence of the community, of people and its lands.[29] Women are thus defined as different from but complementary to men. These sexual values are given equal weight in Igbo and Ibibio cultures. Ideas of sexual equivalence and complementarity echo the interdependence of men and women in reproduction, but also conceal the unequal position of women in society. They function as an ideology.

HOW WOMEN BECAME 'AS MEN': IGBO AND IBIBIO SOCIETIES, 1880–1925

I turn now to a historical outline of how changes in the sexual division of labour in relation to production and distribution took place in the eastern Nigerian economy while religious beliefs and cultural values as they related to men and women appear to have undergone little, if any, alteration. By the nineteen-twenties women had accumulated a wealth which conflicted with 'feminine' values, and with woman's 'inner' ethos. Heavy involvement in production and distribution of palm produce meant that women could no longer concentrate on subsistence agriculture and thus lost sustained preoccupation and contact with the land, whose powers of fertility were so important to women both ideologically and because they were directly related to the biological survival and reproductive continuity of the group. I argue that the evidence available shows that by the late twenties women were impelled to unite in defence of shared economic interests, but the techniques used to assert female solidarity were not economic. Women used the one resource over which they exerted direct, and unambiguous, control— their reproductive powers. Without a formal political voice, and socialized by male control into a dependent relationship with men, which was nevertheless masked by the principle of sexual equivalence, women used their bodies to assert their common womanhood and their

135

right to fair treatment by the (male) administration and warrant chiefs. Men responded to this confrontation in the sexual ideology of their culture, dismissing women's behaviour as 'shocking' and 'obscene'. Demonstrating women operated at times within this sexual ideology when they chose symbols associated with men's rituals.

At present comparatively little is known about social conditions in the Igbo- and Ibibio-speaking hinterland during the early to middle years of the nineteenth century.[30] However, we know something about life in the Igbo and Ibibio settlements that bordered on the river Niger and the entrepôt ports of the Niger delta.[31] Here, the slave trade had already generated 'rich-poor' divisions, which coexisted alongside a fast-fading status system that accorded high value to a long and pure pedigree, and seniority of birth and of descent.[32] Most people, however, worked on the land to produce their means of subsistence. Men and women probably laboured side by side on their farms, sharing some tasks and cooperating in the harvesting of fruits, greens, and other cultivated plants. Men planted and harvested the prestige crop, yams. If a man owned slaves, as was commonly reported for the Niger river and delta communities,[33] his wives and daughters would have been spared much labour on the land. Such women probably spent much of their time in the home, engaging in some retailing of perishables not required by their families.[34] At this time women were not geographically or socially mobile. They were very bound up with the cult of the earth goddess known as Ala among the Igbo, and Isong among the Ibibio. Ala secured the fertility of the land and of women. She blessed people with many children, fruitful harvests, and a peaceful home, as she did in other societies of the savanna—forest zones of West Africa.[35] Women in eastern Nigeria were 'the trees which bear fruit'.[36]

'Legitimate' commerce, that is the overseas trade in palm oil and kernels, expanded rapidly after the eighteen-eighties.[37] By the turn of the century, when the British established the protectorate of southern Nigeria, petty commodity production appears to have been fairly widespread. This meant that people now laboured to produce oil and kernels for sale locally or, more important, for the overseas market (Helleiner 1972: 97). They went on producing subsistence crops as well, but this activity was no longer the sole means of ensuring the reproductive continuity of the society since food supplies could now be obtained also through the market economy. Processing and extraction of the oil was carried out on a small scale by individual producers, men and women. In the early twentieth century, with the establishment of direct British over-rule, the trade was opened up to all and sundry, for people could now travel to buyers in safety over long distances on the roads being built with forced labour.[38] A large number of farmers turned to cash-crop production, and a new generation of traders emerged; the important novelty was that many of them were women.[39] Little if no capital was needed to begin trading, and there were many opportunities for intermediaries. Nevertheless, since large wholesalers operated at an advantage (Hopkins 1973: 125–45), those communities which had specialized in the slave trade entered the era of 'legitimate' commerce with a head-start. They had accumulated the capital which was used to give credit to middlemen and women who in turn made contracts with suppliers in the hinterland. They had also acquired considerable expertise over the years in running regional distribution networks. Three cases in point are the Igbo people of Onitsha and Oguta of the Niger river area, and of the mixed Igbo- and Ibibio-speaking Ngwa-Ohuhu clans of the Aba area.[40] In all of these cases, both women and men emerged as managers of large-scale trading corporations; it was Igbo-speaking women from the Ngwa and Ohuhu clans who led the early riots in the women's war before neighbouring Calabar province became involved.[41]

After 1900, petty commodity production took a new turn with the development of cassava (known as the 'woman's crop') as a cash crop. In some communities like the Afikpo, which were geographically marginal to the wealthier settlements of the oil palm belt, cassava cultivation gave rise to 'profound alterations in the economic and social relations between husbands and wives' (Ottenberg 1959: 215). Elsewhere, the production of cassava as a commodity for sale added to the *de facto* power women were building up as a result of their involvement as producers and distributors in the cash economy.[42] An early colonial observer, A. G. Leonard,[43] wrote in 1906 of the Ibibio, Igbo, and Ijaw peoples of the Niger delta districts:

> . . . in nearly every prosperous community among the interior tribes, particularly, where the women do all the marketing and trading, it is no uncommon thing to see an idol representing the spirit of some woman who, on her departure to the other world, has been elevated to the position of a deity by her household, and in some cases by the community.

Women in the Onitsha area, on the river Niger, are said, at that time, to have transmitted rights of usufruct and management in oil palm trees to their daughters; women also owned and controlled the usufruct of oil palm plantations.[44] And in the Uyo district of Ibibio country, women carried out the following economic activities: they were money-lenders, they bought canoes for transporting palm produce to the beaches of the Calabar and Cross rivers, hired male labour to work their lands and paddle their canoes, bought titles for male children, and paid bridewealth for son's wives (Andreski 1970: 98, 112, 127, 156).

These were truly radical changes in the sexual division of labour and in the distribution of wealth. But women did not exert the same degree of economic power as men for the simple reason that men still controlled the bulk of the economy's capital assets—land and labour—and political power.[45] Perpetuation of male power is evident in the apparent stability of sexual norms during this period. Ethnographers working in eastern Nigeria before the first world war collected data on cultic belief and practice which provides some indirect evidence about the content of sexual values. The material in these early works is consistent with information collected during the nineteen-thirties on Igbo belief. It therefore appears that sexual values did not change significantly between 1880 and 1930. At the turn of the century A. G. Leonard observed that in communities bordering on the river Niger and along the Niger delta, men believed that they possessed fertilizing energy, whereas women were said to contain or conceive energy (Leonard 1906: 342–3). Among the Igbo of Degema division, in the Niger delta, people told P. A. Talbot in 1912–14 that the tortoise represented the 'female qualities of persuasion . . . as opposed to the more forceful male attributes' (Talbot 1927: 6). In the Igbo village-group of Agbaja, Owerri province, people classified the ideal woman in the nineteen-thirties as having a peaceful disposition, as one who mediates successfully in disputes. Medicine used to resolve conflicts was said to be female and cooling, the defensive antidote of male, aggressive, or 'hot' medicine (Green 1964: 91, 255–6).

If women were associated with the home, motherhood, and fertility, men were thought of as the masters and owners of the soil; they controlled public cults and therefore the *ritual* management of reproduction. Men did not, in indigenous belief, have direct control over women's fertility. Male activation is a prerequisite of female reproduction, but cannot guarantee procreation. Male participation is illustrated by the case of the Igbo of one district in Degema division who were observed in the early twentieth century to make three supports in the shape of a phallus for a bride's cooking pot; these supports or *eku* were said to draw the blessing of fertility into the bride.[46] Igbo and Ibibio cosmologies are recorded in the early colonial era as stressing the gender and personality of their gods. The ethnographic literature suggests, however, that of those groups for whom we have information, the Ibibio were more interested than were the Igbo in thinking about the complementary characteristics of their male and female gods.[47]

Ibibio divided up the pantheon into a dominant male section under the creating god Abassi, and a minority female section under Abassi Isu Ma, the mother goddess (also addressed most evocatively as the goddess of love), and Isong, the earth goddess (Talbot 1923: 7–14). The creating god was thought to have three major refractions, which formed a kind of intellectual holy triad. There was Abassi, the creator, Abassi Isu Ma, the mother-figure, and Abassi Obumo, the thunderer—a martial god (Talbot, ibid.). It is possible that Christian influence had diminished the masculinity of the creating god by the early twentieth century when Talbot was conducting his researches. But it seems more plausible that the creating god, Abassi, was less than male on account of his remoteness from man. The same may explain why the Igbo creator,

Chukwu, had none of the aggressive vigour associated with other male godlings.[48] Thus Ibibio cosmology gave the gods, male and female, complementary functions and personalities.

The principle of sexual complementarity [49] sanctioned and reflected the ordering of men and women in Ibibio society into discrete secret societies.[50] Each sexual category had a specific, mystical association with the land.[51] Men's secret societies ruled the country at the turn of the century; they carried out war to defend and extend the territory their people occupied. Women's secret societies, such as the *ebere*, 'women of the land', protected the 'spirit of womanhood' which people thought to be dependent upon the procreative powers of the land.

Ethnographers do not record Igbo culture as having objectified the feminine principle in a great variety of spiritual beings.[52] In this respect Igbo cosmology may have differed from that of their Ibibio neighbours. Instead, Igbo thought about male–female relations in a more profane mode. In the early years of this century, communities living in Degema division, for instance, were fond of making fetish objects known there as *ibudu*. These represented the male and female genitalia; some *ibudu* represented the private parts of both sexes in the one phallic mound (Talbot 1927: 65–8). In many parts of southern Igbo country people would build shrines dedicated to a god, usually the thunderer, Ama-dioha, and his consort, Ala, the earth goddess.[53] These shrines were known as *mbari* houses; beautiful murals sometimes depicted sexual contact and procreation among humans and among animals, and between the two species. A male god, generally Igwe, the sky hero, or Amadioha, the thunderer, was thought to fertilize the earth goddess.[54] On the other hand, people also conceived of the earth as the owner of life and of men. Thus, the role of the sexes in renewing life was defined as complementary: men were balanced against women. Ritual symbolism and cult specialization testify to the significance of the principle of sexual complementarity.

Whatever the mode of articulation of 'masculine' and 'feminine' values, be they ritualized and objectified at the level of the pantheon or expressed in the less sacred, more profane idiom of fetish objects like the Igbo *ibudu*, women's inner belief in the source of their honour as women was invariably encapsulated within cosmologies and institutions controlled by men. In the Igbo case, women articulated their identity through the cult of Ala, the earth goddess, and applied a discrete disciplinary technique which could be used to symbolize women's mystical and reproductive association with Nature. In Ibibio country, women looked to their own secret societies and the goddesses of the earth and motherhood to safeguard their procreative powers.

By the nineteen-twenties women's important role in the prevailing labour-intensive system of palm-oil production and distribution, was established. Over the years some women in many Igbo- and Ibibio-speaking villages had accumulated rights in immovable property. These rights were tantamount to 'ownership'.[55] Since Igbo and Ibibio customary law was based on the principle of male transmission and male control over rights in immovable property, women's rights remained *de facto*.[56] They could not be, and were not, regarded as having general *de jure* status.

The literature suggests that by the nineteen-twenties and thirties men in some Igbo districts of the central oil-palm belt 'pledged' oil-palm trees to women, who then owned the oil they had extracted from the fruits.[57] As a variant of oil-palm-tree 'pledging', men would sometimes 'pledge' the fruits of their trees to women, who then owned the produce, but not the trees. In Igbo customary law, 'pledging' was also used to transfer the usufruct of land, oil-palm trees or their fruits to another person for an indefinite period of time in return for a cash payment. G. I. Jones (1949: 319) writes:

> A person in need of money can borrow it on the security of some of his land; the use of which is transferred to the lender and his heirs until such times as the debt is repaid.

It is interesting to note that some women who were both active and efficiently involved in the palm-produce business are known to have entered into 'pledging' transactions with men who owned trees and land but who needed cash. They must, therefore, have had more liquid assets than these men.

Ethnographers report that in the nineteen-twenties and thirties women owned the kernels, and kept all moneys received from European buyers.[58] Women and men processed oil from the palm fruits by manual extraction; women kept an unspecified proportion of money obtained on selling the oil. Kernels were a highly lucrative source of income for women because after the turn of the century European demand for this commodity remained high. European firms bought the kernels and processed them into cow-cake (Helleiner 1972: 97).

The literature points to men's growing financial dependence upon their women when they had to raise a sum of money quickly. In the early nineteen-twenties women were still important as carriers of oil and kernels from the hinterland to the buyers waiting on their 'beaches' along the Niger delta and on the Cross and Imo rivers. Demand for oil and kernels in the years 1920 to 1928 was still increasing, and more and more were being produced. Information given to the Kingdon Commission of Inquiry tends to confirm that women were a potent element in the economy. It was alleged by one witness to the Commission that women had paid the bulk of the head-tax levied on their men in the previous year.[59] There is, however, no other direct evidence to corroborate this tantalizing hint of many men's financial dependence on their women. The Commissioners certainly accepted that women contributed much to the domestic economy, and that they helped their menfolk pay taxes 'in one way or another' (*Report:* 21). In Agbaja village-group,

Owerri province, women in the nineteen-thirties regarded themselves as the 'food producers and crop owners' (Green 1964: 172); all but one of the twenty crops grown there were cultivated and owned by women.

At the same time as women and men were being drawn into an economic system which required them to use their labour for commodity production, Christian missions stepped up their pressure on people to convert. In the nineteen-twenties a significant proportion of the population had been converted to mission Christianity; this process of religious change was particularly marked in the southern Igbo, and Ibibio, communities of the oil-palm belt.[60] Missions attracted youths anxious for education and a chance for a 'pen-pushing' job. Mature women were generally less receptive,[61] for the colonial system did not offer women posts in the native administration, churches, or trading firms. Furthermore, mission Christianity was strongly opposed to so-called 'pagan' cults, the cult of the earth goddess and the secret societies of Ibibio women (and men) being prime targets for attack. The cults of Ala and Isong were controlled by men in their role of community priests.[62] Mission propaganda against public cults therefore weakened male control over women in this respect; but it may also have undermined female solidarity, so strongly associated with the earth and its powers of fertility.

A DECADE OF PROTEST ENDS IN THE WOMEN'S WAR

In retrospect, the nineteen-twenties emerges as *the* decade of protest during the first forty years of British over-rule. Above all, women became increasingly militant; they thus became politically 'visible' to an extent which was not to be repeated. The better known of the early women's protest movements include the *nwa obolia* (or 'dancing women') movement of 1925, which took place in some parts of Igbo country, and the spirit movement of 1927, which deeply disturbed many villages in Ibibio-land.[63] Women taking part in the *nwa obolia* of 1925 demanded an end to prostitution, better medical facilities, improved fertility, and more safeguards for women traders (*Report:* 19). Only in the 1927 spirit movement do we find no mention by women of economic anxiety about their trading position. This movement, however, was remarkable for its emphasis on cleansing communities of evil practices by destroying idols, and also for women's preoccupation with their powers of reproduction (*Memorandum:* 10–11). Women rioted in Calabar and Oron, in 1925 and 1927 respectively, when they thought that their economic interests were being attacked by new legislation or by other (male) economic groups (ibid.: 12–17). On these latter two occasions, the riots did not spread into other districts. Always, however, women dressed as the 'wild'.

Women rioted in 1929, as earlier, because they believed that the economic interests of their sex were being undermined. Protest turned

141

into rebellion throughout the oil-palm belt because certain short-term events coincided with long-run changes in the sexual division of labour and in the distribution of wealth. Undoubtedly, the knowledge that women who had protested in previous years had not been hurt by the native police added to their sense of personal security and confirmed their awareness of themselves as a distinct section of the population which had common interests. If one local event, the rumour that women were to be taxed, sparked off conflicts springing from the contradiction between women's economic power and their 'inner' beliefs about the dynamic of womanhood, then there was no lack of other local happenings which fuelled the tinder of discontent into flames once the taxation rumour had become generally known. Administrative officers behaved with remarkable insensitivity and lack of care on several occasions. The case of the European doctor who crushed two women to death with his motor-car was mentioned earlier. Finally, women believed that the administration's alleged attempt to tax them was the last straw in a year when the bottom was falling out of the palm-produce market. The trend towards mechanization, although not an openly discussed issue in the late twenties, must also have sharpened women's anxiety.[64] All these short-run events would probably have failed to generate a mass uprising of women had there not been a more fundamental conflict which particularly affected them as a sex. Women expressed their conscious fear that they were becoming 'as men' in the language of reproduction which was associated with the female body and the land. They feared that they were becoming infertile, that more of their children died than in olden times, and that the land itself was 'dying'.

Driven on by their anxiety,[65] women articulated their 'inner' belief in the 'spirit of womanhood':

> We understand that the palm trees and our lands are no longer our own . . . we are told that our lands have been bought over which implies that everything on the land was also bought (*Nigerian Daily Times:* 1930, 14.2).

They declared: 'Government starves us . . . our children die. We ourselves die' (Leith-Ross 1965: 178).

The sexual values of Igbo and Ibibio cultures reaffirmed through rituals, marriage, and child-rearing practices, the unique biological functions of the female sex and, therefore, their different but complementary nature to the male sex. Sexual ideology thus turned women in on themselves, a muted category whose main legitimate weapon was the body, and emphasized the social significance to women of their powers of reproduction.

I have argued that the sexual norms of these cultures were unchanged by the development of a cash economy and did not adjust to the emergence of women as an economic force. This is, perhaps, not surprising given women's inability to achieve a political authority and recognition commensurate with their economic influence. Mission Christianity and colonial rule worked in favour of male domination, rather than the reverse. Men were still the 'masters' and 'owners' of the land (though women largely cared for it and grew their subsistence crops on it), a fact which Ibibio women acted out during the 1929 war when they adopted certain ritual symbols normally identified with male-controlled cults, and the management of fertility.

Ibibio women were seen wearing tails of grass, declaring they were vultures (*Minutes of Evidence:* 7, 41, 43). One ethnographer (Talbot 1923: 163–5) interprets a dance which men performed as members of the *Egbo* secret society (dedicated to the ancestral spirits) to be a simulation of vultures and eagles. Donning short and long tails, men became vultures who symbolized the ancestral spirits. When Ibibio women wore tails during the riots, they were possibly defining themselves as men. Receivers of sacrificial offerings (the warrant chiefs, Native Courts and the trade goods of European firms), and messengers of god, these female vultures went to war as did warriors of old.

The Igbo women's disciplinary technique 'sitting on a man' was not linked with secret societies nor with any ritualized cult of womanhood. Militant women everywhere in the oil-palm belt practised sexual insult, 'shocking' their menfolk. Both Igbo and Ibibio women threw sand (that is: dried-out, barren earth) at their chiefs, while demanding the caps (symbols of office) of the warrant chiefs, and positions as judges, for women.[66] They desired some share in the formal political system.[67]

When men adopted the dress of the 'wild' this symbolized men's power over people and the land. Youths at Ukam, Calabar province, dressed in palm leaves and creepers when they led the revolt there in December 1929. Witnesses to the Kingdon Commission affirmed that this was the dress of warriors (Minutes of Evidence: 20), defenders and managers of the land. It is, then, appropriate that men as 'the owners of the land' and women as the 'trees which bear fruit' should have adorned themselves in the greenery of Nature. But they did so on the basis of ideologically complementary, but materially asymmetrical, roles in society.

CONCLUSION

In this essay I have tried to answer, however partially, several unresolved questions concerning this African case of feminism. Striking similarities between the women's war of 1929, and the southern Cameroon uprising of 1953, suggest how we can explain these questions. Like their Kom sisters, Igbo and Ibibio women united to defend economic interests which they thought to be at risk, and they used bodily insult to demonstrate their pride in themselves as women, and dressed as the 'wild'. My explanation assumes that male domination accounts for the development after 1880 or so of a contradiction between, on the one hand,

143

women's use of their bodies in production and the unprecedented material rewards this brought them during the labour-intensive phase of petty commodity production, and on the other hand women's biosocial functions in reproduction.

Since men controlled the major political and economic resources in these societies, women had assured and certain control only over their reproductive powers. Male dominance therefore directed women to experience the challenge which their new commercial power, resulting from their new role in production, posed to men, as one which eroded women's powers of fertility. They came to fear that they were in danger of losing the asset from which they had traditionally drawn their strength: their power to procreate. They believed that they and the land, from which the means to nourish their children were reproduced, were 'dying'.

Adapting some ideas of Shirley Ardener I have suggested that conception and safe delivery of the foetus was woman's unique secret and the traditional basis of the 'spirit of womanhood'. The sexual ideology of these societies was apparently unaffected by the economic revolution that occurred when petty commodity production became widespread after the eighteen-eighties. Sexual values concerning men's association with activation and ownership of women and the land, and women's identification with the reception of the male essence, sustained women's 'inner' belief that reproduction brought them full maturity and satisfaction. Women were given a cultural identity ('feminine') which placed more emphasis on women's particular biological functions than did men's identity ('masculine') on their biology. It was these values which provided women with the techniques and symbols for demonstrating their fear that they had become 'as men'. They used their bodies to 'insult' men; and they adorned themselves in the 'wild', thereby utilizing the armoury of Nature to convey their belief in the life-giving powers of the land with which they associated their own powers of reproduction. Women's use of their bodies as a disciplinary technique affirms the stability of sexual ideologies throughout the early twentieth century, and the reality of male domination.

The rumour that women were to be taxed was the most publicized single event said to be the cause of the women's rioting. There were also other immediate causes for discontent. The decline of world trade in the depression of 1929 was significant, and the relative decline of women's power in the palm-oil trade due to male command of mechanization and of new administrative techniques was probably influential.[68] Those women who had become 'as men' in so far as they now commanded cash and credit commensurate with that managed by men, were not given the status and political authority of men, and this was a primary source of friction, even though it was *consciously* experienced only by a few really militant women. Certain symbols which were normally associated with male-controlled rituals and male cultural values were

144

sometimes made use of by women in order to emphasize their claims to a share of political power. All these immediate causes were important, but I hope to have demonstrated in this paper that the long-term conditions generating the riots that climaxed a decade of female militancy had their roots in the emergence of female wealth at a time when colonial rule buttressed and strengthened traditional male dominance, and that the latter indirectly determined the forms in which the militancy was expressed.

Acknowledgements

This paper is dedicated with affectionate respect to M. M. Green, for her linguistic and ethnographic work among the Igbo peoples.

An earlier draft of this paper was read by M. M. Green, G. I. Jones, and S. Leith-Ross, who gave me the benefit of their considerable knowledge of Igbo society during the years that followed the Aba riots. Ernest Gellner helped sort out some muddles in my exposition. Participants in an informal women's anthropology workshop at Oxford in 1973 and at a seminar on Sexual Roles held at University College, London, in January 1974 have done much to clarify my understanding of female militancy.

Notes

1 Historical analyses of the women's war include the following: H. Gailey, *The Road to Aba* (1971), gives an historian's view of the background to the riots and draws on the findings of the Kingdon Commission of Inquiry. M. Perham (1937) describes how discontent among women escalated into revolt. She, too, bases her account on the Kingdon Commission of Inquiry (see pp. 206–20). E. A. Afigbo (1966) places the riots in the political context of indigenous reaction to the imposition of colonial rule. He says the riots were a very conservative reaction to the arrival of British rule (p. 539).

2 Mention of the riots in ethnographic studies on the Igbo peoples is made by the following, among others: C. K. Meek (1937: ix–xi, 330–3); S. Leith-Ross (1965: 23–39); M. M. Green (1964: viii–xvi, 3–8); J. Harris (1939–40: 147–8). The slim volume by R. Gore-Clough (1972), a European trader, of his experiences during the heyday of the trade in palm produce contains useful information on how the women seemed to behave, and why, from an expatriate perspective.

3 The complete findings of the Commission of Inquiry, which heard evidence in early 1930 under the chairmanship of Donald Kingdon, were published by the administration as a Blue Book in the same year, called: *Nigeria: Report of the Aba Commission of Inquiry*. The main evidence is given in the *Report of the Commission of Inquiry appointed to Inquire into the Disturbances in the Calabar and Owerri Provinces, December 1929*, hereafter referred to as '*Report*'. The Blue Book also contains several annexures, among which the following are most useful: *Memorandum of the Secretary, Southern Provinces, on the Origin and Causes of the disturbances in the Owerri and Calabar Provinces of 16th January, 1930*, hereafter referred to as '*Memorandum*'; *Minutes of Evidence taken by a Commission of Inquiry to inquire into certain incidents at Opobo, Abak and Utu Etim Ekpo in December, 1929*, hereafter referred to as '*Minutes*'; *Report of Commission of Inquiry appointed to inquire into certain incidents at Opobo, Abak and Utu Etim Ekpo in December, 1929*, hereafter referred to as '*Report of Commission of Inquiry*'.

145

4 Some account of oil palm belt economies is given in D. Forde and R. Scott (1946: 40–78). Data were collected in the nineteen-thirties and forties. See also: A. G. Hopkins (1973: 132–4, 139–41); K. M. Buchanan and J. C. Pugh (1955: 128–31); and the most informative study by a colonial officer of palm-oil production during the nineteen-thirties, namely, A. F. B. Bridges (unpub. 1939: 3–25). J. Harris (1943) has useful data on a local economy, Ozuitem village-group, Owerri Province.

5 See *Report*, Appendix V, *Chronological Table of Events*: 154–6.

6 See *Report*, Annexures IV and V, Appendix III (15) (a) and (b); Opobo Casualty List; Abak and Utu Etim Ekpo Casualty List. Thirty-two women were killed at Opobo, three at Abak, and eighteen at Utu Etim Ekpo, making fifty-three dead in all. The works on the riots mentioned above do not give complete numbers of the deceased. V. Uchendu (1965: 47) gives incorrect figures. E. Afigbo also gives incorrect figures (1966: 555).

7 Other rebellions, or 'disturbances' as they were euphemistically known, were localized, as for instance, the tax riots led by men in Warri province, 1927, or the dancing women's movement of 1925 in Owerri province. In 1949 a new and mass protest movement began which stemmed from the Enugu coalminers' strike of 1949, and then spread into other towns as the nationalist cause was propagated by young, literate, leaders. See *Enquiry into the Disorders in the Eastern Provinces of Nigeria: Proceedings of the Commission, vols. 1 and 2*, 1950.

8 See J. Harris (1939–40: 147). Harris stresses the important contribution of Igbo women in Ozuitem village-group, Bende division, to the exchange economy, and discusses the 'informal' political power of women, such as their custom of 'sitting upon a man' (pp. 143–4, 147).

9 See M. M. Green (1964: 196–214) and J. Harris (1939–40: 147). Green, and witnesses to the Kingdon Commission of Inquiry, suggest that the Igbo practise sexual insult by referring to, or by actually revealing, the sexual organs and buttocks. None of these sources provides any Igbo terms for the sexual organs and buttocks, or explains why obscene gestures should include those associated with the buttocks. However, M. M. Green, who kindly reviewed her field notes for me, states that among the Agbaja Igbo, the word *ohu* (standard Igbo, *oru*) denotes the vulva and vagina. The standard Igbo phrase *oru nsi* extends the vulva and vagina to the anus; *abo*, belly, can also be used loosely to mean the womb or vagina. Green writes that Igbo terminology 'suggests a degree of vagueness in distinguishing parts of the body. And how far does the unsophisticated Igbo analysis of the body correspond with the English, or even assume that the anatomy and physiology are identical? . . . I don't know whether Igbo women think chiefly of the vagina or of the womb, or of the female organs in general, but my overall impression . . . is that child-bearing is the important consideration'. Green observed several cases of cliterodectomy during her fieldwork, and suggests that 'this messing up of the sexual orifice might . . . throw women's attention rather on to the womb'. She asked an elderly woman the reason for the girls' operation, and her note of 1 December 1935 records the following: 'She said people say that unless a girl cut she will not be able to bear children. I asked what way? Would she not be able to deliver a child or is it that when she goes to her husband he would not be able to conceive her. She says she could not go to her husband, i.e. the second of the two things I said.' Although J. Van Allen cites Green (pp. 170–1), in support of her analysis, it is noteworthy that Green herself does not use the term 'sitting on a man' to describe the women's use of sexual insult to crush offenders (see pp. 201–2 for examples of sexually lewd songs, not normally recited in public). M. M. Green concludes her account of female disciplinary techniques in Agbaja village-group, Okigwi division, Owerri pro-

vince, with the warning: 'It would probably be unwise to interpret too literally the statement that "all married women of Agbaja" cooperated' (p. 214). J. Harris (ibid.: 147) discussed women's sanctions under the label 'sitting upon a man' used by Ozuitem Igbo. S. Leith-Ross (1965) has a footnote on p. 25 about the practice, which people were not eager in the nineteen-thirties to discuss with her. V. Uchendu (1965) describes Igbo society from an almost completely masculine perspective. He gives no information at all on 'informal' processes of control exercised by women, despite the early interest of ethnographers in Igbo women.

10 Young palm leaves and ferns symbolize both fertility and masculine actions such as courage in war, and aggressive defence of the interests of one's own settlement if threatened by another. Known as '*eyei*' among Igbo, young palm leaves were used in inter-town diplomacy to represent peace or war; they also symbolized the life-essence generated by communal 'rites of passage', secret society rites, and harvest festivals (see M. Ekandem 1955: 53–63). Among the Etche Igbo of Degema, young palm leaves symbolized manhood, rain, children, and fruitfulness of the land and of women. The same word *omu mu* is used to express fruitfulness and the act of giving birth (see P. A. Talbot 1927: 40). Ibibio women either wore young palm leaves or *nkpatat*, a climbing creeper, on their heads; the head was the symbol of the source of life (see Meek, ibid.: 39). When Ibibio women fear they are barren, they may be initiated into the *nyama* secret society. They wear a raphia necklet, dyed red, are naked from the waist up, and their trunks are daubed with green dye (see Jeffreys 1956: 15–27).

11 These societies and other jural institutions were denied jural powers as native administration was imposed on indigenous political institutions. In 1906 Lord Lugard wrote the following guidance to his political officers: 'Some few societies existed no doubt for purposes of fetish worship combined with human sacrifices, enslaving and other crimes—and for these complete suppression is the only course which can be adopted. But there are many others whose origin and main purpose supplies a want—probably by exercising discipline and control, and by promoting cohesion. In such cases it is better policy to purge them of their undesirable characteristics and accretions and to utilize them, than to attempt ineffectually to suppress them' (Kirk-Greene 1965: 79). The administration wanted to strip 'native' institutions of any powers which might make pacification difficult. In 1933 the administration issued Ordinance 44. Section 8, *An Ordinance to Make Better Provision for the Administration of Justice and the Constitution of Native Courts in the Protectorate*, excluded any 'native tribunal' from exercising judicial powers. This document is listed by Margery Perham (1937: 365–8). The ban on indigenous judicial proceedings, and hence of effective secret societies and women's informal sanctions, was not fully implemented until after 1933. Nevertheless, the administration and missions had kept up a continuous attack against these institutions from 1901.

12 D. A. Talbot (1915: 190). The wife of the colonial officer and brilliant ethnographer P. A. Talbot, D. A. Talbot left a unique record of the customs and beliefs of Ibibio women in Oron and Eket districts. It was pointed out to her by a (male) literary friend that 'although men have taught us much of late years concerning primitive man, primitive woman is still unknown save through the medium of masculine influence' (p. 2).

13 S. Ardener (above). Describing the Kom uprising of 1953 in the southern Cameroon, and the Bakweri practice of '*titi ikoli*', Shirley Ardener argues that female militancy may reveal a profound preoccupation with the symbol of female honour—the body and more especially the vagina. She says that, forming as they do a mute category, when women unite to defend certain of their interests which

147

they believe reflect back on women's sexual identity, they may use those weapons which are most conveniently available to them: their bodies. Obscenity, or revealing what should normally be hidden, has been practised by these women as a disciplinary technique. Sexual organs and their surrounds (e.g. the buttocks) can be made visible to the naked eye (unlike, of course, the reproductive organs). Shirley Ardener suggests that some 'vulgar' gestures may communicate women's pride in their 'hidden' source of honour, symbolized for Bakweri by the vagina. In Igbo and Ibibio cultures, women, I suggest, focus on the womb and on the reproductive process generally. Shirley Ardener's work demonstrates that economic anxieties and bodily insult are sometimes associated by female militants in southern Cameroon; my material on eastern Nigeria confirms this correlation of variables. It was Edwin Ardener who made the original point that in the eyes of the men women among the Bakweri of Cameroon persist in fusing into Nature, whence originate their reproductive powers. In his words:

> 'Since these powers are for women far from being marginal, but are of their essence as women, it would seem that a woman's model of the world would also treat them as central' (1972: 143, and above).

14 M. M. Green (1964: 203) recounts the obscene gestures of women in Agbaja when protesting women's rights. J. Harris (1939–40) describes women's disciplinary techniques in Ozuitem. These included boycotts of offending women, refusal to cook for husbands, and so forth. Harris describes women rioting in 1929, carrying fern-covered sticks, 'symbols of the protection of the female "ancestors"' (p. 148). To my knowledge, Igbo had no *cult* of the ancestors and ancestresses of women, belief being distinct from institutionalized worship. There is an extensive but not informed discussion of secret societies in eastern Nigeria in *Memorandum* (pp. 1–8). *Minutes of Evidence* (pp. 4–43) contains eye-witness accounts by men of how women dressed as the 'wild', daubed their bodies with clay or vegetable dye, and danced rhythmically.

15 A common statement. See, for instance, J. Van Allen (ibid.: 175; *Report*: 75). This despite the fact that men actually took an active part in the looting of factories; they led the Ukam revolt of 4 December 1929; and often lined the roads, matchets in hand. See *Report* (pp. 24–34, 57, 79). The epithet 'passive' was presumably used because men were not the leaders, the initiators, of the revolt against colonial rule (see *Report*, p. 75).

16 See *Report of a Commission of Inquiry* [the Birrel-Gray Commission] (p. 11).

17 *Report* (pp. 59, 63); men helped loot at Abak, the Imo river station, and elsewhere.

18 See *Report* (p. 105). Authors who do not countenance this suggestion are Van Allen (1972: 175–6); and H. Gailey (1971: 131). Leith-Ross (1965: 21–2) affirms the vigorous autonomy of Igbo women and their non-servile position in society despite the male view that men are lords and masters of all.

19 R. Gore-Clough (1972: 88–9) writes that in Opobo men actively encouraged the women to riot, calling 'on the juju priests to help'. He says that 'the male population took the opportunity of engineering the riots as a lever to get the tax on the men removed also' (p. 101), an opinion shared by Nigerian journalists writing in 1930 about the women's war (see *Nigerian Daily Times*, 24.3.1930). Evidence such as the above fits in with the findings of the Commission of Inquiry, that men in some areas did either initiate revolts or, more commonly, help women loot factories. The Commission admit the men's tacit support for their womenfolk (see *Report*, p. 106).

20 See M. M. Green (1964: 217–18). R. Henderson (1972: 311–14, 484, 495–6)

describes women's trading and political associations in the Igbo settlement of Onitsha during the late nineteenth century. The hierarchy of offices is identical with that described by G. Basden (1938: 204–10) for women's societies among the Igbo of Onitsha and Awka in the early twentieth century. Basden says women had their own 'committee or club which legislates for the women independently of the men'. The women elect their own officials who work under a 'Queen'. She is the official counterpart of the *Obi* or 'King'. The Queen, *Omu*, is never the King's consort.

M. M. Green (1964: 217–26), gives a vivid account of one kind of women's society in Umueke village of Agbaja village-group. Women born in Umueke formed a *mkiri*, a meeting, whose officials included these: the chairwoman or *Mama*; gun-bearers clad in thick, dark blue blouses and pillbox hats, pink and green, carrying miniature guns over their shoulders; policewomen similarly attired; a 'D.C.'; and a *Nwa Beke*, white woman, who 'stands out in one's mind, sometimes for the ferocity of her expression, sometimes for her clothes—a pink silk dress with an orange Tam O'Shanter on one occasion and horn-rimmed spectacles with a white blob on each lens.' Green adds, 'She gave one much food for thought' (pp. 218, 225–6). S. Leith-Ross (1965: 105–10, 163–5), describes Igbo women's councils in Nneato and Nguru but gives no information regarding offices. There is no detailed information on the principal women's secret societies among the Ibibio, the *ebere* and the *iban isong* or Women of the Land society. D. A. Talbot (1915: 189–96), describes the main rites of these societies but gives no information on internal organization, offices and the like. F. Butt-Thompson (1929), collates material collected by early travellers and administrative officials in the British colonies. A rather fragmentary collection of data on an inevitably inscrutable institution.

21 I can find no information on marketing associations among the Ibibio in the literature. But it seems likely that they would have had such interest groupings.

22 See my 'Sitting on a man: Colonialism and the Lost Political Institutions of Igbo Women: A reply to Judith Van Allen' (1973).

23 See Ifeka-Moller 1973, and above, note 20. It is obvious from the above information that women were not allocated a formal status within the political system; they had no offices which carried judicial, executive, or legislative powers. Sheila Rowbotham (1973: 49–66) discusses the status of women in industrial Britain from a socialist perspective.

24 R. Henderson (1972), is very clear on this point for the old settlement of Onitsha during the late nineteenth century.

25 F. Butt-Thompson (1929: 27–34) contains an account of the principal grades and officials of the men's *egbo* (Efik and Ibibio) and *okonko* (Igbo) secret societies. *Okonko* is of mixed membership and has little of the restrictive marks of a secret society, being more a masking society connected with *mmuo* masquerades in honour of ancestral spirits and their promoters, the *ayaka*. See p. 247 for a sketch of the women's titles and offices in the *okonko* society; the Queen or *omu*, that is the head of the women, wears a man's hat when carrying out her role as supervisor of women's business in the markets. P. A. Talbot (1926: 781–2) has a description of the *okonko* society or club, but he gives no information about offices. The same is true of D. A. Talbot's study of Ibibio women's rituals and associations (1915).

26 A point made to me by G. I. Jones in a personal communication (1973) and evident in the *Report* (pp. 18–20) and *Memorandum* (pp. 10–13).

27 As described by S. Leith-Ross (1965: 25, fn. 1, 106–9) and by M. M. Green (1964: 198–209).

28 For additional information regarding activation and reception see M. M. Green (1964: 91, 225–6) for a southern Igbo village-group. P. A. Talbot (1927: 99–102, 111) describes the 'feminine' and 'male' principles of life that must be honoured through sacrifice of human life and wrestling matches if the yams and corn are to grow bountifully. The yam cults described took place among the Ikwerri Igbo of Degema division. Sacred groves in Eket country, Ibibio-land, included: 'A little hut, representing the family, hearth and home . . . Holy stones or rocks in conjunction with a pool, a lake or earth itself—all typifying motherhood or fertility' see P. A. Talbot (1923: 9–10). An Awka Igbo proverb has it: 'Woman is the house'. See N. W. Thomas (1913, vol. 3: 34).

29 In the nineteen-thirties Meek observed in the Igbo district of Agwu, Onitsha province, that women prayed thus to the female cult of *njoku-ede*, the cocoyam spirit: '. . . men are producers while women are consumers' (p. 35). An Igbo proverb affirms: 'Woman never reigns', quoted by A. G. Leonard (1906: 75), who does not indicate in which part of Igbo country this proverb is commonly retailed. See notes 55–7 below for information regarding ownership of land, which was customarily vested in men. Women, on the other hand, saw themselves as carriers of fertilized energy, of new life. In the words of the Kingdon Commission of Inquiry: 'But though the origin of the recent movement was political, in the eyes of the women it seems to have become invested with a kind of religious sanction. The very thought, which after the Okugo incident became, and still remains in the minds of many, a settled conviction that women "the trees which bear the fruit" were to be taxed, stirred them to the depths of their being' (cited in *Report*, p. 19).

30 S. Ottenberg (1958) describes the Aro-dominated trading 'empire' of the nineteenth century, and G. I. Jones (1963) contains an introductory chapter on conditions in the interior (see ch. 2).

31 But see the scholarly and evocative account of Elizabeth Isichei (1973), which describes changing conditions among the Igbo of the river Niger and delta areas during this early period.

32 See G. I. Jones (1963: 16–19); E. Isichei (1973: 106–7); and R. Henderson (1972: 105–56).

33 See E. Isichei (1973: 64–8, 89); and P. A. Talbot (1931: 288–95).

34 As described for the turn of the century by two Ibibio women in Iris Andreski (1970: 140–8); and for the Igbo of the river Niger see E. Isichei (1973: 74–6).

35 Three examples are the Tallensi of northern Ghana, studied in the nineteenthirties by M. Fortes (1945: 171–7); the Ashanti of southern Ghana among whom the earth is not a deity but an important spiritual force with the power of fertility, see K. A. Busia (1954: 195–6); and the Yoruba of southwestern Nigeria who recognize the earth goddess under the name *Orisha oko*, but who do not concentrate on worshipping this deity above most others since they are urban-based farmers and craftsmen by tradition. See D. Forde (1951: 30).

36 As described in note 29 above; *Report*, p. 19.

37 A. G. Hopkins (1973: 127–34); A. Latham (1970: 80).

38 See *Memorandum* (p. 43). The repeal of the Roads & Rivers Ordinance in the mid-twenties deprived warrant chiefs of an important power over young men. Instead of forced labour, taxation was introduced. Also, see E. Morel (1912: 53–4).

39 Confirmed by G. I. Jones in a personal communication (1973). This evidence

150

runs counter to the accepted view that men monopolized the lucrative long-distance trade. See A. G. Hopkins (1973: 58–60).

40 The Ngwa-Ohuhu clans covered the administrative districts of Bende, Owerrinta, Aba, Nguru, Oloko, and Umuahia. Situated alongside slave-trading routes, Ngwa and Ohuhu entered 'legitimate' commerce as experienced middlemen and women. D. Forde and G. I. Jones (1950: 43–4), say that Ngwa and Ohuhu are a mixture of Asa Igbo, Igbo-speaking Anang, Ibibio, and Ibibio-speaking Anang. The *Report* (p. 9) testifies to 'Ngwa solidarity' during the riots, and a picture emerges of Ngwa traders (women) travelling the region to spread the message of revolt (pp. 14, 18). Wealthy Ngwa women practised 'woman-to-woman' marriage, according to V. Uchendu (1965: 187–8).

41 Ngwa-Ohuhu women also resided in the trading village of Azumini, which comprised Ngwa, Opobo, and Bonny settlers (see Report: 118–19). Near by were several Ibibio settlements whose women traders spread the taxation rumour to adjacent Abak.

42 It should, however, be remembered that women's new-found wealth was not distributed evenly throughout Igbo and Ibibio communities. Rather, particular clans or village-groups emerged by the nineteen-twenties as commercial specialists who commanded the heights of the exchange economy. However, not all Ngwa and Ohuhu groups were wealthy commercial specialists. S. Leith-Ross (1965: 135–40) reports that in the mid-thirties in the Ngwa settlement of Nguru, which was directly involved in the riots of 1929, women were relatively impoverished, confining themselves to local retailing of palm oil which they had themselves produced. Also, D. Forde and R. Scott (1946: 69–70, 77) stress that 'hungry' communities could be found throughout the oil palm belt. However, for many Igbo people, among whom cassava was being intensively cultivated at this time, it was probably the case that, as among the Mba-Ise of Owerri division: 'The position of women *vis-à-vis* their husbands' lands gains strength in this area because the women's crops, especially cassava and cocoyam, have completely eclipsed yam as staple products' (see E. Ardener 1954: 87).

43 A. G. Leonard (1906: 216). The exact meaning of 'deity' is arguable but it does suggest high regard for women.

44 Helen Chukwuma-Peters (personal communication, 1973). In *Omu Okwei: Merchant Queen of Ossomari*, Felicia Ekejiuba (1966) emphasizes the way in which Madame Okwei used marriage alliances and kinship connections to build up her Onitsha-based 'trading empire' of the early twentieth century. R. Gore-Clough (1972) has useful eye-witness accounts of women traders in the Niger delta during the same period. P. A. Talbot (1926: 678) recorded that: 'Since women do the greater part of the trading, they are often wealthier than the male members of the household, especially in ornaments, cloths, flocks and herds.' After the nineteen-twenties women's material power declined for reasons discussed in this essay.

45 By the early twentieth century the local economy in eastern Nigeria comprised four important sectors: craft production and services, carried out in the main by certain clans; production of cassava for local sale and domestic consumption; production of oil and kernels for the Nigerian and overseas markets; and production of yams, which had important prestige functions (see Forde and Jones 1950: 39–49, 81–3; Forde and Scott 1946: 40–4). Men controlled production of all commodities except cassava (which, for a time, was regarded as 'a woman's crop'), kernels, and certain sectors of the distribution and sale of semi-processed palm produce. In an agrarian economy, men were given a head-start by their jural status as owners of the land, in their capacity as representatives of the

ancestors of their patrilines. Men held rights of ownership and management over lineage lands and oil palm trees; see, for instance, G. I. Jones (1949: 309–16) who recounts land-holding practices among several Igbo groups. S. N. Obi (1963: Ch. 2) also has a helpful account of rights over land. E. Ardener (1959: 114) emphasizes that: '. . . while formal ownership of land is vested only in men, the day-to-day management of the land is in the hands of their wives, who acquire clear and definite rights of usufruct.' *De facto* female rights of use, and rights of ownership through leasehold, pledging, and purchase transactions developed within an ideology of male ownership over the land. Despite the inroads made by women between 1880 and 1920 on the principle of male ownership, land on the whole continued to be controlled by men, whether by transmission of rights in the patriline or by sale to a man who would then become a *de facto* member of the community. In other words, men controlled the resource giving most economic advantages in the long run. On account of male dominance, and the jural standing of men *vis-à-vis* immovable property, they could switch from producing yams to selling palm oil if the market looked promising. Women did not have these kinds of options open to them; their resources were fewer, limited in the main to cash gained from marketing and distribution profits (see Harris 1943–4: 302–3). In Ozuitem, Owerri province, it used to be said that women had owned both oil and kernels, until trade in palm produce became profitable (see Forde and Scott, ibid.: 70, fn. 2). And in the nineteen-twenties rioting women demanded that men should not invade women's monopoly of cassava production; which demand suggests than in lean times men were indeed involved in cassava growing (see *Memorandum*: 11).

46 Described very vividly by P. A. Talbot (1927: 82–3, 88).

47 The principal deity of Agbaja was said by informants to be of masculine and feminine gender (see M. M. Green 1946: 187). Agbaja is somewhat unusual, in comparison with other Igbo groups for whom we have records, because the people did not select one of the pantheon for the role of a creator god (see pp. 51–2). On the whole, Igbo did not attribute to one god dual sexual characteristics; they paired off one god with another of the opposite sex. Ala, the only major female goddess, was commonly married to Amadioha, the thunderer, or to Chukwu, the creator; she was also on occasions defined as the daughter of these gods in their fatherly dimension (see Green 1964: 99–102, for a brief and not very helpful account of offences against Ala). More illuminating is C. K. Meek's discussion of Igbo cosmology and, indirectly, of ideas about the relationships between gods of different gender. See Meek (pp. 54–61) for descriptions of belief about the ancestors' position *vis-à-vis* Ala, the earth. For a mission-based account of Onitsha and Awka Igbo belief in the early twentieth century see G. Basden (1938: 34–52, 98–109) where he describes some of the 'kinship' relations between the gods and goddesses. P. A. Talbot (1923: 1–30, 170–82) describes Eket Ibibio cosmology and, indirectly, sexual dualism.

48 R. Horton argues that a shift in indigenous belief towards a monolatric cult influences the speed at which people will later convert to Christianity. This intellectual change accomplished, the way is open for people to go over to Mission Christianity (Horton 1971: 103). See also my critique of Horton's explanation of conversion (Ifeka-Moller 1974).

49 Eva Gillies reports a strikingly similar case in Ogori culture, eastern Kabba Yoruba country (unpublished paper 'Sexual Symmetry in Ogori', given at a seminar on sexual roles held at University College London, in 1974). Other instances were reported (in the same seminar) for the Wik-mungkan, Australia, by David McKnight, and for the Hadza, Tanzania, by James Woodburn.

50 P. A. Talbot (1923: 170–89) describes the importance of the *egbo* secret society

for men as members of patrilineal corporations and successors to the ancestors; the secret society of Idiong, a divining god; and the secret society of Ekong, the war god. P. A. Talbot (1926, vol. 2: 63) outlines the major symbols of Isong (the earth goddess), Ete Abassi (the 'father', creator, god) and Eka Abassi, or Abassi Isu Ma (the mother goddess).

51 Ibid. (p. 512) and D. A. Talbot (1915: 189–92).

52 But note the one recorded exception, given in note 47 above.

53 P. A. Talbot (1927); Chapter II and III describe *mbari* houses in Owerri and Etche districts of Igbo country.

54 Ibid.; also C. K. Meek (1937: 24) for belief about Ala in Awgu area, Igbo country.

55 G. I. Jones (1949: 315–16) writes of the southern Cross river, and northeastern Igbo that:

> Land is normally owned and inherited by men. . . . Where a householder lacks sufficient houseland of his own to supply the needs of his wives, he endeavours, if he is wealthy enough, to rent or obtain in other ways the additional land they require. In many cases, however, he is unable to do this and the women themselves can acquire property in land in their own right, obtaining it by gift, for rent, on pledge or by outright purchase. Ibo custom debars a woman from absolute ownership of property and should she leave her husband or his successor he is entitled to all her property. As long as she remains in his household, however, the property is hers and she can dispose of it as she likes during her lifetime. On her death it is inherited by her sons. . . .

Obi (1963: 69–70) is of the opinion that women may *own* land in their own right, having acquired land with their own money or by inheritance or gift. Women rarely inherit land. G. I. Jones (ibid.) and D. Forde and R. Scott (1946) support the view that women in general did not exert *de jure* rights of ownership over land in their own person, since they held these rights indirectly through a male proxy, and were therefore restricted to *de facto* ownership. Obi, however, agrees with C. K. Meek in arguing that the 'rights and interests thus secured [e.g. by purchase of land] are hers personally in both legal theory and actual practice' (p. 70). I have abided by the view of G. I. Jones and others for this reason: customary law, which stresses the *de jure* status of male transmission and ownership, was probably based on the pre-commodity economy and division of labour. When women emerged in the early twentieth century as a potent economic force, *de facto* adjustments were made to precedent that accommodated some women's acquisition of rights of ownership over immovable property.

56 Edwin Ardener (1959: 114) quoted in note 45 above. Earlier (1954: 88), Ardener said of the same village-group: 'Women speak of the land they "own", sons speak of their "mother's land", and although it is understood that this is not true ownership as men can own, it is also conceded that the women have strong claims over the land they manage, and cannot be excluded from using them as long as they remain wives.'

57 See Edwin Ardener (1953: 900). In Mba-Ise, at the heart of the oil palm belt, people 'pledged' (i.e. pawned) oil palm trees in return for a sum of money. 'The most common means by which women obtain oil palms is in pledge. In any pledge transaction a woman will usually be accompanied by her husband, son or senior man who will speak for her, it being held, but not as strongly as when land is pledged, that women cannot act on their own behalf—although many able widows prove otherwise.'

58 See A. Martin (1956: 4); D. Forde and G. I. Jones (1950: 13–14).

59 *Report* (25, 105). S. Leith-Ross, in a personal communication (1973), tells me she heard no mention of women paying a share of men's tax in 1928. She says, however, that she did not inquire into this point.

60 See figures given by P. A. Talbot (1926, vol. 4: 120–6). These are based on the (incomplete) census of Nigeria conducted in 1921.

61 As discussed by S. Leith-Ross (1965: 169–70), who says that in the mid nine-teen-thirties, Nguru old folk held firmly to traditional religious practices, youths being the most fervent proselytizers of Christianity. J. Messenger (1959: 290–1) writes that among the Anang Ibibio mature women and unmarried girls have always given more durable support to mission and syncretist Christian churches than men. Messenger's researches of the nineteen-fifties are supported by figures for converts in the same area by the Primitive Methodist Mission during 1920, when youths and women predominated among catechumens. See *77th Annual Report* (1920: 32). For other areas, however, I have records which point to relative lack of interest among women. In the Qua Ibo area of Ibibio country, a majority of the 1,268 attending a holy communion service at Etinam before the first world war were youths (see R. M'Keown 1912: 127). Ekechi reports that in Onitsha town, at the turn of the century, the first converts were invariably boys, or slaves, and other lowly categories (see F. K. Ekechi 1971: 15, 215).

62 For the Igbo cult of Ala, the earth goddess, see C. K. Meek (1937: 24–32). Meek's material on the cult relates, in the main, to Owerri, Awgu, Nsukka. The Ala cult among the Southern Igbo at Ikwerri and Etche is described by P. A. Talbot (1932: 19–27). Talbot's observations relate to the period 1914–16. The cult of Isong, the Ibibio earth goddess is similarly described by P. A. Talbot (1923: 3–8, 27), for the Ibibio of Eket and Oron districts, Talbot wrote up his records of Ibibio culture in 1914.

63 Of these movements only one known to historians, the so-called Spirit Move-ment of 1927, was apparently without *explicit* economic and political grievances. Women's protest movements were either explicitly connected with trading practices, as in the Calabar and Oron market riots of 1925 and 1927 respectively, which are extensively discussed in *Memorandum* (pp. 10–13), or women protested against injustice in a ritualistic fashion, as in the 1925 dancing women's move-ment and the 1929 women's war (see ibid., and *Report*: 19). Women participating in the 1925 *nwa obolia* (dancing women's) protest demanded better sanitation, an end to abortions and miscarriages, more children, and improvements in trad-ing practices. They also attacked the Native Courts. P. A. Talbot records an earlier instance of female militancy at Abak in Ibibio country. Women alleged they were aborting foetuses 'unnaturally', that many children were dying, and that crops were failing to grow. Representatives of the afflicted women were sent to the then underground oracle of the Aro Chukwu Igbo (see P. A. Talbot 1927: 51).

64 G. I. Jones (personal communication, 1973).

65 Confirmed by M. M. Green (personal communication, 1973).

66 See *Report* (14–18). In one district of Owerri province, the Ngwa area of Umu-aro, women rushed the Native Court:

> dressed in rags with leaves tied round their heads but without sticks, and said that all the chiefs must leave or there would be trouble. Some sat on the benches and imitated the chiefs, while other pretended to be Court Messengers. Eventually they drove the chiefs out and danced and sang round the Native

Court until evening. The burden of their song was that the Court Clerks and Messengers and all strangers should leave their town (see *Report*: 61).

S. Leith-Ross (1965: 165) heard Igbo women in the nineteen-thirties reiterating their belief that the Commission of Inquiry had promised they should be appointed judges. This had not happened and they wanted to know why.

67 See S. Leith-Ross (note 66 above), and *Report* (p. 57). Nguru women demonstrating at Owerri told the administrative officer present: 'We said that even District Officers were changed periodically. We said that we wished the relations between us and Government to be as cordial as those existing between us and the Reverend Fathers. If there is cooperation between us and Government we shall be able to select new men to take the place of those chiefs who have been oppressing us.' See also *Memorandum* (p. 13), where women rioting at Calabar market in 1925 told the Resident that 'women shared equally with the men matters that concerned the welfare of the country'. On other occasions in the women's war, they acted as chiefs; and declared they were indeed chiefs (eee *Report*: 61–2).

68 An important aspect of the women's war, emerging economic class differentials among women, has not been discussed here. An already long essay would have been unduly complicated by introducing this problem. I have concentrated on female militancy *per se*, women being a class with inferior rights to men, who yet toiled hard to earn their daily bread. I have therefore passed over the economic divisions which petty commodity production inevitably introduced among a formerly more homogeneous category. The transition to production for exchange naturally generated class divisions among women on account of their relationship to the means of production, as it did among men. E. Boserup (1970: 20–3) argues that female labour in cash economies which produce semi-processed or raw materials leads to more work for women. Women witnesses to the Kingdon Commission cited in the *Report* (p. 11) complained that some of their number, unlike their wealthy sisters, depended on their husbands for support—'We, women, do not make oil or have any means to look after ourselves' (see also note 42 above).

References

AFIGBO, E. A. 1966. Revolution and Reaction in E. Nigeria: 1900–29. *Journal of the Historical Society of Nigeria* 3 (3).

ALLEN, J. VAN 1972. 'Sitting on a Man': Colonialism and the Lost Political Institutions of Igbo Women. *Canadian Journal of African Studies* 6 (2).

ANDRESKI, I. 1970. *Old Wives Tales*. London: Routledge & Kegan Paul.

ARDENER, E. 1953. A Rural Oil-Palm Industry. *West Africa* (1909), (1910), 26 September, 3 October 1953.

— 1954. The Kinship Terminology of a Group of Southern Ibo. *Africa* 24 (2).

— 1959. Lineage and Locality among the Mba-Ise Ibo. *Africa* 29 (2).

— 1972. Belief and the Problem of Women. In J. S. La Fontaine (ed.), *The Interpretation of Ritual*. London: Tavistock; and above.

ARDENER, S. 1973. Sexual Insult and Female Militancy. *Man* 8 (3); and above.

BASDEN, G. T. 1938. *Niger Ibos*. London: Cass.

BOSERUP, E. 1970. *Woman's Role in Economic Development*. London: Allen and Unwin.

BRIDGES, A. F. B. 1939. Report on Oil Palm Survey, Ibo, Ibibio and Cross River Areas (Unpublished).

BUCHANAN, K. M., and PUGH, J. C. 1955. *Land and People in Nigeria*. London: London University Press.

Caroline Ifeka-Moller

BUSIA, K. 1954. The Ashanti. In D. Forde (ed.), *African Worlds*. London: I.A.I. for Oxford University Press.

BUTT-THOMPSON, F. 1929. *West African Secret Societies*. Witherby.

EKANDEM, M. J. 1955. The Use of Plants as Symbols in Ibibio and Ibo Country. *Nigerian Field* **20** (2)

EKECHI, F. 1971. *Missionary Enterprise and Rivalry in Igboland*. London: Cass.

EKEJIUBA, F. 1966. Omu Okwei: Merchant Queen of Ossomari, *Nigeria* **90**.

EKUNDARE, R. O. 1973. *An Economic History of Nigeria 1860–1960*. London: Methuen.

FORDE, D. 1951. *The Yoruba-Speaking Peoples of South-Western Nigeria*. London: I.A.I./Oxford University Press.

FORDE, D. (ed.) 1954. *African Worlds*. London: I.A.I./Oxford University Press.

FORDE, D., and JONES, G. I. 1950. *The Ibo and Ibibio-speaking Peoples of South-Eastern Nigeria*. London: I.A.I./Oxford University Press.

FORDE, D., and SCOTT, R. 1946. *The Native Economies of Nigeria*, Vol. 1. London: Faber and Faber.

FORTES, M. 1945. *The Dynamics of Clanship*. London: I.A.I./Oxford University Press.

GAILEY, H. 1971. *The Road to Aba*. London: University of London Press.

GORE-CLOUGH, R. 1972. *Oil Rivers Trader: Memories of Iboland*. London: Hurst.

GREEN, M. M. 1964. *Igbo Village Affairs* (1st edn, London: Sidgwick and Jackson, 1946; 2nd edn London: Cass, 1964).

HARRIS, J. 1939–40. The Position of Women in a Nigerian Society. *Trans. N.Y. Acad. Sci.* ser. II, **2** (5).

— 1944. Some Aspects of the Economics of Sixteen Ibo Individuals. *Africa* **14** (6).

HELLEINER, G. 1972. *Peasant Agriculture, Government and Economic Growth in Nigeria*. Newhaven, Conn.: Yale University Press.

HENDERSON, R. N. 1972. *The King in Every Man*. Newhaven, Conn.: Yale University Press.

HOPKINS, A. G. 1973. *An Economic History of West Africa*. London: Longmans.

HORTON, R. 1971. African Conversion. *Africa* **61** (2).

IFEKA-MOLLER, C. 1973. 'Sitting on a Man': Colonialism and the Lost Political Institutions of Igbo Women: A Reply to Judith Van Allen. *Canadian Journal of African Studies* **7** (2).

— 1974 White Power: Social Structural Factors in Conversion to Christianity, Eastern Nigeria, 1921–1966. *Canadian Journal of African Studies* **8** (1).

ISICHEI, E. 1973. *The Ibo People and the Europeans*. London: Faber and Faber.

JEFFREYS, M. D. 1956. The Nyama Society of the Ibibio Women. *African Studies* **15** (1).

JONES, G. I. 1949. Ibo Land Tenure. *Africa* **19** (4).

— 1963. *The Trading States of the Oil Rivers*. London: I.A.I./Oxford University Press.

KIRK-GREENE, A. H. M. 1965. *The Principles of Native Administration in Nigeria*. Oxford: Oxford University Press.

LATHAM, A. J. 1970. Old Calabar 1600–1891; The Economic Impact of the West upon a Traditional Society (Ph.D. thesis University of Birmingham).

LEITH-ROSS, S. 1965. *African Women*. (1st edn, London: Faber and Faber, 1939; 2nd edn London: Routledge and Kegan Paul, 1965).

LEONARD, A. G. 1906. *The Lower Niger and Its Tribes*. London: Macmillan.

LIEBER, J. W. 1971. *Efik and Ibibio Villages* (Human Ecology and Education Series, Vol. 2, S.E. State, Occasional Publications, No. 13, University of Ibadan).

M'KEOWN, R. L. 1912. *Twenty-Five Years in Qua Ibo*. Belfast.

MARTIN, A. 1956. *The Oil Palm Economy of the Ibibio Farmer*. Nigeria: Ibadan University.

MEEK, C. K. 1937. *Law and Authority in a Nigerian Tribe*. Oxford: Oxford University Press.

156

MESSENGER, J. H. 1959. Religious Acculturation among the Anang Ibibio. In G. Bascom and M. Herskovits (eds.), *Continuity and Culture Change in African Cultures*. Chicago: University of Chicago Press.

MOREL, E. D. 1912. *Nigeria: its Peoples and Problems*. London.

NAIR, K. 1972. *Politics and Society in South Eastern Nigeria: 1841–1906*. London: Cass.

NIGERIA 1930. Report of the Aba Commission of Inquiry. Lagos.
Report of the Commission of Inquiry appointed to Inquire into the Disturbances in the Calabar and Owerri Provinces, December, 1929;
Annexure I: Memorandum of the Secretary, Southern Provinces, as to the Origin and Causes of the Disturbances in the Owerri and Calabar Provinces of 16th January, 1930;
Annexure II: Minutes of Evidence taken by a Commission of Inquiry to Inquire into Certain Incidents at Opobo, Abak and Utu Etim Ekpo in December, 1929;
Annexure III: Report of the Commission of Inquiry appointed to Inquire into Certain Incidents at Opobo, Abak and Utu Etim Ekpo in December, 1929 (Sessional Paper, No. 12 of 1930);
Annexure IV: Opobo Casualty List;
Annexure V: Abak and Utu Etim Ekpo Casualty List.

— 1930. *Nigerian Daily Times*. Lagos.

— 1950. Enquiry into the Disturbances in the Eastern Provinces of Nigeria: Proceedings of the Commission of Inquiry. London: H.M.S.O., Vols. 1 and 2.

OBI, S. N. C. 1963. *On the Ibo Law of Property*. London: Butterworth.

OTTENBERG, P. 1959. The Changing Economic Position of Women among the Afikpo Ibo. In G. Bascom and M. Herskovits (eds.), *Continuity and Culture Change in African Cultures*. Chicago: University of Chicago Press.

OTTENBERG, S. 1958. Ibo Oracles and Inter-Group Relations. *Southwestern Journal of Anthropology* **14** (3).

PERHAM, M. 1937. *Native Administration in Nigeria*. Oxford: Oxford University Press.

PRIMITIVE METHODIST MISSIONARY SOCIETY. 1920. 77th Annual Report. London.

RICHARDS, A. I. 1956. *Chisungu: A Girl's Initiation Ceremony among the Bemba of Northern Rhodesia*. London: Faber and Faber.

ROWBOTHAM, S. 1973. *Woman's Consciousness, Man's World*. Harmondsworth: Penguin.

TALBOT, D. A. 1915. *Woman's Mysteries of a Primitive People*. London: Cassell.

TALBOT, P. A. 1923. *Life in Southern Nigeria*. London: Cass.

— 1926. *The Peoples of Southern Nigeria*, Vols. 1, 2, 3, 4. Oxford: Oxford University Press.

— 1927. *Some Nigerian Fertility Cults*. Oxford: Oxford University Press.

— 1932. *Tribes of the Niger Delta*. London: Cass.

THOMAS, N. W. 1913. *Anthropological Report on the Ibo-speaking Peoples of Nigeria, Part III, Proverbs, Narratives, Vocabularies and Grammar*. London: Harrison.

UCHENDU, V. 1965. *The Igbo of South-East Nigeria*. New York: Holt, Reinhart, Winston.

— 1965. Concubinage among Ngwa Ibo of Southern Nigeria. *Africa* **35** (2).

Name Index

Acton, T. A. 65–6, 83n, 85
Adams, B. 82n, 84n
Adler, I. 125n, 125
Afigbo, E. A. 145n, 146n, 155
Alexander, J. 48, 51n, 52
Allen, J. Van 132–3, 148n, 155
Andreski, I. 137, 150n, 155
Ardener, E. W. vii–ix, xi–xiv, xxiin,
 xxiiin, xxiii, 1, 6, 7, 13, 14, 16n, 16,
 19, 26, 37, 44–6, 49, 50n, 51n, 52, 69,
 70, 74, 83n, 85, 101–2, 104, 125n, 125,
 127, 148n, 151n–3n, 155
Ardener, E. W., Ardener, S. G., and
 Warmington, W. A. 7, 13, 16, 19,
 26
Ardener, S. G. vii, ix, xi, xx, 52n, 52,
 83n, 84n, 85, 101–4, 124, 125n, 127,
 133, 144, 147n, 148n, 155

Basden, G. T. 149n, 152n, 155
Bastide, R. 84n, 85
Beattie, J. viii
Beauvoir, S. de 45–6, 52, 84n, 85
Bell, V. 55, 85
Blair, J. xxiii
Bond, B. 51n
Borrow, G. 56, 60, 77–8, 84n, 85
Boserup, E. 155n, 155
Bovin, M. 16n, 16
Bowen, E. S. 16n, 16
Bridges, A. F. B. 146n, 155
Brittain, V. 44, 52
Buchanan, K. M., and Pugh, J. C. 146n,
 155
Busia, K. A. 150n, 156
Butt-Thompson, F. 149n, 156

Callan, H. viii, x, xv, xvii, 50n, 52, 100,
 104
Callaway, H. xxiii
Chilver, E. M. 20
Chilver, E. M., and Kaberry, P. M. 36,
 52

Chukwuma-Peters, H. 151n
Clébert, J. P. 77, 81, 83n, 85
Comte, A. 108

De Vos, G. 44, 50n
Douglas, M. 5, 14, 16, 41, 45, 48, 51n,
 52, 61, 83n, 84n, 85
Du Boulay, J. 84n, 85
Dumont, L. 106–9, 125
Durkheim, E. 108

Edgerton, R. B., and Conant, F. P. 42,
 52
Ekandem, M. 147n, 156
Ekechi, F. K. 154n, 156
Ekejiuba, F. 151n, 156
Ekundare, R. O. 156
Endeley, Dr 38–40
Evans-Pritchard, E. E. 1, 16, 40–1, 52,
 114

Figes, E. 45, 50n, 52
Firestone, S. 45–6, 51n, 52
Fonteyn, Dame M. 107
Forde, D. 150n, 156
Forde, D., and Jones, G. I. 151n, 154n,
 156
Forde, D., and Scott, R. 146, 151n–3n,
 156
Fortes, M. 150n, 156
Fox, R. 25
Freud, S. 45, 50n, 79, 108
Friedan, B. 44, 52

Gailey, H. 145n, 148n, 156
Gellner, E. 145
Gillies, E. 152n
Goffman, E. 56, 85, 89, 91, 103n, 104
Gore-Clough, R. 133, 145n, 148n, 151n,
 156
Green, M. M. 20, 128, 132, 138, 141,
 145, 145n–50n, 152n, 154n, 156
Greer, G. 42, 44, 46–9, 50n, 52

159

Hardman, C. xii, 22, 27
Harris, J. 132–3, 145n–8n, 152n, 156
Hastrup, K. xxiii
Helleiner, G. 136, 140, 156
Henderson, R. N. 148n–50n, 156
Hertz, R. 24, 27
Hindes Groome, F. 56, 85
Hope, B. 42
Hopkins, A. G. 137, 146n, 150n, 151n, 156
Horton, R. 152n, 156

Ifeka-Moller, C. viii, x, xi, xiii, xv, xvi, xxiin, 20, 149n, 152n, 156
Isichei, E. 150n, 156
Ittmann, J. 8, 16n, 16

Jeffreys, M. D. 147n, 156
Jones, G. I. 140, 145, 149n, 150n, 152n–154n, 156
Jung, C. G. 119

Kaberry, P. M. 15n, 20, 27
Kenyatta, J. 87
Kingdon, D. 145n
Kirk-Greene, A. H. M. 147n, 156

La Fontaine, J. S. vii, xxiii, 15n, 16n, 20, 25, 67, 85
Laing, R. D. 26n, 83n, 85
Lambert, H. E. 41, 53
Lane, M. 108
Latham, A. 150n, 156
Lawrence, D. H. 56, 85
Leach, E. R. 5, 16, 108, 125
Leith-Ross, S. 20, 142, 145, 147n–51n, 154n, 155n, 156
Leonard, A. G. 137–8, 150n, 151n, 156
Lévi-Strauss, C. xiii, 2, 5, 6, 8, 14, 17, 23–4, 45, 70, 79, 83n, 85
Lewis, I. M. 50n, 53
Lieber, J. W. 156
Lienhardt, P. viii
Lugard, Lord 147n

McKenzie, F. 47, 53
Mackenzie, M. 48
M'Keown, R. L. 154n, 156
Maguire, M. 22, 27
Malinowski, B. 108
Martin, A. 154n, 156
Marx, K. 108
Mathieu, N.-C. 19, 21, 24–5, 26n, 27
McKnight, D. 152n
Mead, M. 20, 47

Meek, C. K. 145n, 147n, 150n, 152n–4n, 156
Merimée, P. 56, 85
Messenger, J. H. 154n, 157
Millett, K. 47, 50n, 52, 84n, 85
Miss World, 42, 47
Mitchell, J. 9, 53
Morel, E. 150n, 157
Murphy, P. J., and Kempf, A. F. 125n, 125

Nair, K. 157
Needham, R. 4, 17, 24, 27
Nkwain, F. 36–7, 50n, 52n, 53

Oakley, A. xxiiin, xxiii
Obermeyer, G. 103
Obi, S. N. C. 152n, 157
O'Faolain, J., and Marines, L. 50n, 53
Okely, J. viii, x, xii, xiii, 59, 60, 70, 75, 82n, 85
Ortner, S. 26n, 27
Ottenberg, P. 137, 157
Ottenberg, S. 150n, 157

Parsons, T. 47
Peers, A. 109–11, 114, 125
Perham, M. 145n, 147n, 157

Radcliffe-Brown, A. R. 108
Reik, T. 51n
Richards, A. I. vii, 1, 13, 15n, 17, 20, 157n
Ritzenthaler, E. R. 36–7, 50n, 53
Rivière, P. G. 108, 125
Rousseau, J.-J. 24
Rowbotham, S. xx, xxiii, 149n, 157

Saint John of the Cross, 105, 109–10, 119, 123, 125
Saint Paul, 115, 118
Saint Teresa of Avila, 105, 110–11, 114, 118–19, 124n, 125
Sampson, J. 56, 85
Sandford, J. 57, 85
Satow, Sir E. 89–90, 93, 104
Sibisi, H. xxiii
Smart, B. C., and Crofton, H. T. 66, 84n, 85
Solomon, 123
Steady, F. 40, 43
Steane, C. 15n
Stone, B. G. 15n, 17
Strathern, M. 50n, 51n, 53

Sutherland, A. 83n, 85
Symons, A. 56, 85

Talbot, D. A. 128, 147n, 149n, 153n, 157
Talbot, P. A. 138–9, 143, 147n, 149n, 150n–4n, 157
Thom, M. 83n
Thomas, N. W. 150, 157
Thompson, T. W. 62–5, 85–6
Tiger, L. 25, 45, 50n, 53
Turner, V. W. 13, 17, 84n, 85

Uchendu, V. 146n, 147n, 151n, 157

Van Gennep, A. 13

Wade, V. 52n, 53
Wellard, J. 50n, 53
Williams, D. viii, x, xvii, xviii, 103
Wilson, B. 108, 125
Wood, J. R., and Serres, J. 90, 93, 104
Wood, M. F. 59, 86
Woodburn, J. 61, 152n
Woolf, V. 19, 27

Subject Index

abortion, 51n
animality, 48
  see also boundaries; nature/culture;
    wild
anlu, 36–40, 43, 46
anomie, 96
anthropology, vii–viii, xii, xxi, 1, 26n,
  105, 108, 124–5, 128
  female anthropologists, 1, 2, 15, 19–
    21, 50n
  and historical reconstruction, 127
  and studies of religious phenomena,
    123
  and studies of women, 20, 69
articulateness, *see under* inarticulateness
Ashanti, 150n
Association of Social Anthropologists,
  Decennial Conference, viii
Azande, 40–1

Bakweri, vii, 1, 7, 24, 29, 51n
  demographic changes, 10
  division of labour, sexual, 7, 8
  ecology, 7, 13
  elephant dance, male, 14, 51n
  European goods, 11, 14
  kin groups, 46, 51n
  male/female views of Bakweri society,
    19
  marital conflict, 19
  marriage, 12–13
  myth, 6
  nature/culture, notions of, 7
  plantation camps, 30
    migrants, 13
  residence pattern, village, 7, 12
  sexual insult to women, 30
    judicial procedure against in Colon-
      ial period, 31–5
    traditional sanctions, 30
    see also '*titi ikoli*'
  water spirit (mermaid) cult, ix, 1, 6, 7
    liengu doctors, 11, 12

liengu language, 9–12
  rites, 9–12
    male/female view of, 8, 12
  wild, 7, 8, 12, 13, 35
    see also boundaries; nature/culture
  zombie beliefs, 8, 13
Balong, ix, 35–6
belief, 4, 8, 10, 13, 117, 127, 142
Bemba, vii, 67
binary discriminations, 23–4
biological functions, 24
biological needs, 108
biologism, 24, 26n
biology, xviii, 2, 3, 5, 12, 24–5, 52n, 69,
  123, 135, 142, 144
body,
  symbolism, 11, 39, 43, 47, 60, 63–4,
    67–8, 83n, 84n, 127, 133, 135, 142,
    148n
  as weapon, 142, 148n
  see also sexual insult; sexual parts,
    female
Bororo, 24
boundaries, 2, 5, 13, 14, 79, 81–2, 83n
  ethnic, 61, 79
  see also nature/culture
bounding problem, 13, 23, 25
  male/female views on, 6
bricolage (*bricoleur*), xiii, 8

Carmelite nuns, *see under* nuns
caste system, 106–7
  see also hierarchy
categories, xiii, xiv
  markers of, xviii
  see also boundaries; symbolism; taboo
change, xvii, 30, 31, 38, 46, 102
  see also women's war (E. Nigeria)
charter myths, 99
children, 5, 14, 22
Civil Service, British, 89
classes, dominant/exploited, 21
communication system, 22

162

conceptual system, xvii
condensation, symbolic, 13
conformity, 87
conservatism, xvii
cosmology, 107–9, 113, 119–20, 138–9, 152n
  see also nuns
criminals, 22
culture, 23, 25, 87
  total, 87
  see also nature/culture
culture contact, 74

dance, 13, 30, 35, 37–8, 41, 50n, 77, 120, 132, 141, 143
deference, 43, 91
definition, 23
defloration, 65, 67
deodorants, 47–8
deviants, 56
dignity, honour, pride, ix, xiin, 47, 48, 127
  see also sexual insult
Diplomatic Service (British)
  Embassy, social life of, 88, 90
  wives of diplomats, x, xv, 51n, 87, 89
    dedication, premiss of, xv, 87, 98, 100, 102
    independent employment, possibility of, 96–8, 103
    official slots, 93
    position of, paradoxes in, 88, 97–8, 100
    rank among, 89–92, 96
    relation to Diplomatic Service, 88
Diplomatic Service Wives' Association, 90, 92
division of labour, 7, 8, 135
divorce frequency, 4, 61
dominant group, xii–xv, xvii, xxiiin, 43, 51n
  see also muted group
dominant ideology, xv
dominant model, xii, xxi, xxiin, xxiiin, 3
dominant structure, xxi–xxii, xxiin, 19, 22, 24, 124
Duala, 8

ethnocentrism, 66
ethnographers, 2–4, 15, 26n, 44, 128
ethnography, functionalist, deficiencies of, 4
ethologistic determinism, 25
ethos, 135
etiquette, 90

events, xi, xiii, xviii, xix, 51n, 52n
  see also s-structures
experience, xiv, xx, 20, 22–3, 45, 88, 122, 144
exploitation, 44, 71
expression, mode of, xx, 42–3, 47, 49

family, 88
female model, ix, xi, xv, xvi, xix, 3, 6, 7, 14, 44, 46, 51n, 70, 124
  congruence between, xix
  see also femineity; male models; muted groups
female solidarity, 132, 135, 141
femineity, 46–8, 51n, 102, 124
  see also femininity
femininity, 44, 46–7, 49, 51n, 72, 102, 135
feminism, 44, 49, 68, 99, 127, 132, 143
  literature of, 19
  see also women's protest movements
fertility, 12, 13, 68, 127, 138, 141, 143–4, 147n
fieldwork, 1, 4, 16n, 69, 87–8
folk biology, 99
Fulani, 36, 38
functionalism, 4, 12, 108
  liberationist hostility to, 47

gesture, 49, 129
  see also body symbolism
Gisu, 67
Gorgio (non-Gypsy), 82n
  see also Gypsy
group theory, 116, 123
groups, recruitment to, xvii
Gypsy, x
  body, ideas of, 60, 67
  cooking, 61, 63–4
  economic life, 58–62
  Gypsy/Gorgio boundary, 79, 81–2
  as muted group, xii–xiii, xxiin
  pollution, ideas of, xii, 55, 59–60, 62–64, 68, 80
    childbirth, 66–8
    menstruation, 65–7, 84n
  prostitution, 57, 78–81
  purity, ideas on, 61, 65, 67–8, 75
  sedentarization, 71
  sex, ideas on, 63–5, 68, 76
  stereotypes
    Gorgio of Gypsy women, 55–6, 76–7
    Gorgio of Gypsy men, 56
    Gypsy of Gorgio, 57, 60–1, 78, 80

Gypsy—*continued*
  women
    manipulating male models, 57, 81
    'Calling', 58–9, 62–4, 68, 70–1,
      83n
    ideal behaviour, according to Gypsy
      males, 57–8
    view of Gorgio females, 55, 57, 80

Hadza, 61
handedness, 24
hierarchy, 91, 100, 107–8, 134
human action, 106
human identity, 45, 47–8, 121
  see also identity; nature/culture
humankind/non-human, 14

Ibibio, xi, 128–9, 132, 136–7, 147n
  religion, 136, 138–9
    changes in, modern, 141
  secret societies
    female, 133, 139, 141
    male, 139, 149n
  sexual values of, 142
  see also women's war (E. Nigeria)
ideal, 55, 81
identity, xvi, 46, 48, 71, 127, 144
  see also human identity; self-identifi-
    cation
ideology, xv, xxi, xxiin, 99–100, 135,
    143
  dominant, 22
  sexual, 135–6, 142, 144
Igbo, Ibo, xi, xv, 19, 127–9, 132, 134,
    147n
  religion, 136, 138–9, 152n
    changes in, modern, 141
  secret societies, male, 149n
  sexual values of, 142
  see also women's war (E. Nigeria)
Ijaw, 137
inarticulateness, viii, xii
  and non-linguistic symbolism, ix
  male/female compared, 2, 3, 14, 21,
    44, 50n, 101
  see also female models; muted group;
    women's war (E. Nigeria)
individualism, 107, 109
instrumental/expressive, 44
insult, *see under* sexual insult
interpreters, 2, 3, 128
inversion, 5, 49

Kikuyu, 41, 43, 50n
kilipat, 42

Kole, 8
Kom, ix, 36, 46, 147n
  women's rebellion, 143
  see also sexual insult

language, viii, ix, xv, 9–12, 25, 105–6
  see also mode of expression; semantic
    field; semantics
Lele, 41, 51n
liminality, 65, 84n
liturgy, liturgical space, 106, 108–9, 110
London Women's Anthropology Work-
    shop, 69

male domination, vii, xxi, 134, 144–5,
    152n
male models, ix, 2–7, 14, 24, 44, 51n,
    52, 70, 74, 81
  see also female models; dominant
    groups
mankind/womankind, 14
marginality, 6, 7, 57
marriage, 13, 57, 85, 124
marxism, and concept of world structure,
    25
marxist analysis, 22
mathematics, non-metrical, 125n
measurement, xviii
men's models, *see under* male models
menstruation, 62, 65–6, 84n
metalanguage, 3
metanoia, 118, 120
metaphor, 23–4
militancy, female, xx, 21, 29, 36–7, 46,
    49, 127, 141, 144–5
  see also women's movements;
    women's war (E. Nigeria); sexual
    insult
Miss World Competition, 47
mode of production, 22, 127, 134–5,
    138, 144
mode of specification, xv, 26n, 51n
model, x–xiii, xv–xvii, xx, xxiin, 24, 44–
    46, 52n, 92, 101, 116, 125n
  bounded, 2, 3, 6
  conscious, 94, 100
  counterpart, xii, xiii, xvii, xxiin,
    xxiiin
  degree of 'fit', xii, 51n
  dominant, xii, xxiin, 3
  ethnographic, 2
  ideal, xviii
    primacy of, xviii
  surface/deep, xvii
    disjuncture, xv, xvi

see also female models; male models; structures
multivalency, in symbolism, 13
muted group, xii–xv, xvii, xix, xxi, xxiin, xxiiin, 22, 24, 25n, 51n, 147n
  children as, 22
  conservatism of, xvii
  criminals as, 22
  female social anthropologists as, 21
  see also dominant group; inarticulateness
myths, ix, 3, 5, 6, 99
  about women, 91–2, 103n

names, 9, 12
nature/culture, 5, 14, 23, 25, 48
  Bakweri scheme, 7, 48
  Gypsy scheme, 56, 61–2
  Lévi-Strauss on, 5, 14
  see also wild
Naturmensch, 6
ndong, 35–6, 46
negritude, negro pride, 46, 49
nudity, *see under* body
nuns, Carmelite nuns, x, xvii, xviii
  anonymity, concept of, 106
  as 'closed' group, 123
  contemplation, 105, 123
  cosmology, 107, 109, 113, 119–20
    structural aspects of,
      above/below, 117
      birth/death, 118
      inside/outside, 118
      male/female, 110, 118–19
      space and time, 113–16
  daily round, 111–13, 115
  economic life of, 111–12, 124
  hierarchy, 107
  historical origins of Order, 105, 110
  language of, 106
  metanoia, 118, 120
  non-individualism of, 107, 109
  partnership, 110
  prayer, 111–13, 117, 120
  relation to Christ, 122–3
  relation to God, 110, 118–19
  relation to other women, 121–2
  seclusion, 107
  silence, 112, 114
  solitude, 110–12
  vows of poverty, chastity, obedience, 119–20

objectivity, 87–8

obscenity, vulgarity, ix, 30, 40–3, 129, 132, 148n
  and female dignity, ix, 47
  see also sexual insult
observation/statements about observation, 4
observers, vii
Oli, 8
oppression, xxi
ostracism, 37, 39, 40, 43
overdetermination, xii–xiii, xv, xxiin, 49

p-structures, xiv, xx, 26n, 46, 51n, 115–116
  difficulty of statement in language, xv
  paradigmatic, 115
  see also p-structures
participant observation, 87
perception, vii, xii–xvi, xx, 21, 22, 24, 44, 88, 93, 102, 133
Pokot, 42
political space, xvi
politics, xvi, 6, 134
pollution, xii, 5, 14, 37, 48, 50n, 51n, 55, 61, 83n
  see also Gypsy; purity; taboo
polysemy, symbolic, 13
populations, viii, xxi, 1, 123, 125n
possession, 50n
primate evolution, 101
privacy, 106–7
programmatic statements, 49
programme, xiv
protocol, 89
psychological impulses, individual, 107
psychology, 119
psycho-social transformation, 98, 100
puberty, vii, 12–13
purity, x, xii, 61, 65
  see also pollution
Pygmies, 61

race, 83n, 84n
rank, 89–92, 96, 134
  distinguished from authority, 91
rape, 50n
rationality, 108
reality, 4, 24–5
  female, 46
  separate, of the sexes, 19
  see also perception
religion, 50n, 61, 107, 123, 152n
reproductive powers, female, xxiin, 7, 142, 144
  see also fertility

restricted code, 96
ridicule, 5, 38, 42, 49
rites (rituals), vii, ix, 1, 8, 11, 63, 66–8, 70, 84n, 133, 136, 138
  Bakweri, 6, 9–13
  Chisungu (Bemba), 1, 13
  fertility, 12
  nubility, 12
  of passage, 10, 13, 65, 67, 84n, 147n
  puberty, vii
  purity, x
  reduced, 10
  see also pollution
role model, 87

s-structures, xiii–xv, xx, 26n, 51n
  see also events
scale, unevenness of, 102
schizoid situation, 83n
seclusion, 9, 11, 107
  see also rites
'secular', 106, 121–2
self/not-self, 23
self-denial, 121
self-identification, self-image, xxiin–xxiii, 15, 81, 87, 92, 98, 100, 127
  see also femineity
semantic field, 34, 101, 119, 124n
semantics, 102, 117
semiological elements, 25
set theory, 123
sex/gender, xviii
sexes, relations between, xviii, 1, 14, 23, 45–6, 51n, 69, 127, 133, 135, 139
  fantasies, 55, 81
  see also female models; male models; muted group; women's protest movements; women's war (E. Nigeria)
sexual discrimination, 69, 83n
sexual insult,
  in Africa, 40–2, 127, 144, 146n, 148n
  Bakweri, 30–5
  Balong, 35–6
  Kom, 36–40, 52n
  see also obscenity
sexual parts, female, 29–34, 36, 41–2, 47–8, 50n, 51n, 64, 68, 84n, 127, 146n, 147n, 148n
Sierra Leone, 40, 43, 51n
simultaneities, xxiiin
social 'etymology', 43
socialization, xxiiin, 67, 69, 84n, 135
society/culture, 23
socio-intellectual structures, 25

sociolinguistics, 96
sociology, 108
statistics, 20
stereotypes, xiv, 44, 55, 81
  see also Gypsy
structural analysis, 109
structural dominance, 24
structural levels, deep/surface, 48, 101, 104n
structures
  deep, underlying, xix, 49, 52n, 116
  as definers of reality, 22
  as language, 25
  see also dominant structure; p-structures; s-structures
swearing, 43
symbolic behaviour, 49
symbolic force, 43
symbolic reversal, 12
  see also inversion
symbolic sets, 13
symbolic structures, 4
symbolic systems, 42–3
  contradictions in, 13
symbolism, ix, xxii, 12, 15, 42–4, 47, 147n
  militant, 127
  non-linguistic, ix
  studies of, 4–5
  total nature of, 13
  Turnerian approach to, 13
syntagmatic, xiii, 115
  see also s-structures
system, 8, 13, 42–3, 108

taboo, 5, 9, 10, 14, 43, 49, 61–2, 66, 77, 81
Tallensi, 150n
Tanga, 8
template, 8, 10, 37
titi ikoli, 29–36, 46–7, 49
tokenism, 134
topology, 123
total institution, 89, 103n
transformational links, xv
translation, 105, 119

unconscious, xiv, xv, 44, 93
universals, xvii, 23, 49

voluntary work, 96

Wik-mungkan, 152n
wild, 14, 16n, 23–4, 26n, 61, 83n, 133, 141

Bakweri, 6–8, 12–13, 35
male wild, 14–15, 83n, 143
see also nature/culture
wives, x, 71, 98, 101
see also Diplomatic Service (British)
womanhood, 51n, 135, 142, 144
women, vii–ix, xviii, 44–5, 84n, 101, 122, 127
and anthropologists, viii, 1, 2, 15, 20, 50n
as inarticulate, xii
biological definition of, xviii
see also inarticulateness
as intellectual category, xviii
in literature, 19
myths about, 91–2, 103n
position of, studies of, xxi, 1
in African towns, 16n
problem of, 1–3, 101
see also female models; Gypsy; women's movements; women's war (E. Nigeria)
Women's Anthropology Group Seminar (Oxford), viii, xxiii, 83n, 103n
women's models, *see under* female models
women's protest movements, viii, ix, 29, 46–9, 69, 133, 141, 154n
women's rights/women's liberation, xx, 43–4, 47
see also women's war (E. Nigeria)

women's secrets, 30, 33–4, 41, 43, 48, 51n
women's war (E. Nigeria), xi, xv, 19, 127, 141
economic change and the sexual division of labour, xvi, 135, 137–9, 140, 143–4
economic sources, 132, 134, 142
evidence on, 128–9, 132–3, 145n–6n
male/female as producer/reproducer, 127, 134–5, 138, 144
men's part in, 133–4, 148n
political aspects of, 134
religious factors, 141
sexes, relations between, 127, 135, 137, 139, 142, 144–5
political, xvi, 134
taxation, xv, 127, 131, 143, 144
women as producers, 135, 142, 144
see also Ibibio; Igbo
women's war (Cameroon), *see under* '*anlu*'
world structures, 22, 24
as reality reducing, 25
as self-defining, 23
totalitarian tendency of, 25
world view, xix, 16n
Wovea, 8

Yasa, 8
Yoruba, 150n, 152n